Mediterranean Migration and the Labour Markets

This book focuses on issues that are relevant for the Euro-Mediterranean Partnership. The depth and the extension of the current political crisis in the area have changed the perspectives of conventional Euro-Mediterranean integration policies. The book provides the grounds for new patterns of analysis and addresses policy guidelines which are able to respond to the dramatic challenges that Mediterranean regions are facing.

By implementing a multidisciplinary approach, the volume uncovers the structural determinants of migrations in the area: territorial and social imbalances, climate change, unemployment, weak institutions, poor governance, lack of efficient redistributive policies. Each chapter proposes innovative and rich analyses of the socio-economic conditions of all Mediterranean countries. The prevailing evidence suggests that while the North–South imbalances persist inside the basin, the recent world economic and financial crises have deepened social, intergenerational and gender inequalities. These inequalities cross all territories both nationally and internationally and affect the living conditions of large segments of population in Southern and Eastern Mediterranean countries. To bridge these gaps, it is necessary to strengthen territorial cohesion, reduce income differentials and improve the access of marginal areas to basic infrastructure. These long-term goals can be achieved through an inclusive development model for which young people and women can enjoy the same opportunities of education and work.

Offering innovative and practical guidelines for future programs and policies, this book is essential reading for policy makers, researchers at policy think tanks as well as academics and postgraduate students of Mediterranean studies and Economic Policy. The general policy recipes, provided to govern migration flows, make useful reading for national and international research centres and major governmental agencies interested in migration issues.

Salvatore Capasso is the Director of the Institute of Studies on Mediterranean Societies and Full Professor of Economic Policy at the University of Naples Parthenope. His research interests are in the fields of Economic Development and Financial Economics. He is author of a large number of scientific publications in international journals.

Eugenia Ferragina was first researcher at the Institute of Studies on Mediterranean Societies of the CNR and contract professor of Economics and Institutions of the Mediterranean countries at the University of Naples 'L'Orientale'. She is the author of many publications in national and international journals.

Routledge Studies in Labour Economics

Youth and the Crisis
Unemployment, Education and Health in Europe
Edited by Gianluigi Coppola and Niall O'Higgins

Workers and the Global Informal Economy
Interdisciplinary Perspectives
Edited by Supriya Routh and Vando Borghi

The Political Economy of Employment Relations
Alternative Theory and Practice
Aslihan Aykac

The Economics of Trade Unions
A Study of a Research Field and Its Findings
Hristos Doucouliagos, Richard B. Freeman and Patrice Laroche

Young People and the Labour Market
A Comparative Perspective
Floro Caroleo, Olga Demidova, Enrico Marelli and Marcello Signorelli

Women's Economic Empowerment in Turkey
Edited by Onur Burak Çelik and Meltem İnce Yenilmez

A Comparative Perspective of Women's Economic Empowerment
Edited by Meltem İnce Yenilmez and Onur Burak Çelik

Mediterranean Migration and the Labour Markets
Policies for Growth and Social Development in the Mediterranean Area
Edited by Salvatore Capasso and Eugenia Ferragina

For more information about this series, please visit: www.routledge.com/ Routledge-Studies-in-Seventeenth-Century-Philosophy/book-series/SE0420

Mediterranean Migration and the Labour Markets

Policies for Growth and Social Development in the Mediterranean Area

Edited by Salvatore Capasso
and Eugenia Ferragina

Routledge
Taylor & Francis Group

LONDON AND NEW YORK

First published 2020
by Routledge
2 Park Square, Milton Park, Abingdon, Oxon OX14 4RN

and by Routledge
605 Third Avenue, New York, NY 10017

First issued in paperback 2021

Routledge is an imprint of the Taylor & Francis Group, an informa business

British Library Cataloguing-in-Publication Data
A catalogue record for this book is available from the British Library

Library of Congress Cataloging-in-Publication Data
A catalog record for this book has been requested

ISBN 13: 978-0-367-78512-3 (pbk)
ISBN 13: 978-1-138-55734-5 (hbk)

Typeset in Bembo
by Apex CoVantage LLC

This book is dedicated to Eugenia. She conceived it and worked on it valiantly during her relentless illness, succeeding against all odds in bringing her project to life. She was sadly not able to see the finished product, but left it to our trusted hands and eyes. Though no longer present in our lives, she has left her devoted fingerprints all over this collective labour of love.

Contents

Figures

Maps

Tables

Contributors

Roger Albinyana, European Institute of the Mediterranean, IEMED and University of Barcelona (Spain)

Corrado Bonifazi, Institute for Research on Population and Social Policies, Italian National Research Council, IRPPS-CNR (Italy)

Salvatore Capasso, Institute of Studies on Mediterranean Societies, Italian National Research Council, ISSM-CNR and University of Naples PARTHENOPE (Italy)

Saïd Chahi, University Hassan II (Morocco)

Fátima Fernández, University of Santiago de Compostela (Spain) and University Hassan II (Morocco)

Anna M. Ferragina, University of Salerno (Italy)

Eugenia Ferragina, Institute of Studies on Mediterranean Societies, Italian National Research Council, ISSM-CNR (Italy)

Giorgia Giovannetti, University of Florence (Italy)

Bichara Khader, University of Louvain (Belgium)

Mauro Lanati, Migration Policy Centre, Robert Schuman Centre for Advanced Studies, European University Institute (Italy)

Ivan Martin, Migration Policy Centre, Robert Schuman Centre for Advanced Studies, European University Institute (Italy)

Giulia Nunziante, University of Rome Tor Vergata (Italy)

Yolanda Pena-Boquete, AYeconomics Research Centre, University of Santiago de Compostela (Spain)

Desirée A. L. Quagliarotti, Institute of Studies on Mediterranean Societies, Italian National Research Council, ISSM-CNR (Italy)

Paolo Quercia, University of Perugia and Center for Near Abroad Strategic Studies (Italy)

Dolores Riveiro, University of Santiago de Compostela (Spain)

Alessandro Romagnoli, University of Bologna (Italy)

Salvatore Strozza, University of Naples "Federico II" (Italy)

Erol Taymaz, Middle East Technical University (Turkey)

Alessandra Venturini, University of Turin (Italy)

Barbara Zagaglia, Marche Polytechnic University (Italy)

Marco Zupi, Centre for Politics and International Studies, CESPI (Italy)

Acknowledgements

The editors wish to acknowledge the financial support of the Union for the Mediterranean Secretariat (UfMS) through its Cooperation Agreement with the Institute of Studies on Mediterranean Societies (ISSM), signed in May 2016. Additionally, we would like to thank the ISSM for its technical support.

Mediterranean migration between territorial imbalances and structural changes in labour markets

Introduction

I should have written this introduction with Eugenia Ferragina. She made a huge effort to follow this project until her last supplies of energy finally ebbed away and she succumbed to a cruel illness. She loved her work and the idea of contributing to a better world through research. Her world revolved around the study of the Mediterranean Region: she displayed dedication and enthusiasm possessed by very few, and which even fewer can transmit to others. The editing of this book was largely the result of her efforts and the fulfilment of her passion.

In recent decades, the Mediterranean region, torn apart by a number of crises, has experienced a series of profound and substantial geopolitical changes. Causes and effects of these changes mingle and fuse in a complex set of phenomena whose understanding requires in-depth investigation and interdisciplinary analysis. The Grand Recession, the Arab Spring and wars in the Middle East have undermined the well-being of the economies in the area and have put enormous pressure on welfare systems: labour markets have been hard hit, with the result that South–North migrations in the Mediterranean have substantially increased.

It is far from easy to determine the causes and consequences of migrations. This is even more difficult in a fragile conflict-fraught environment, in which economic and political variables are strictly interrelated and reinforce each other: territorial and social imbalances, climate change, unemployment, weak institutions, poor governance and lack of efficient redistribution policies may all, to a different extent, put pressure on populations and lead to an increase in migration flows.

This book aims to provide the basis for developing new patterns of analysis and drawing up policy guidelines to respond to the dramatic migration challenges that Mediterranean regions currently face. Each chapter proposes innovative and multidimensional analyses of the socio-economic conditions in the area. The baseline argument is that social, intergenerational and gender inequalities are major drivers of migrations. These inequalities cross territories and borders and affect the living conditions of large segments of populations in Southern and Eastern Mediterranean countries. To bridge these gaps, it would appear necessary to strengthen territorial cohesion, reduce income inequalities and improve access of marginal areas to basic infrastructure. To achieve these long-term goals, an inclusive model for economic development needs to be forged, a model able to ensure the same opportunities of education and work especially to young people and to women.

This book is a collection of original essays by academics and experts on Mediterranean migration, and on its causes and effects. The essays set out a new vision for Mediterranean space where neighbour relationships are conceived as two-faceted challenges that can be overcome by common knowledge on major issues and a shared effort to set up a more comprehensive understanding of critical situations. This vision is necessary to bolster the role of the EU and to empower non-EU Mediterranean countries.

After describing the geopolitical changes that have framed Mediterranean migrations in recent decades (Chapters 1 and 2), the book analyzes different push factors of migrations: demographics (Chapters 3 and 4), economic imbalances (Chapter 5), labour markets (Chapters 6 and 7) and the environment (Chapter 8). Chapters 9 and 10 study the effects of migrations on origin and destination countries, and Chapter 11 delineates the possible future of migration dynamics. Let us now describe each chapter content in more detail.

Chapter 1 shows that far from having purely economic consequences, the recent financial crisis has undermined political stability in many countries and has compromised the geopolitical environment in the Mediterranean area, to the point that several historically circumscribed regional problems have modified their nature, growing in magnitude, deteriorating in quality and intensifying in their geographic outreach. The consequences of these radical changes is a rather new migratory phenomenon which cannot simply be framed within the old economic-humanitarian interpretation but rather within a broader politico-strategic conceptual vision, a vision that needs to encompass the issue of security. Starting from this premise, Chapter 1 identifies the keys to reinterpreting and understanding the nature of recent migration flows in the relationship between the multiple levels of intra- and inter-State security issues. The debate on the migration-security nexus needs to incorporate a new geopolitical dimension and take on board the political and socio-economic changes that have emerged in the last 20 years in the Southern Mediterranean countries. The idea is that the response to migration flows in destination countries should wisely balance solidarity, integration, rule of law, human safety as well as social and state security.

In this new context of far-reaching institutional and socio-economic change, greater Mediterranean regional integration has been perceived as a tool for decreasing territorial imbalances in the area, and has become one of the main objectives of Euro-Mediterranean policies over the last two decades. Around the basin, governments have attempted to restore the conditions for balanced growth through the search for socio-economic and political stability: in this sense, the Barcelona Process appeared to be a turning point and a generous European attempt to promote development and mutual understanding within the Mediterranean. And yet, to date, although some steps forward have been made, the Euro-Mediterranean area is still far from the targets set by the Barcelona Process and the levels of regional integration in the area remain similar to the levels recorded in the 1960s.

Chapter 2 examines the possible effects of greater economic integration and analyzes the actual steps to be taken in this direction. In particular, the chapter considers paradigmatic the path followed by Morocco in its search for greater international integration after the post-colonial period. The analysis suggests that Moroccan international policy has been heavily influenced by the process of construction of the European Union (EU) not only in the projects concerning the North–South dialogue, but also in South–South projects of collaboration. The Moroccan experience shows that the missed targets of greater labour mobility and more intense agricultural trade among Southern countries have generated a social fracture that has turned Euro-Mediterranean affairs into a laboratory of crisis management. Beyond the Moroccan case and on a more general scale, the chapter points out that all the attempts to enhance Euro-Mediterranean integration have been substantially unsuccessful. The evident interrelation between foreign policy affairs and any process of economic integration suggests the need of a really comprehensive approach to provide an effective policy for facilitating the flows of goods, capital and people across borders.

Migrations and labour market conditions are strictly interrelated: one of the main reasons for people to move is the lack of job opportunities. Yet, at a deeper level, the state of the economy itself is heavily influenced by demographics. In the long run, the distance between labour supply and demand, and the pressure in the labour market, is shaped by demographic forces. Chapter 3 focuses on demographics in Mediterranean countries and studies the possible long-run effects of population dynamics. Unlike the Northern countries, the Southern Mediterranean countries are still experiencing substantial population growth that will continue into the near future: by the year 2030, the working age population will have increased by around 19 million in Egypt, 6.3 million in Algeria, 4.5 million in Morocco, 1.2 Mauritania, 1.1 million in Libya and 0.8 million in Tunisia.

However, depending on the participation rates, the actual increase in effective labour supply will diverge from the increase in the working age population. Chapter 3 portrays three different scenarios – a baseline scenario, which assumes constant labour force participation rates at current levels; an intermediate scenario that emerges if the International Labour Organization forecast activity rates prevail; and an optimistic scenario that depicts the dynamics of labour markets should the maximum increase in labour force be reached. The results show that, whatever the scenario regarding the participation rate, in most countries, it will be necessary to guarantee employment to an increasing number of people until 2030, especially for those in the mature age groups (45–54 and 55–64 years). Moreover, the labour supply would ensure greater participation of women with only a radical transformation of labour markets, as happens in scenario 3. However, if participation rates were to remain stable at the current levels, the gender gap would worsen over time. Chapter 4 focuses on gender issues in the labour market. As might be expected, in Southern Mediterranean countries, women's conditions in the labour markets are particularly vulnerable. In these countries relative to those with similar levels of GPD per capita, women continue to experience higher rates of unemployment and lower rates of employment. Yet education rates have improved considerably in the last decade and are now at relatively high levels, particularly among younger women. Educational attainments have raised hopes and increased expectations of higher possibility of employment and social mobility, but to date, such expectations are unfulfilled. In this context, the so-called feminization of migration, that is, the migration of women independently of men, risks turning into a new frontier of discrimination, violence and abuse against girls and women, and forces us to look beyond the idea of empowerment as just context specific. In analytical terms, the chapter addresses women's empowerment and migration from and to Southern Mediterranean countries on three levels: (a) legality, (b) empirical facts and practices, (c) subjective perceptions, opinions and attitudes. To be meaningful and to portray the facts in the correct light, descriptions should cover all three levels. Otherwise, the data would fail to provide either complete characterization of women's empowerment or a comprehensive description of the socio-economic context. After all, institutions are a very important factor to understand women's position in a complex social reality.

Income inequalities and wage rate differentials are a major cause of migration flows. People tend naturally to move from countries with low per capita income and low wage rates to more affluent economies with higher income and wages. Moreover, since the wage rate is positively related to the average and marginal productivity of labour, migration also tends to reduce productivity differentials. The outflow of people moving from low wage–low productivity countries tends to increase productivity in the country of origin and have beneficial effects on growth. As well as influencing migration flows, spatial differentials also influence firms' clustering and the geography of production and capital productivity. Chapter 5 attempts to describe the process of firms' clustering and the effect of firm location on productivity and the innovation process. The chapter focuses on Turkey for the specific features of this economy but most of the results may be generalized. By developing a new index of agglomeration, the study shows that a greater agglomeration is generally linked to higher levels of efficiency and productivity. The explanation is that the use of similar production technologies facilitates positive knowledge exchanges and through positive spillovers firms in the same industry benefit from a reduced spatial distance between them. The lesson is that sectoral distance and geographic distance matter since they facilitate the absorption of knowledge. Spatial agglomeration also affects the efficacy of foreign direct investment on the economy. The policy implication is that a comprehensive and coordinated industrial policy in the Mediterranean may deliver high levels of efficiency and boost productivity and innovation.

Socio-economic imbalances, demographic pressures and a stagnant economy in most of the Mediterranean countries are the leading cause of high employment rates, particularly among young people (Chapter 6). Hence, although labour market policies on their own cannot be a solution to unemployment, the design of efficient labour policies is the first step governments can take to reduce unemployment. The next two chapters analyze different types of labour market policies: whereas Chapter 6 studies the nature and efficacy of active labour market policies (ALMPs), Chapter 7 analyzes employment protection legislation (EPL) and unemployment insurance (UI). In recent years, Southern Mediterranean countries have effectively introduced, designed and executed a number of ALMPs under the same rules as most EU countries to improve workers' employability. In these countries, often a wide range of different institutions and organizations, such as ministries and agencies, non-governmental organizations (NGOs) or even the private sector, have the responsibility to design and implement ALMPs. This complex governance, combined with lack of funding, may explain why ALMPs have not been properly executed or monitored. That said, there are no holistic solutions to tackling the severe challenge of unemployment, especially among youngsters. The first important step towards a higher level of youth employment across borders would be regional cooperation at the Euro-Mediterranean level.

After careful analysis of ALMPs implemented in the Mediterranean countries in recent years, Chapter 7 studies the nature of EPL and UI. EPL and UI are policy tools through which governments attempt to provide a supporting income to workers moving from one job to another. These policy instruments focus on different objectives of workers' protection and have their own features and limits. Their objectives sometimes overlap, but they are not substitutes. More specifically, UI is worker oriented and provides periodical benefits for a limited fixed duration, whereas severance payment (EPL) schemes are job oriented and provide a lump sum payment based on employers' liability. Since severance payment depends on the individual firm, in practice, it may be not delivered to workers. In general, South-Eastern Mediterranean countries, like other developing countries, show higher levels of EPL and lower levels of UI in comparison to EU-Mediterranean countries, although the latter have reduced labour market rigidities since the Great Recession. In line with other studies, Chapter 7 points out that workers' protection may not be appropriate for most developing economies since it merely covers the small formal sector, given that the share of the informal economy and the level of self-employment in these countries may be extremely large. Ultimately, lack of enforcement offers little worker protection even in the formal sector in almost all Southern

Mediterranean countries while regional disparities are such that, in these countries, it is impossible to implement a universal institutional design to protect workers. Results and data provided in Chapter 7 lay the ground for future analysis of the effect of labour institutions on economic performance.

Chapter 8 attempts to explain migrations and changes in labour markets by moving away from economic factors and concentrating on the effects of climate and environment changes. Increasing flows of forced migration are a response to sudden climate hazards. In practice, climate change is likely to lead to sea-level rise and to exacerbate aridity in the south Mediterranean region as temperatures increase, affecting the potential to grow food and creating a potential flow of environmental migrants. People tend to migrate from more vulnerable to less vulnerable countries, confirming that migration can be an effective adaptation strategy to environmental risks. It should be pointed out, however, that exposure to climate and environmental stress does not necessarily mean that those under such stress would necessarily migrate. It is often the combined effect of climate change and socio-economic stress that causes people to migrate. Supporting adaptive capacity in its broadest meaning is a valuable anthropic response to the challenges of climate change in the Mediterranean region.

A further important issue that needs to be analyzed in greater depth is the impact of migration on the socio-economic systems of the countries of origin and destination. The next chapters pursue this objective. In particular, Chapter 9 studies the possible effects of migration on the economic growth of the country of origin and analyses the potential benefits and damage of (highly) qualified migration in the destination country. The chapter shows that, in Mediterranean countries, migration generally favours the growth of exports in the country of origin, whereas skilled migration favours the development of products with a higher technological content. As a result, although skilled emigration reduces the level of human capital, it also favours the production of goods with higher technological content and sustains the employment of more skilled workers, making a virtuous circle of development possible. These arguments provide the basis to reassess the impact of skilled migration, the so-called brain drain. Migration seems to be less harmful to the country of origin, since it is likely to trigger production and the trade of goods with higher technological content, thereby favouring growth and skilled employment. In other words, it is a process that potentially leads to a brain gain. In general, Chapter 9 shows that, in the case of the Mediterranean countries, skilled migrants can positively affect the high-quality goods trade. This, in turn, contributes positively to the ongoing debate on 'skilled migrations' whose benefits are known in terms of larger remittances, higher propensity to invest in their homeland, increased human capital and important contacts for development of their country.

In contrast, Chapter 10 explores the impact of migrations on destination countries, typically the Northern Mediterranean EU countries. In the second half of the 1990s and the early years of the new millennium, the Northern

Mediterranean countries (Italy, Spain, Portugal and Greece) became the main European pole of attraction for international migratory flows. Despite the general perception, the European Commission estimates that these flows of migration have remained stable in recent decades at around 5 million per year. The composition of migration, however, has changed profoundly: the number of refugees and asylum seekers has increased, as has the number of skilled migrants. The increase in the share of skilled labour raises once again the debate on the consequences of the brain drain. It is often argued that the migration of skilled labour reduces human capital in the country of origin and has a negative impact on productivity and growth. Moreover, education is a very costly investment which is lost whenever skilled workers move somewhere else. However, skilled migration may have a positive impact on the destination country for contrasting reasons. In recent years there has been extensive discussion on the effects of skilled migration; the debate is ongoing but many questions remain open. One of these is the effect of migration on trade. Chapter 10 argues that by influencing the demand for goods with a high technological content, skilled migration favours the trade in these goods between origin and destination countries. Hence skilled migration may positively impact the production of goods with high technological content and boost growth in both countries. The evidence shows that this is particularly true in the Mediterranean.

The last chapter of the book, Chapter 11, attempts to outline the future of Mediterranean migrations. In recent years, the European Union has dealt with the 'migration problem' mainly by focusing on 'security issues' (forgetting the economic role of migrants), and the general perception is that the EU will in future build only on the idea of a 'countercyclical labour force supply' (temporary workers crossing back and forth adjusting to the labour supply). Indeed, the framework of the *European Agenda for the Integration of Third Country Nationals* mainly focuses on problems related to the labour force. The most pressing challenges to managing the problem are the following: (a) the low employment levels of migrants (especially of migrant women); (b) the rising unemployment of migrants and the high levels of 'over-qualification'; and (3) the increasing risks of social exclusion, the gaps in educational achievement and public concerns with the lack of integration of migrants. Moreover, the design of migration policies to tackle such issues has been entrusted to local administrations and not to Community legislation. Yet migrations are typically a response to economic imbalances and Chapter 11 highlights the most pressurizing divergences in the Mediterranean countries. The baseline idea is that the 'migration problem' needs a unified solution and a new Euro-Mediterranean partnership which should emerge from the awareness that promoting the development of 'different level economies' requires a real multilateral approach, a shared commitment to manage all common economic problems (starting from migration) and a structured investment plan. In addition, all these policy suggestions call for new forms of economic cooperation in the Mediterranean based on country-specific development objectives.

Chapter 1

Migrating in the global vacuum

How globalization has securitized regional market migration flows

Paolo Quercia

Introduction: avoiding 'how we lost the Mediterranean?' as a future scenario

There is a tendency among international and geopolitical scholars to cyclically underestimate the challenges and structural transformations occurring under their eyes and to explain these cognitive failures by recurring to nostalgic narratives of 'why we lost' something. We have seen such an approach several times in recent decades where the 'lost' object, from time to time, was represented by the Balkans, or Turkey, or Russia, or China and so on. This tendency of being geopolitically short-sighted and then geopolitically regretful is clearly an aspect of the present times, in which the West has visibly lost the leadership of world affairs, or governance as it is mostly called nowadays.

It will come as no surprise if, in a few years' time, we will see books and conferences dedicated to weeping over the topic of 'how we lost the Mediterranean' constructing a regretful narrative on why Mediterranean political and economic integration has been abandoned and the sea and its shores have been sealed to insulate the States from the negative outcomes of a regional system lurched out of control. Almost a decade has passed since the Mediterranean geopolitical region experienced an unprecedented level of disruption and destabilization, both within and beyond the borders of the coastal states. The vulnerabilities of many Mediterranean societies and economies have been exacerbated by the profound changes in the international system and in international relations, whose character, praxis and grammar has been departing more than substantially from the old post-war system.

The transformation of international relations is a worldwide phenomenon, but in a unique region like the Mediterranean, this has resulted in the rise of an exceptional multilevel set of challenges, absorbing instability and insecurity from many sub-regions of its 2.5 million square kilometres. Historically, one of the functions of the Mediterranean has been to absorb the geopolitical shocks from its sub-regions, retarding and attenuating its effects on the whole system. In the last 20 years, and especially in the last decade, the shocks have intensified in number, severity and frequency especially since many statehoods weakened or failed in Africa, Asia and the Middle East. No other world space, no other intercontinental sea is facing so many interconnected challenges and confronting such a variety of instability and threats. Threats that are concentrating and incubating in this fragile 'Sea between lands', posing a new set of challenges and asymmetric risks to the coastal states.

Paradoxically, this process of de-structuring of the Mediterranean geopolitical space was clearly evident a decade ago, in the very same year when the Euro-Mediterranean Union was launched, on 13 July, 2018. Since its inception in Paris ten years ago, many things have changed for the worse in the Mediterranean, to the point that the Declaration of Barcelona – another diplomatic document signed 20 years ago and full of promises of stability, security, peace and prosperity for the whole of the Euro-Mediterranean space – appears a very distant dream of a geopolitical age long past.

Political involution, the rise of insecurity over stability and the decline of many ideals of social and economic progress not only has been a feature of the southern shore of the Mediterranean but also has affected the more affluent, better-off northern shores. The same European Union, once proud and superior in its material and moral achievements, has started to shake under internal and external pressures, exacerbated by its incapacity to respond to the collapse of the security environment in its proximity and for the difficulties of its economic model. The economic and social collapse of Greece, probably the most Mediterranean country of the Union, is a clear case in point. The EU can hardly today be called 'prosperous, secure and free', as was proudly announced in 2003 in Solana's European Security Strategy and a huge number of internal and external crises are placing at risk the very social and political fabric of the Union.

The transformation of Mediterranean geopolitical space: the key question of collapsing statehoods and the mutating nature of migration flows

The long-term effects of globalization on weak and fragile statehoods, the reduction of State Development Aid and the retreat of the great powers – who had supported and sustained for decades dozens of inefficient and ineffective governments and leadership – have transformed the Euro-Mediterranean space into a new de-structured environment. The imbalances in statehood, democracy and economic development have become today a problem of systemic stability and sustainability. Dramatic gaps in primary economic and social needs have increased the likelihood of internal conflict or external intervention in many countries of the enlarged Mediterranean. In the last decade, no region of the Southern or South-Eastern Mediterranean has been spared by turmoil, revolts, conflicts and unrest: from the Maghreb (Libya and Tunisia) to the Mashreq (Egypt and Syria), to the Black Sea (Ukraine and Georgia), up to the countries of the enlarged Mediterranean, like Somalia and Yemen. Those countries that were spared the most acute turbulence were unable to avoid the collateral spillovers, like refugee flows and many other negative effects. The Mediterranean space has been capsuled by a great Mediterranean region of crisis whose borderless territories are generating and amplifying an extremely wide-ranging set of security threats and challenges, most of which are of a non-military but asymmetric nature.

In this context, the geopolitical environment of the Southern and Eastern Mediterranean has dramatically deteriorated, to the point that several traditional transnational regional problems (e.g. smuggling and trafficking, radical pan-Islamism, weakening of statecraft and sovereignty, inadequate border control and rule of law) have transformed their local nature, growing in magnitude, deteriorating in quality and intensifying in their geographic outreach.

At the heart of this process of deterioration of the geopolitical environment around the Mediterranean and the rise in asymmetric and hybrid actors (and threats), there is the process of the progressive de-structuring of a growing number of states of the Northern Mediterranean and sub-Saharan Africa (Mühlberger 2015) and the rise of private criminal cartels built on tribal loyalty and sometimes on radical religious identities (a process that has been called jihadi-gangsterism, see among others Aall and Crocker 2017). The magnitude and consequences of this process of deconstructing the State in Africa and reconstructing the spoiled sovereignty on a non-state basis has been clearly underestimated and their negative effects have been miscalculated by European and Western governments, analysts and scholars. Very often, the weakening of the old authoritarian post-colonial regimes and of the old state structures in Northern and sub-Saharan Africa has been welcomed and actively promoted as a stage of a process of modernization and development and as a sign of the inevitable route of regime and social change towards more democratic, liberal-minded and inclusive models. This has been mostly the case, for example, of the various movements that have shaken the political map of the Southern Mediterranean countries during and after 2011 and that have been popularly referred to as the Arab Spring.

The migration crisis is often overestimated as regards its impact on internal security and social cohesion of the receiving countries, but at the same time, it is underestimated for the long-term effect on international security and regional stability.

From a Mediterranean point of view, we should focus on the great connection between the new transcontinental migration flows across the Mediterranean and the collapse of statehood in Africa: two aspects that cannot be separated, and in this hybrid nature of migration lies the new nexus between migrations and security. It is quite evident that the integration of failed and failing states in different continents is a new geopolitical driver that has deeply transformed the very old migration phenomena across the Mediterranean; more than economic poverty, underdevelopment or political repression, it is the collapse of statehood in the Sahel–Maghreb continuum that has changed substantially the legal and security background where the old migrations were taking place. The main consequence of this systemic transformation is that we should emancipate from looking to migratory phenomena only with the old economic-humanitarian approach and we should frame it in a broader political-strategic conceptual vision. For this outlook to be balanced, there is a need to discuss how to include in it the concept of security. We define this new standpoint as the 'question of international migration security', to stress the need to upgrade migration studies, to include the relation between the multiple levels of infra- and inter-State security. This is a conceptual shift necessary to understand and govern the new phenomenon of transnational mass migration to Europe: a process that prominent European scholars, like the recently departed Schwarz (2017), have labelled as '*Die neue Völkerwanderung nach Europa*' to stress the different nature of the present migration crisis *vis-à-vis* the old migration movements.

It is important to stress that this growing, awkward, relation between security and migration is not a structural one but a contingent one, since it is the result of a unique geopolitical environment characterized by the overlapping of two distinct crises: the global migration crisis and the regional security crisis. Moreover, these external crises have to be confronted with the internal political and economic-financial crisis of the European Union. The convergence of these four crises is shaping a completely new scenario which should be addressed with new conceptual and political instruments: short-sighted management of these four processes and their interconnections will inevitably result in the considerable risk of a fatal blow to the entire European political project.

The 'new' relation between migration and security is not a connection of the two concepts *per se* but it derives from three fundamental attributes of the new migrations occurring in the current Euro-Mediterranean scenario: magnitude, quality and speed. Increasing magnitude, decreasing quality and escalating speed have transformed the grassroots migration phenomena into something different, whose real nature is substantially unknown. Moreover, to add problems to problems, the security nexus is further strengthened by the fact that the migration flows heading towards Europe are intersecting a number of regional and local security crises around the Mediterranean that have contributed to change the rules of the mass movement of people across Africa.

The nature of the many security crises in Africa is increasingly of an intra-state nature (Heidelberg Institute for International Conflict Research 2017) and their rise in number has been facilitated by the emergence and consolidation of old and new non-state actors. Such actors have taken over ample peripheral spaces with weak or no sovereignty, crafting new and alternative forms of territorial governance (Cerny and Prichard 2017) that are transnational in their nature. We call this 'transnational networks of sovereignty' that are cooperating to roll back the territorial control of centralized governments, creating neo-feudal zones of local ownership with global outreach. These networks of non-state actors are disconnected by the government and state-based international system and are interacting disrespectfully of their nature (criminal, religious, ethnic, ideological, terrorist, tribal, business, irredentist/insurgent) in pragmatic cooperation aiming to achieve a simple goal: make profits through the erosion of the residual control of central governments over territory, population and resources. A process that triggers, in a domino effect, further deterioration of the regional security, affecting deeply the geopolitics of the Mediterranean and resulting potentially detrimental for North–South relations.

It is important to understand that even if mass migration towards Europe is occurring in a growing geopolitical vacuum, this vacuum is not neutral but determines the quality and quantity of the migration flows, favouring illegal and criminalized migrations versus the legal ones. The way people migrate has a transformative effect on the character and nature of the phenomena. This means that in today's Euro-Mediterranean environment, it is mostly inappropriate to resume the 20-year-old debate on possible connections between security and migration. Quite the reverse, today's issue is to acknowledge that migrations that occur across insecure and lawless areas inevitably have a security nexus and may become, therefore, an international and internal security challenge. The old debate on the security nexus, therefore, should be updated to the new geopolitical framework that has emerged in the last 20 years and which is radically changing the connotations and the fundamentals of migration flows, mass movement of populations and even relations among states.

There is, therefore, an evident need for scholars and experts in international relations to update the old narratives and ideological positions pro- or anti-migrations as well as the functionalist approaches to this phenomenon, returning to a more political vision of contemporary international relations and, with it, of migration policies. More specifically, scholars need to increase their efforts to bridge the gaps between two different approaches to migration: the economic-humanitarian approach and the political-strategic one. Only a joint approach that connects human security with state security is useful for a political understanding of the reality and for shaping an effective response to the negative effects of global migrations: a response that must balance solidarity, integration, rule of law and human security as well social and state security of the receiving countries.

A sea sinking in the sand: great migrations in the great vacuum

One of the factors that is progressively transforming the migratory crisis into a crisis of European security is the fact that these human flows pass through a series of ungoverned but interconnected areas extending for more than 2,000 kilometres from the external borders of the European Union. The crossing of this region has become, in our opinion, a hallmark of the post-statual migration flows after 2011, singling them out as different social and historical phenomena in a way that they can hardly be associated with the traditional migration processes (like the intra-European migrations or the migration from Europe to Northern and Southern America or even with the traditional inter-Mediterranean flow of workers and *Gastarbeiter*).

The vacuum factor is emerging as a game changer of many socio-political phenomena, including migrations. This geopolitical vacuum edging into the Central Mediterranean has created several vulnerabilities in the social and economic exchanges and integration between the two shores of the Mediterranean, and intra-Mediterranean human migration has been absorbed into the more global – and less circular – transcontinental movements of peoples. With the destruction of Libya and the failing of many other States around it, ungoverned territories have merged, with the vertical fusion of three different horizontal geopolitical regions: the Sahel/Sahara strip, the Cyrenaic-Tripolitan Libyan coastal strip (including Libyan territorial waters) and Mediterranean international waters.

This immense politically and geographically diverse portion of the African continent is being integrated by new drivers unleashed in African post-statual globalization, transforming it into a gigantic geopolitical cone that channels the negative externalities produced by failing statehood in Africa into the Central Mediterranean towards the European Union magnet.

This fusion-region is a huge and undefined space, with blurred contours, that starts at the southern borders of Algeria, Libya and Egypt and at the northern ones of Mali, Niger, Chad and Sudan. The Central Mediterranean/Horn of Africa corridor, for example, is changing the historical and natural borders of the Mediterranean, challenging most of the old integration strategies and policies.

This expanding African vacuum is becoming similar to maritime spaces: vast areas with no sovereignty and low or no governance, centered on the Sahel Region,[1] whose fragility has been greatly shaken by the collapse of the Libyan state following the civil war, and gravitating towards the international waters of the Central Mediterranean. And the more the statehood is eroded the greater are the similarities between maritime spaces and the Sahel. A sea of sand where global interconnections are transforming traditional anarchy, freedom and tribal sovereignty, often the only form of organized control over territory, into global gangsterism.

In the 2,000 kilometres that separate Agadez in Niger (or Gao in Mali, or Dongala in Sudan) from Lampedusa, there are no structured government centres capable of exercising the monopoly of the use of force or projecting their power to enforce laws, control borders or deliver public goods. This vast territory is surviving in a pre-modern but globalized condition, in which nomadic or semi-nomadic tribes, traditionally engaged in small border smuggling of cigarettes, petrol, weapons and drugs, have become powerful international actors that are operating different kinds of illegal transnational flows.

These tribes and other non-state actors are involved in a complex power-sharing game with the central governments for legitimacy, resources, control over territory and delivery of basic public goods in marginal areas. The economics of the migration movements and the immense cash flow that it produces in poor and underdeveloped areas have greatly empowered these non-state actors; although stateless, unrecognized and poorly equipped they gained access and capacity of control of the European Union borders, demonstrating their ability to guarantee the mass transfer of millions of migrants from sub-Saharan Africa, Asia and the Middle East into the European Union, often in violation of national and international laws and obliging EU member states to indiscriminately open their borders. It is clearly a situation with few or no historical precedents, which European governments have long underestimated and overlooked.

The Mediterranean and the growing anarchy of international waters

The anarchy of the Sahara and much of the Sahel is putting under extraordinary pressure the relative disorder of international waters that have traditionally enjoyed a certain level of international anarchy, the opposite side of the coin to freedom of navigation, with no specific authority with the capacity to exercise effective forms of control and policing.[2] Historically, the precarious stability of large ungoverned spaces such as international waters was largely mitigated by the assumption that this space was enclosed, with very few exceptions, by coastlines and territorial waters controlled by sovereign states, in a way that the lawless of the seas was substantially an exception to the principle of statehood and every phenomenon that was taking place in the high waters was happening in this anarchic dimension only temporarily, until being inevitably brought under territorial forms of government.[3] The situation has gradually changed with the erosion of sovereignty and failed states, the increase in economic and technological capacity of private actors and the emergence of transnational organized crime that has found in international waters one of the most powerful factors of expansion of their activities. Criminal cartels are able to access and operate in international waters through failed states or by corrupting weak states nominally holders of maritime sovereignty, obtaining easy access to the benefits of international waters and its 'privileges' that the states originally granted only for themselves. The growing lawlessness of international waters[4] is another crucial element in understanding the new dimension of migration in the Mediterranean.

Final remarks: the concept of migration security

Migration security is a new approach to migration studies that focuses on studying the different security dimensions of illegal migration flows. It can be differentiated in three different and autonomous branches:

- the **level of internal security** of the states of arrival of illegal migration flows. This is, the level of homeland security or – using an increasingly shrunken view of security in vogue today – of so-called urban security. It includes, among others, issues of growing importance connected to integration process and its possible multiple failures: political or religious radicalization of diasporas; ethno-criminality; the rise of xenophobic or racist movements; ethnic, religious or political conflict among different diaspora groups; the manipulation of diasporas by countries of origin for political or security reasons.

- the level of **security of flows** in the transit countries and in the non-governed areas crossed on the way to the Mediterranean. This level deals mostly with the topic of human security of migrants, fighting against the criminalization of the transit, human trafficking and smuggling, slavery, forced labour, kidnapping for ransom, organ trafficking, prostitution and other forms of abuses and exploitation against migrants.

- the level of **security/insecurity in the countries of origin**. This level deals with the study of the links between migration and conflicts and other causes of instability and insecurity that may contribute to originate the flows. The functioning, size, management, security and socio-economic sustainability of refugee camps in conflict and neighbouring areas and the role played by NGOs and international organizations is also part of this level.

The enormous flow of illegal migrations to Europe has increasingly led to the vertical integration of these three dimensions of migratory security, adding to them the level of transnational interconnections, almost an exclusive domain of criminal organizations. The challenge posed by organized crime is an age-old phenomenon but the challenge that transnational crime brings to the sovereignty of states today is largely a new challenge, especially when it overlaps with the risks of uncontrolled demographic pressures. This is a challenge which, if not managed and contained, becomes a threat to the very existence of many states that, without the power to control access to their territory, lose their legitimacy and motivation to exist.

The uncontrolled, illegal, massive and continuous access to a state's territory of foreign citizens breaches that exclusive legal relationship that exists between state, people and territory and that lies at the base of the constitutional legitimacy and order of every sovereign State, and that is expressed through the mechanism of citizenship. This problem is very clear to international organizations dealing with migration issues, such as the International Organization for Migration, which reiterates that illegal immigration poses a challenge to state authority when it involves the mobilization of vast economic resources that erode ability to govern and represent effective threats to national sovereignty.

The perception of migratory security changes from country to country, but it is certainly a multilateral issue of increasing complexity. What is certain is that no state can face it alone. The control of contemporary migratory phenomena and the process of making them reasonably secure means that creating 'secure migration processes' both for human beings and for states should be a common goal of all European and Mediterranean countries. In the current international context, for a number of reasons, effective control of borders can no longer be achieved by a single country. In this field, the European Union has been a pioneer in harmonizing its external borders and even created a body of European border guards and a single visa policy. The migration crisis and European external security have put this construction in danger and today discussing migration security – or how to organize sustainable, secure and safe migrations to Europe – among European countries has become a strategic necessity.

It is evident that the European migration crisis is not simply a humanitarian emergence but probably the most severe geopolitical challenge to European security and stability and one of the main geopolitical issues of the 21st century. The magnitude of the phenomenon makes it not only an issue of humanitarian security and State security, but its importance reaches the core of international relations as well as relations between civilizations and religions.

The need to create the environment for safe and secure migrations both for human beings and states is a common goal across the Mediterranean. The sooner this normal situation is restored in the Euro-Mediterranean space, the easier it will be to develop new agreements for circular migration among the countries of the region, as was envisaged in the EU summit of La Valletta of November 2015 and in the Conclusion of the European Council of the same year.

Notes

1 A transition zone in progressive Saharization that etymologically means 'sea, coastline'.
2 The almost anarchic nature of the high seas, a fundamental condition for avoiding abuses of sovereignty that could endanger the cardinal principle of freedom of the seas and the principle of perfect equality and complete independence of all States, is well known.
3 Since life at sea is not possible, the ungoverned space of the international waters was, in fact, a temporary privilege that the States allowed each other, creating a global common from which everyone benefits through traffic, while the negative externalities where minimalized by the States' territorial waters responsibility.
4 The topic was widely studied after 9/11 by many scholars and analysts and investigated by journalists, especially during the surge of maritime piracy in the Horn of Africa between 2008 and 2013. A good overview of the problem is in Langewiesche W., 'Anarchy at Sea', *The Atlantic*, September 2003.

References

Aall, P.R., and Crocker, C.A., 2017. *The Fabric of Peace in Africa, Looking Beyond the State.* Waterloo: Center for International Governance Innovation.
Cerny, P.G., and Prichard, A., 2017. The New Anarchy: Globalisation and Fragmentation in World Politics. *Journal of International Political Theory*, 13 (3), 378–394.
Heidelberg Institute for International Conflict Research, 2017. *Conflict Barometer 2017.* Heidelberg: Heidelberg Institute for International Conflict Research.
Langewiesche, W., 2003. Anarchy at Sea. *The Atlantic*.
Mühlberger, W., 2015. *The State of Arab Statehood. Reflections on Failure, Resilience and Collapse.* European Institute of the Mediterranean.
Schwarz, H.P., 2017. *Die neue Völkerwanderung nach Europa. Über den Verlust politischer Kontrolle und moralischer Gewissheiten.* München: Deutsche Verlags-Anstalt. The concept of Völkerwanderung can be translated as 'mass movement of peoples'.

Chapter 2

The Euro-Mediterranean regional and sub-regional integration

The role of the EU in the Moroccan path of regional integration

Fátima Fernández, Saïd Chahi and Dolores Riveiro

Introduction

Regional integration has persistently been outlined as one of the main ambitions of Euro-Mediterranean policies over the last two decades. According to the European Commission:

> Regional integration is the process of overcoming barriers that divide neighbouring countries, by common accord, and of jointly managing shared resources and assets. Essentially, it is a process by which groups of countries liberalise trade, creating a common market for goods, people, capital and services.[1]

When bringing such a debate to the Mediterranean area, diagnoses about regional integration take 1995 as a turning point, and the ambitions asserted in the Barcelona Declaration as a measure for its achievements. From this perspective, the Barcelona Process appears as a generous European attempt to overcome structural gaps in the Mediterranean Basin by promoting development and mutual understanding. To a certain extent, the conception of the Euro-Mediterranean project as a benevolent proposal enacted by an international 'force for good' (Barbé and Johansson-Nogués 2008; Whitman 2011) exempts the EU from any responsibility or blame regarding the unsuccessful goals of what is seen as a facultative choice to raise prosperity beyond its borders.[2]

Formally, the initiative behind Euro-Mediterranean integration has been held by the European Community as a strategy to encourage economic development, security and stability of the whole area. As stated in the Barcelona Declaration, the ultimate ambition of economic and financial cooperation was to create 'an area of shared prosperity' by accelerating sustainable socio-economic development, improving the living conditions of their populations and encouraging regional cooperation and integration.[3] With such objectives on paper, European foreign policies have gained renewed impetus since the 1990s, explicitly assuming the relevance of Maghreb to the European project.[4]

However, a historical insight into this matter reveals that the underlying reasons of this initiative respond to a foreign policy approach that is rooted in the economic and political relations established during the colonial period. In this regard, this work critically reviews the process of Euro-Mediterranean integration focussing on Maghreb countries, with particular attention to the case of Morocco. By putting into question conventional views of North–South asymmetries as neutral facts stimulating the European will to improve conviviality, we identify a multilayered bargain between private and public actors on both shores around domains of mutual interest and within a shared quest for legitimacy. To this extent, we argue that current imbalances are also to be regarded as an outcome of European choices over time.

Many authors link the Euro-Mediterranean shift of the European Economic Community (EEC) within the framework of its southward enlargement in the 1980s and its consequences for the European markets (Guth and Aeikens 1980; El-Malki 2000; Sanchez 2003; Darbot-Trupiano 2007). True, but not new. Correlation between European expansion and reforms in EU's strategies towards the Mediterranean has been a constant pattern since the 1960s. That being so, it is hardly surprising that such changes fit better with intra-European wavering challenges than with the official aim to achieve regional integration.

Be that as it may, more than 20 years after the Barcelona turning point, there is wide consensus on the fact that the Euro-Mediterranean area cannot be defined as an integrated region.[5] Seen from the Southern shore, the regional dimension is still harder to appraise. The North–South flows that prevail in the whole area, with particular intensity in the Maghreb, are mostly built on a set of long-standing bilateral economic relations that follow a structure of hubs-and-spokes (De Ville and Reynaert 2010). Besides, the successive initiatives implemented since the 1980s with a myriad of Southern partners are far from having improved the situation. The failure of these projects has boosted research on the welfare losses of unachieved integration, with a strong accent on the costs of non–Maghreb (Bchir et al. 2006; Achy 2007). Nonetheless, in comparison, limited efforts have been made so far to investigate the root causes of non-integration (World Bank, 2006; African Development Bank, 2012, UNECA, 2013).

Taking into account the intricate relationship between economic integration and foreign policy affairs, this chapter aims to analyze the interplay among the different frameworks that coexist in this context through the particular case of Morocco. Since its independence, Morocco has experimented with different options of regional integration in all the possible directions allowed by its geopolitical and economic position. Nonetheless, the Moroccan economy cannot be said to be truly integrated with any of the regions in question (Aït Amara 1995; Martínez 2008; WB 2010; Zouiri 2010; Stora 2011; Biad 2013; Bichara 2013).

Our findings show that the Moroccan path of international integration is intimately linked to the process of construction of the European Union, which largely influenced its decisions and outcomes regarding North–South and South–South projects. With an actor-centred approach that takes into account the dialectic between internal and external affairs, as well as the relationship between public and private interests, it explains how independent Morocco followed a path of 'peripheral reconnection' to Europe whereby its international exchanges and geopolitical strategies were progressively installed into the Mediterranean orbit of the Community. For greater clarity, the Moroccan path of regional integration is explained in three periods whose central disruptions are defined by the Moroccan debt crisis in the 1980s and by the outset of the Barcelona Process a few years after the sanction of the Arab Maghreb Union (AMU; 1989).

Notwithstanding, before any further consideration, it is essential to clarify that the lack of integration in the Mediterranean area does not mean that results have not been achieved. Indeed, the evolution of Euromed relations since the very Treaty of Rome (1957) shows a number of outcomes often attributed to processes of economic integration, such as those regarding trade, foreign direct investment (FDI) or tariff and non-tariff barriers among participating countries. In the same vein, it should not be implied that low levels of regional integration mean a lack of economic relations. As an example, although Moroccan integration within the Euro-Mediterranean area cannot be said to have been successful, its exchanges within the area account for around 60% of its total trade. However, the weight of the EU on such flows remains similar to the figures of 1960, a time when no Association Agreement existed between both partners. Besides, France and Spain, its former *métropoles*, capture the vast majority of the flows.

In this regard, the outcomes of Moroccan regional choices suggest that a sort of geopolitical dilemma binds economic relations in the Mediterranean. Whereas choosing the EU as a privileged partner implies accepting its conditions, disregarding its rules of the game might endanger economies whose foreign trade grew up spurred by European demand. Therefore, our research shows that the role of preferential agreements in the continuity of economic relations prior to decolonization is directly related to this state of affairs. In more general terms, these findings suggest that the role of EU affairs on the shape of Euro-Mediterranean relations should be carefully considered when assessing the current level of economic integration among countries in this area (Schimmelfennig 2007).

After this introduction, the chapter is organized as follows. The next section deals with the state of regional integration in the Mediterranean with a focus on its links with the colonial legacy, independence processes and the inception of the EEC. The following section addresses the integration initiatives endorsed by Morocco since independence and within the framework of Euro-Mediterranean relations. The last section summarizes the main conclusions and opens the floor to key points of debate that should be carefully noted when making policy recommendations.

Euro-Mediterranean regional integration: the colonial legacy and the binding nature of North–South imbalances

More than 20 years after the outset of the Barcelona Process, the limited extent of its achievements (De Ville and Reynaert 2010) has not blurred its perception as a major turning point in Mediterranean affairs. Although the Euromed Association was not an unprecedented initiative and would not attain any of its main goals,[6,7] its establishment remains the cornerstone of North–South dialogue and integration in the Mediterranean. In this regard, the most powerful asset of this framework seems to be its ability to prevail over time and reality as a promise of stability and shared prosperity. However, the whole history of the European Union happens to be closely linked to the Mediterranean. Accordingly, the key features defining the current structure of Euro-Mediterranean relations date from long before the 1990s.

The construction of the Common Market ran parallel to a process that could be described as 'economic disintegration' between European countries and their former colonial settlements. The need to remodel the colonial legacy within the new regional framework was especially relevant in the case of France, whose colonial concerns would largely determine the structure and functioning of Euro-Mediterranean relations. Indeed, while decolonization gained momentum within the UN, France would struggle for the maintenance of privileged relations with its Maghreb dominions within the EEC by asserting their historical significance (Calandri 2012). Consequently, the Treaty of Rome (1957) endowed the country with the right to decide unilaterally on its preferential commercial treatment of the former Protectorates of Morocco and Tunisia and recognized Algeria's belonging to the EEC as a French department.[8,9] These provisions granted the continuity of former relations until new circumstances pushed all the actors involved to renegotiate their statuses.

The asymmetric nature of the bargain and geopolitical disruptions in the area engendered a new impasse in the 1960s. On the one hand, the independence of Algeria,[10] UK's demand for accession and the reinforcement of integration through the Common Agricultural Policy (CAP) and the Common External Tariff (CET) imposed the renegotiation of Euro-Maghreb relations.[11] This process would culminate in the signature of two separate Association Agreements with Morocco and Tunisia in 1969 while the status of Algeria remained unsolved. On the other hand, a variety of alliances with other Mediterranean countries would trigger a heterogeneous mixture of agreements around EEC borders.[12] By the beginning of the 1970s, four different types of agreements coexisted in Euro-Mediterranean relations with no apparent underlying strategy.[13] To solve this situation, the EEC designed the Global Mediterranean Policy (GMP) to give coherence and a more political profile to its relations with Third Mediterranean countries. The trade and cooperation agreements that followed this policy consolidated a hub-and-spokes scheme (Escribano

2006) based on North–South agreements whose bilateralism consisted of a 'one region–one country' imbalance.[14]

The third enlargement of the EEC evidenced once again the contingent nature of the structuring mechanisms of Euro-Mediterranean policies, which varied according to fluctuating Northern interests. After the inclusion of Greece, Portugal and Spain in the CAP, the EEC became a surplus market in most of the agricultural goods traded by its neighbours (Martin 1988). Besides, bilateral fisheries agreements between Spain and Morocco inherited from the colonial period (Holgado and Ostos 2002) were transferred into the EEC framework. Thus, the reinforcement of self-sufficiency and the decline of the *Trente Glorieuses* called again for a new approach to Mediterranean foreign affairs. To warrant the mastering of sensitive flows of goods and people while preserving the upper hand in Mediterranean matters, subsequent European policy instruments would focus on strategic dialogue, standards regulation, non-tariff barriers and a pragmatic use of financial cooperation. Accordingly, the Dialogue 5 + 5 European Council in Lisbon (1992) reaffirmed the importance of Euro-Mediterranean relations in general and, in particular, the essential role of the Maghreb for the ambitious project of the European Union.[15] On this basis, the Renovated Mediterranean Policy was provided with a greater budget to finance local development and to support Structural Adjustment Plans in host countries, but no significant progress in Euro-Mediterranean integration occurred.

The binding nature of regional imbalances ably explains the comprehensive breadth of the European approach since the Barcelona Declaration (1995). Security and economic concerns in Southern countries compelled Northern actors to react to protect their economic interests and avert any risk of expansion. Despite the widening scope of Association Agreements,[16] the idea of regionalism was progressively diverted from quantitative to qualitative issues. The degree of adaptation to the *acquis communautaire* became the benchmark of Mediterranean integration while long-lasting demands on labour mobility and agricultural trade were systematically postponed.

Triggered by regional expansion, intra-European hegemonic quarrels and growing contradictions between Membership and Partnership have overfilled since 2004 the Mediterranean spaghetti bowl.[17] The ENP, originally addressing the new eastern borders of the EU and applied then to the south due to French insistence, would not smooth either the vertical or the core-periphery nature of the European approach in the Mediterranean. Its strategy to turn bilateral relations into a multilateral framework relied on the expansion of the *acquis communautaire* to eventually establish a Pan-Euro-Mediterranean system of rules of origin (RoO). In 2008, the French proposal of the Union for the Mediterranean (UfM) sought to apply a more pragmatic strategy that restricted the management of Mediterranean affairs to Mediterranean countries by boosting the role of key stakeholders in the area.[18] The failure to establish a distinct sub-region and the eventual enactment of a further Mediterranean framework comprising all the Members of the EU summarizes well the uncertain margins of the region.

By placing firms at the heart of the project, the UfM aimed to boost cooperation in sectors like energy, business development, transport and the environment. Focussing on micro-economic integration, it appeared as a forum gathering private initiative and public decision-makers whose co-presidency was shared between a Northern and a Southern partner. However, economic crisis further contributed to the hesitant start of a project whose geographical limits, core missions and sources of financing were difficult to grasp. Thus, despite continuous advocacy of friendship and shared prosperity, the shape and functioning of the ENP and the UfM owe more to intra-European dialectic than to cross-border dialogue with Southern and Eastern neighbours. The quest for equity regarding the geopolitical weight of Member countries scattered Southern specificities all along the borders of the continental area. Hence, rather than a Euro-Mediterranean framework, there is a European framework around the Mediterranean. As a consequence, only specific sectors in specific countries manage to match with the terms of the Euro-Mediterranean region.

Regardless of the outcome, it is worth noting that the whole set of North–South regional frameworks enacted in the Mediterranean Basin since the Treaty of Rome resulted from and contributed to current European hegemony in the area. This assertion does not imply a lack of agency by Southern Mediterranean neighbours. Instead, it aims to place current imbalances within a historical path and a socio-political structure that takes into account the context and terms of regional negotiation. In this vein, the wide variety of initiatives implemented in the area seem to arise from the shared willingness of the various actors on both sides of the Mediterranean to maintain their status quo and to legitimate their position throughout changing circumstances. The case of Morocco illustrates it quite accurately.

The Moroccan path of regional integration: the role of the European Union

On the grounds of their geographical proximity, EU-Moroccan economic relations are far from a recent affair. During the second half of the 19th century, a number of commercial treaties were signed that opened the country to the advance of European capitalism.[19] The main lever of European trade penetration in Morocco was the treaty concluded with England in 1856, whereby European products reached the concession of a 10% ad valorem duty on entry. The growing European economic thrust paved the way for the establishment of a Protectorate in Morocco. At the beginning of the twentieth century, the French colonial administration controlled most of the country while Spanish rule prevailed in the North and the South.

Structural transformations overturned the foundations of the Moroccan socio-economic organization. The French colonial administration favoured the establishment and expansion of dependent capitalism in the agricultural, industrial and mining sectors. Thus, placed in the orbit of the *métropole*, the Moroccan economy evolved according to the needs of the former both concerning production and trade.

After independence, the nature of the relations woven with Europe would not undergo any radical change. European integration would run smoothly over the path of colonial experience, the new terms of cooperation being tailored to its own preferences. Moroccan integration with Europe would then be conceived as a process of peripheral reconnection (Deblock and Regnault 2009). In the aforementioned process, three key phases can be distinguished, each lasting approximately 20 years.

From independence to Moroccanization

The development project promoted by independent Morocco in the early 1960s was designed against a backdrop of confrontations between the partisans of economic disjunction and those defending stronger ties with France (Oualalou 1980). Fuelled by strong nationalist sentiments, it pursued an economic policy of rupture with the colonial legacy, aiming to achieve economic independence and to regain command over the necessary decision mechanisms for autonomous development (El Aoufi 1990).

Two milestones marked this first phase: the 1960–1964 Five-Year Plan and the Moroccanization Act of 2 March 1973. Between the two, the conclusion, in 1969, of an Association Agreement between Morocco and the EEC expressed, on the basis of preferential relations,[20] the willingness of both parties to reinforce their links through geographical and historical factors (Essebbani 2008).

The 1960–1964 Plan, prioritizing the quest for economic empowerment, industrialization and agrarian reform, was abandoned before its completion. The reasons for its failure, often attributed to a financial crisis, owe much to what Oualalou (1980) defined as an 'alliance between the indigenous reactionary forces and representatives of neo-colonial economic and political interests' that favoured foreign control over the national economy. In this regard, 'during the Sixties, French colonial interests in agriculture, mining, trade and industry were not affected' (Oualalou 1980). Under the influence of the World Bank's recommendations, the following Plans of 1965–1967 and 1968–1972 encouraged Moroccan integration into the international market. National economic policy triggered the primacy of phosphate and agricultural exports, the promotion of tourism, the liberalization of foreign trade and the granting of advantages to attract foreign capital (mainly through Investment Codes).

In line with this liberal tendency, Morocco signed an Association Agreement on 31 March 1969 with the EEC to ensure the allocation of its products onto European markets. This five-year agreement had a purely commercial content and enabled the parties to grant each other advantages with a view to creating a Free Trade Area.[21] However, Association with the EEC did not manage either to help diversifying Morocco's foreign trade or to fulfil expectations about export gains. On the contrary, its results confirm

> the maintenance of the geographical concentration of foreign trade, the stagnation of financial resources coming from the exports covered by the agreement, and the fall in the share of Communitarian imports from Morocco compared to those coming from competitor countries.
>
> (Oualalou 1980)

The underlying reasons are to be found in the political will to gradually enlarge the Europe of the Six. The EEC project advanced by the Treaty of Rome gave primacy to the integration of European economies, which did not exclude the quest for European hegemony in the Mediterranean Basin. Accordingly, the nature of the relations established by the EEC with Morocco was limited to trade and tailored to the objectives of the Community project. Besides, Association policies maintained open channels for exploiting the colonial heritage and preserved the prominence of European capitals, namely French, in Morocco.

Coinciding with the first EEC enlargement, Morocco undertook in 1973, when the EEC expanded to nine Member States, both the Moroccanization of many economic activities and the negotiation of a new agreement with Europe to overcome the limits of the 1969 arrangement. The process of recovering the assets held by foreigners during the Protectorate had been in force since 1956, but 'from 1956 to 1973, it remains hampered while foreign presence undergoes hardly any significant modification' (El Aoufi 1990). Paradoxically, the conspicuous influence of foreign capital on the agricultural, mining, industrial, banking and insurance sectors hitherto (Lamodiere 1977) did not prevent a sharp decline in private – namely foreign – investment that would reach even the 1973–1977 Plan. Consequently, the institutional Moroccanization of 1973 intended to enable Moroccan citizens to recover part of the national assets owned by foreigners. The final goal was to spur development through investment and a more equitable redistribution of income. However, its results remained limited. Contrary to expectations, foreign capital retained major interests in the secondary and tertiary sectors, whereas high-level positions in administration and large indigenous capital-owners captured most of the gains on the national side (Berrada 1988). More precisely, the effects of Moroccanization on foreign assets were significant only for small individual capitalists established in Morocco. French groups could sell part of the shares of their subsidiaries to nationals. Henceforth, not only did their financial risks decrease, but also they could benefit from significant liquid resources and secure their presence in Morocco (El Aoufi 1990). As a result, a renewed alliance between foreign and indigenous capital favoured the maintenance of the former *status quo* between Morocco and Europe.

Concerning foreign affairs, bilateral negotiations for a new agreement took place in a European context of economic recession and unemployment. The comprehensive Cooperation Agreement that followed in April 1976 was concluded for an undefined period and dealt simultaneously with commercial, technical, financial and labour aspects. Nevertheless, the primacy accorded to Community goals imposed a restrictive export policy on Morocco. In fact, the future accession of countries in Southern Europe (Greece, Spain and Portugal) and the extension of European concessions to other Mediterranean countries (Israel, Turkey and Egypt) would severely hinder Morocco's export capacities. In short, although the 1976 Agreement is considered more advantageous than its 1969 predecessor, its concept of cooperation lost most of its significance within the framework of an unbalanced relationship where the primacy of European interests prevailed to the detriment of Moroccan priorities.

Certainly, the terms of the commercial, financial and technical cooperation enacted by the agreement denoted the biased nature of Morocco–EEC cooperation. On the one hand, trade provisions were hampered by the mechanisms set by the CAP and by the anti-competitive nature of an ever-growing Community market.[22] On the other, inadequate funding for financial, technical and social cooperation reduced such pillars to sterile assistance from an increasingly watertight Europe. In sum, this pattern of peripheral reconnection did not entail any dramatic disruption in the previous North–South balance of power. Most important, it nourished a path of post-colonial integration based on inequality and dependency, especially at the financial level. The consequences of such a situation would became apparent in the 1980s when a deep debt crisis would wreck the Moroccan economy during its second phase of integration into the EEC (Berrada, 2017).

From the Structural Adjustment Plan (SAP) to the Arab Maghreb Union (AMU)

On the wavelength of the debt crisis that would hit international economic relations in the 1980s, the Moroccan economy would face a period of extreme difficulty that would last almost two decades. The combination of unfavourable conditions during the second half of the 1970s, both internally and externally, was to generate a severe financial crisis that mortgaged the Moroccan economy for more than a decade. At the domestic level, Moroccanization enhanced the rise of a new oligarchy whose access to all economic sectors and stable alliances with foreign capital added up to its preferential access to European markets. Global economic trends, together with the multiplication of Investment Codes, tax incentives and fiscal exemptions, pushed the State budget into chronic deficit deadlocks. At the external level, in the wake of the oil shock, Morocco lived a phosphate shock entailing a four-fold increase in prices in 1974 and 1975. Ephemeral as it was, the sudden growth of Moroccan resources spurred euphoria and its already ambitious Five-Year Plan was revised upwards (El Ktiri and Akesbi 1987). Later on, in a context of growing public deficit aggravated by the reduction in tax revenues and phosphate prices, European recycling of overabundant petrodollars facilitated the massive Moroccan recourse to international credit. The result was a staggering rise in external public debt. The steep rise in external debt during the 1975–1985 decade, as Table 2.1 shows, had a heavy impact on public finances.

Indeed, between 1975 and 1985, the stock of debt increased almost sevenfold, from US$2.37 billion to US$15.80 billion, and the debt ratio nearly four-fold, from 26.61% to over 102.5%. The ensuing deterioration in debt service and the weight of the debt on public finances, which, as Table 2.1 shows, became unbearable from 1979 onwards, reveal the depth of the financial crisis that the Moroccan economy was facing. Its intensity gradually increased with a debt ratio rising from less than 50% in 1979 to more than 102% in 1985.

The technical assistance offered by the financial institutions of Bretton Woods, which had constantly accompanied Moroccan authorities since the abandonment of the 1960–1964 Plan, led to the implementation of a Structural Adjustment Plan in 1983. Based on fiscal austerity measures, it sought to achieve debt control. However, by 1990, public debt had worsened to almost US$23.47 billion and debt servicing alienated one third of the country's foreign exchange earnings (Tlemçani 1991). Debt began to decline steadily from 1992 when a series of long-lasting rescheduling operations officially ceased.

At the peak of the Moroccan crisis, the financial pillar of the 1976 Cooperation Agreement remained more nominal than real. Considering that Moroccan debt was inherently bilateral and concentrated on individual European countries (France, Spain, Germany, Italy), the EEC could have played an active role in Moroccan financial recovery. However, the scant exploitation of initiatives such as debt conversion into investments or the allocation of financial assistance for the creation of joint ventures confirms the limited extent of the European contribution. More specifically, 'the Community's approach to

Table 2.1 Evolution of external debt and its burden, 1975–1985

Year	External debt in billions ($)	Debt service (% of X)	Debt service in billions ($)	External debt (%) GDP
1975	2.37	6.70	0.17	26.61
1976	3.10	10.22	0.23	33.40
1977	5.34	14.52	0.35	44.76
1978	6.61	22.86	0.66	50.10
1979	7.89	26.55	0.97	49.60
1980	9.26	33.34	1.45	49.25
1981	10.20	38.42	1.57	66.75
1982	12.10	45.36	1.72	78.52
1983	12.80	40.27	1.55	77.77
1984	13.70	27.83	1.08	86.97
1985	15.89	34.62	1.43	102.54

Source: Data from IMF

structural adjustment was belated, since it only began to take this aspect into account in its relations with developing countries after the conclusion of the Lomé IV Convention in 1989' (Essebbani 2008). Together with its Maghreb neighbours, Morocco tried during the same year to revive an old project of Maghreb regional integration. Formerly conceived as a project against French colonialism, the idea of Maghreb unity had reached strong popularity in the aftermath of decolonization. However, the differences between post-colonial regimes and the rise of border conflicts would relegate regionalism to a second-ary place. Despite a number of bilateral and trilateral meetings and the signature of around 40 bilateral agreements after 1956 (Santucci 1972), regional goals would decay after Algerian independence to be replaced by long-lasting border disputes.

Sanctioned by the Marrakesh Treaty on 17 February 1989, the AMU sought 30 years later to face both the external enclosure and internal enlargement of the EEC, which was progressively undermining Maghreb commercial interests. Nonetheless, the blatant lack of maturity of intra-Maghreb relations became apparent in 1994, when exchanges between Algeria and Morocco were hampered by the closure of borders between the two countries. At the same time, the new Euro-Mediterranean framework of the EU was beginning to take shape. Con-ceived as the southern border of the Union, the Maghreb region was endowed with a security mission devolved mainly to its three central countries (Morocco, Algeria, Tunisia), contrary to the AMU's South–South vision of a Maghreb region formed by five countries (Mauritania, Morocco, Algeria, Libya and Tunisia).

Since the Barcelona process

As Maghreb ambitions began to fade, *open regionalism* spread all over the Medi-terranean.[23] Conforming with this trend, Morocco deployed during the 1990s an extensive programme of domestic and external measures that would boost its role as a valuable interlocutor in North–South relations (Dkhissi 2015; Akesbi 2017). On the one hand, a vast record of privatizations accompanied the repeal of the 'Moroccanization' Act (1993), the implementation of a new Investment Code (1995) complying with international standards and a number of mon-etary and financial reforms (El Aoufi et al. 2005; Achy 2013; Berrada 2016; El Mataoui 2017; Oubenal and Zeroual 2017). On the other, trade liberalization with the EU continued through the signing of an Association Agreement in 1996 whose main red lines lay on the limits imposed by CAP (Akesbi 2015).

Along with this trend, an effort to diversify its partners and products led the country to sign a number of North–South and South–South bilateral and regional agreements. Concerning bilateral integration, free trade agreements (FTAs) with the United Arab Emirates, Turkey and the United States came into effect between 2003 and 2006.[24] According to Fernandez-Molina (2016), the latter responds to a pattern of triangular games whereby Morocco tries to bal-ance its foreign relations with Northern hegemons, namely the US and the EU.

In this respect, the causality of integration ought not to be limited to economic reasons in general, or to trade or capital flows in particular, as is often the case.

In the last two decades, growing EU fearful discourses about migrations, instability or terrorism would enhance Moroccan means for negotiation and consolidate its prior status in Euro-Mediterranean policies (Jaidi and Martín 2010; Remiro and Martínez 2012). The accession of Mohamed VI to the throne in 1999 would intensify this trend by enacting a foreign approach based on what Irene Fernandez-Molina (2016) defines as a '(neoliberal) economistic and pragmatic thrust' relying on the concept of economic diplomacy and upholding its privileged relationship with the EU. Helped by its geographical position, the Moroccan international approach has increasingly relied on a strategic use of micro-, meso- and macro-economic agreements whose scope overcomes the straightforward logic of trade liberalization and growth. The following figures sum up the major trends derived from these shifts.

After the Association Agreement entered into force in 2000, Moroccan international exchanges experienced a progressive increase until the drop of 2008. After overcoming the crisis, growth resumed with a certain vigour. Nevertheless, despite all the agreements and integration processes it has sanctioned, Moroccan trade followed a less robust path than the average middle-income developing country (see Figure 2.1).

In addition, the growing gap between imports and exports is wider in the Moroccan case than it is for the rest of its partners (see Figure 2.1). As a consequence, the lower dynamism of exports compared with imports has entailed a progressive worsening of the trade balance, which was accentuated after the economic crisis (see Figure 2.2).

Seen from a regional perspective, Moroccan exchanges are marked by continuity. As for Euro-Mediterranean relations, the Barcelona Process sought to establish, by 2010, a Mediterranean Free Trade Zone stemming from the accumulation of North–South bilateral agreements. However, no major changes have occurred in terms of trade composition, direction or barriers within the new framework. As shown in Figure 2.3 and Figure 2.4, the main trading partners of Moroccan exchanges remain, by and large, its two former *métropoles*, which were also behind the largest amount of incoming FDI towards recently privatized sectors (Berrada 2010). In contrast, the weight of South–South regional areas on Moroccan trade has maintained an almost negligible role.

Indeed, the increase of Moroccan trade derives essentially from greater exchanges with France and Spain that entailed the aforementioned worsening of the Moroccan trade balance (see Figure 2.2).

Regarding South–South arrangements, the initiative that raised most expectations was the Agadir Agreement. Sanctioned in 2004 by Morocco, Tunisia, Egypt and Jordan, it was open to Arab Mediterranean countries bound to the European Union through an Association or an FTA. The ultimate goal was the establishment of a Mediterranean Free Trade Area that coalesced with the guidelines of the Great Arab Free Trade Area signed in 1997. However, its provisions regarding the

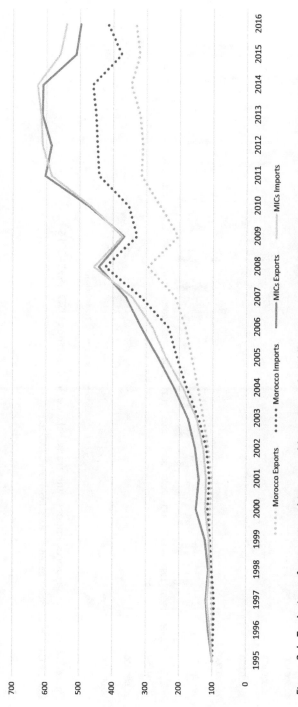

Figure 2.1 Evolution of exports and imports, Morocco and middle-income developing countries (index, 1995 = 100)

Source: Own elaboration based on data from UNCTADstat

····· Morocco Exports   ····· Morocco Imports   —— MICs Exports   —— MICs Imports

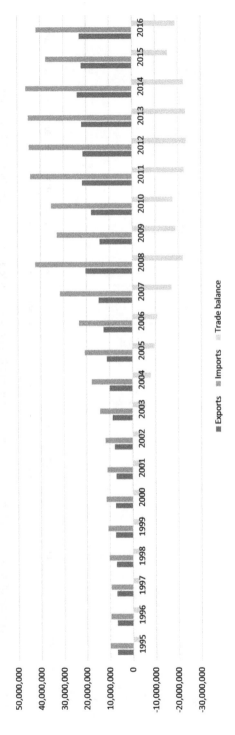

Figure 2.2 Morocco: exports, imports and trade balance, in thousands USD, 1995–2016

Source: Own elaboration based on data from UNCTADstat

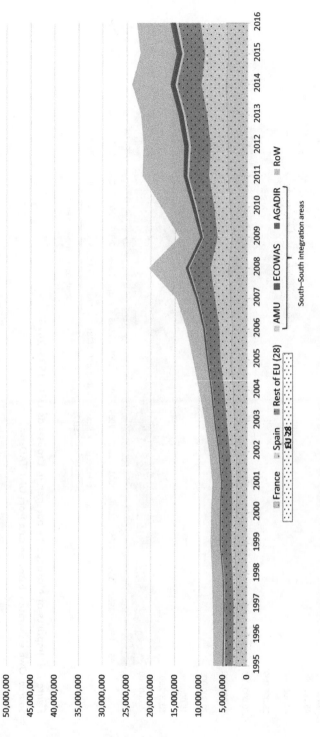

Figure 2.3 Exports of Morocco by partner, in thousands USD, 1995–2016

Source: Own elaboration based on data from UNCTADstat

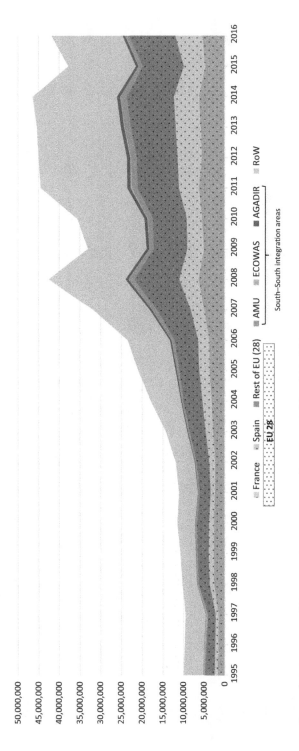

Figure 2.4 Imports of Morocco by partner, in thousands USD, 1995–2016

Source: Own elaboration based on data from UNCTADstat

Pan-Euro-Mediterranean system of rules of origin, following the European *acquis communautaire*, spanned doubts about their compatibility (Zorob 2008). Regardless of these aspects, its outcomes in terms of trade flows and enlargement have been somewhat disappointing to date (see Figure 2.5a,b and Figure 2.6a,b).[25]

In recent years, Moroccan political discourse and economic diplomacy have enacted a decided shift towards Africa. On the political side, its return to the African Union in January 2017 was preceded by an intense campaign of official visits and bilateral economic agreements. Such arrangements comprised financial aid, investment or sectorial projects, focussing on partners that remained

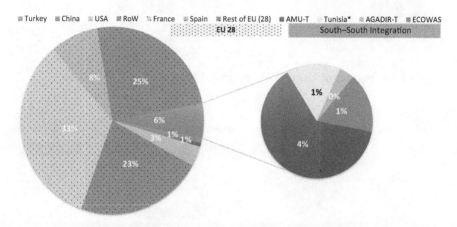

Figure 2.5a Exports of Morocco by partner, 1995

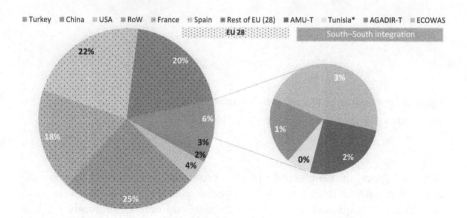

Figure 2.5b Exports of Morocco by partner, 2015

Source: Own elaboration based on data from UNCTADstat

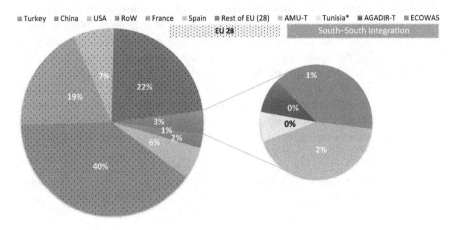

Figure 2.6a Imports of Morocco by partner, 1995

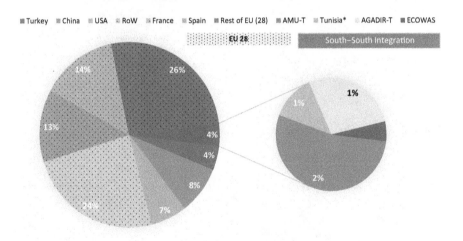

Figure 2.6b Imports of Morocco by partner, 2015

Source: Own elaboration based on data from UNCTADstat

skeptical about its readmission. In the economic field, having ratified the death of the AMU during the King's official speech before the African Summit, Morocco requested its admission to the Economic Community of West African States (ECOWAS) less than one month later. A strong emphasis on its African roots, features and plans has since captured growing aspects of Moroccan public and private affairs.

Although the dynamism shown by Moroccan exports towards the region confirm the potential gains of this request (see Figure 2.5 and Figure 2.6), Morocco's belonging to the Euro-Mediterranean area raised concerns about its accession among Members of the region. On the one hand, a preliminary report released at the Abuja Summit on the 16 December 2017 warned about potential collisions among the different regional frameworks in which Morocco takes part.[26] On the other, a number of private actors in countries like Nigeria (the strongest economy the region) have expressed their opposition to Moroccan accession by arguing the threat posed by its relationship with the EU.[27] According to their view, through the intermediation of Morocco, EU countries might be able to introduce their goods advantageously into the area. Indeed, from the standpoint of international political economy, Morocco's recent opening towards Africa holds a few features to be taken into account:

First, it appears as a strategic choice to replace the unlikely integration of the AMU. The chronic failure of the Maghreb association is a strong argument in favour of the redeployment of Moroccan trade and investment towards the continent.

Second, it is part of a South–South cooperation perspective that responds more closely to the expectations of developing countries, especially in view of the impacts of the crisis of 2008.

Last, but not least, as suggested by Nigerian reactions to its request before the ECOWAS, it is not necessarily taking place to the detriment of the EU or against the structural limits inherent to the nature of their relationship. On behalf of its status as a Euro-Mediterranean hub, Morocco's opening towards Africa might act as a bridge to the African market. Nonetheless, would this new role bring new compensation to the limits of the Association Agreements with the EU?

A priori, one may be tempted to answer affirmatively if considering Morocco's return to the AU and the number of agreements signed with various African countries. Moreover, the deployment of investment flows to Africa has been greatly facilitated by the relevant choice of sectors concerned. Integration has been pursued through a match between the needs of African countries and the maturity of sectors in which Morocco has a relatively solid experience (e.g. phosphate fertilizers, banking and insurance activities, real estate and public works, pharmaceutical products). Regardless of the outcomes of such an affair, it seems clear that in the analysis of the complex interactions between North–South and South–South frameworks experienced by Morocco, the presence of the EU is never negligible.

Where does Morocco stand now?

The conventional approach to economic integration suggests that successful processes of integration will drive involved countries to an increase of welfare through the potential static and dynamic trade effects for specialization, investment, FDI, income, employment and, all in all, for economic growth (Balassa

1961; El-Agra 1988; Baldwin and Venables 1995; Jovanovic 2005). As noted earlier, low levels of regional integration do not mean a lack of economic relations. So the absence of integration in the Mediterranean area does not mean that results have not been achieved in terms of trade, as shown earlier, or other economic variables.

Regarding Morocco's economic performance over the period, Moroccan gross domestic product (GDP) increased from 1995 to 2016, both in absolute terms and in per capita terms. Compared with the countries from its income group (middle-income developing countries, MIDC) or with its main trading partner (the EU), we see that Moroccan growth rates, which are very volatile, have been higher than those for the EU, especially after the crisis, but have been on average lower than for the other MIDCs (Figure 2.7).

A similar behaviour is shown by GDP per capita (Figure 2.8): its growth was also lower in Morocco than for other MIDCs and higher than for the EU, especially after the crisis.

Compared with the EU, there was a slight rapprochement, since the Moroccan GDP per capita moved from the 6.4% of that of the EU28 in 1995 to 9.5% in 2016. But this ought not to be interpreted as a great success, because it does not derive from the favourable evolution of Morocco, but rather from the stagnation of the EU after 2008. Nevertheless, in 2016, the GDP per capita of Morocco (at constant US dollars of 2010) was $3400 against $35884 in EU28 or $41,300 in the EU15. Consequently, the North–South gap continues to be wide and GDP growth is not sufficient to reduce it. When we compare Morocco with the MIDCs, although the per capita income of Morocco continues to be higher than the MIDC average ($3400 versus $2178 in 2016), the difference is narrowing: if in 1995, the GDP per capita of the MIDC was 61.8% of that of Morocco, it was 64% in 2016.

As for economic growth, although it may be linked in part to the growth of trade, it cannot be directly attributed to the process of economic integration, as it has been shown. In the same vein, the relatively favourable evolution of GDP and per capita GDP must not be interpreted directly as an improvement in economic development and welfare, which depends on more dynamics than output.

To that extent, the Human Development Index (HDI) from the UN Development Programme (UNDP) tries to balance the focus on economic growth with other dimensions that have to do with national policy choices and with the way they influence people's capabilities. Life expectancy at birth, years of schooling and gross national income (GNI) are the main variables taken into consideration.

Data concerning Morocco show a remarkable improvement since 1990, from 0.489 to 0.647 in 2015. In fact, the last report available situates Morocco in the 123rd position in a list that currently has 188 countries. However, HDI evolution was not as dynamic as GDP per capita (Figure 2.9). Between 1995 and 2015, the average annual growth was 1.6% for HDI and 4.3% for GDP per

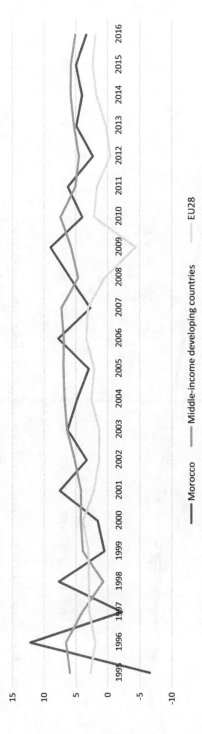

Figure 2.7 GDP annual average growth rate, 1995–2016

Source: Own elaboration based on data from UNCTADstat

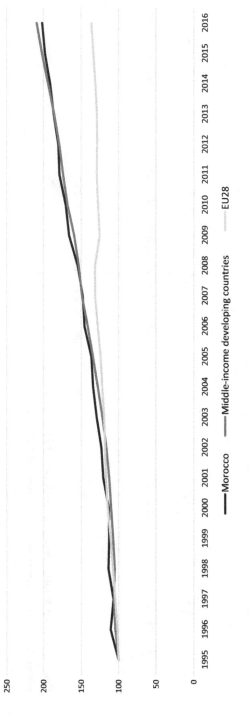

Figure 2.8 Evolution of GDP per capita, USD at constant (2010) prices (index, 1995 = 100)

Source: Own elaboration based on data from UNCTADstat

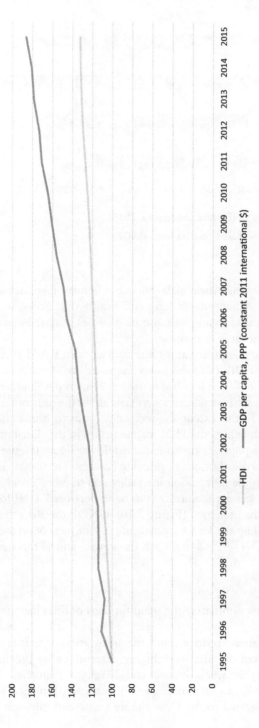

Figure 2.9 Evolution of Morocco's GDP and HDI (index, 1995 = 100)

Source: Own elaboration based on data from UNDP and WBDI

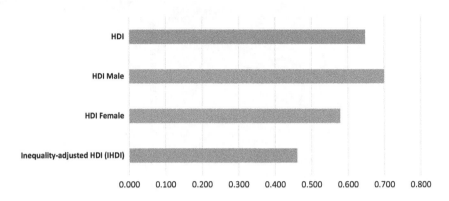

Figure 2.10 Morocco's HDI and inequality, 2015
Source: Own elaboration based on data from UNDP

capita. Results are nowhere near as favourable when we take into account not just the three HDI dimensions (a long and healthy life, access to knowledge and a decent standard of living), but also inequalities in distribution across the population regarding these dimensions.

As regards income inequality, according to data from World Bank Development Indicators (WBDI), the Gini index increased in Morocco from 39.5 in 1998 to 40.7 in 2006. When looking further at human development data provided by the UNPD, other striking features arise about the distribution of welfare within the country. To this extent, the inequality-adjusted human development index (IHDI), which adjusts the HDI for inequality in the distribution of each dimension across the population, shows a much lower figure (Figure 2.10), confirming that unequal distribution is a growing constraint to welfare in Morocco.

In addition to income distribution inequality and to other already mentioned dimensions of HDI, gender inequality is to be underscored: HDI for women is significantly lower than for men (Figure 2.10). UNDP for 2015 shows that the mean years of schooling are 3.8 for women and 6.4 for men. Moreover, estimated GNI per capita (in 2011 PPP $) is $3.388 for women and $11.091 for men.

Conclusions

The following points summarize the main findings of this chapter:

- Euro-Mediterranean relations and the integration agreements signed in the area in recent decades were highly determined by previous colonial ties, particularly between France and Maghreb countries. Being safeguarded by the Treaty of Rome (1957), bilateral privileged relationships have been transferred to the Community framework through Association

Agreements since 1969. Consequently, the nature of asymmetric power relations in Euro-Mediterranean area integration has to be understood within a broader framework that goes beyond the Barcelona Process.

- The humanitarian and financial approach of the Euro-Mediterranean initiatives derives primarily from a pragmatic choice, rather from the generous approach of a 'force for good' seeking for mutual prosperity. It is the wavering needs and interests of the European markets due to successive phases of enlargement rather than intra-Mediterranean dialogue which has determined the shape and scope of Euro-Mediterranean integration. In this regard, it is worth considering the binding nature of Mediterranean imbalances, which ought not to be seen as a neutral fact originating such frameworks, but rather as a result of them.
- Although trade has increased in the Euro-Mediterranean area since 2000, structure and composition of the flows have not experienced substantial changes, which calls into question the existence of advances in regional integration. Indeed, rather than referring to a Euro-Mediterranean framework, it would be more accurate to talk about a European framework in the Mediterranean Basin. Southern countries are invited to participate in different ways, but their margin of decision consisting of whether to engage and, if so, to what extent.
- Despite being an open economy and having signed a number of integration agreements with Northern and Southern countries and regions since its independence, Morocco cannot be said to be truly integrated with any region around its area of influence.
- Moroccan dependency on the European market has been maintained since the colonial period through a set of Association Agreements that accomplished a process of peripheral reconnection whereby Moroccan development is bound to the political decisions and economic performance of the EU. By legitimating former privileged relations with France and extending them to the EU framework, Moroccan economic structure and international exchanges remained anchored to the Mediterranean orbit of the EU. In spite of the variety of agreements signed by Morocco since then, France and Spain remain its major trade partners. In this regard, the slow path of economic recovery in Europe, particularly in countries like Spain, has a direct impact on the growth of Moroccan export
- The dominant role played by the European Union is apparent in Moroccan decisions of integration even when the Community is not directly involved. Triangular games to balance power relations, as well as the search for alternatives that replace or complement the influence of the EU, have been a constant strategy since the 1990s. Nevertheless, the lack of integration resulting from such attempts does not mean an absence of effects. In fact, some of those outcomes might coincide with those predicted by theories of economic integration, but it is also undeniable that many others overcome the limits of orthodox postulates on this topic.

- Morocco's GDP increased from 1995 to 2016 both in absolute terms and in per capita terms. However, economic growth, although linked in part to trade growth, cannot be directly attributed to the process of economic integration.
- HDI improved from 1995 to 2016, though its evolution was not as dynamic as GDP per capita. Moreover, the inequality-adjusted HDI shows worse figures for Morocco than its position in the HDI ranking suggests. Neither can it be affirmed that the effects of trade and growth have been distributed equally in the country, nor can it be supposed that the good performance of Moroccan trade after the last economic crisis has pushed the country towards a more egalitarian path of development.

These are the policy implications:

- At the bilateral level, the current impasse of the Deep and Comprehensive Free Trade Agreement with Morocco, as well as the mitigating achievements of the ENP, are only but a few outcomes of the unbalanced nature of Mediterranean relations. Furthermore, the instability derived from the contested validity of agricultural and fishery agreements proves the ambiguous legitimacy of a structure of exchanges rooted in colonial relations. To this extent, a solid bilateral framework is to be sought through arrangements whose terms are neither contingent on European internal affairs, nor exclusively guided by the will to preserve long-standing relations of mutual interdependence.
- At the regional level, the overlapping initiatives to foster South–South integration through North–South integration are far from meeting their goals. Attempts to enhance Euro-Mediterranean integration should give a higher priority to the needs and features of Southern countries than they do to harmonization with EU standards and red lines.
- Finally, given the evident interrelation between foreign policy affairs and economic integration, a really comprehensive approach is needed that offers a coherent and solid framework to the flows of goods, capital and people. Beyond economic effects, the requests unfulfilled by Southern countries have generated a great social fracture that has turned Euro-Mediterranean affairs into a laboratory of crisis management.

Notes

1 https://ec.europa.eu/europeaid/sectors/economic-growth/regional-integration_en
2 https://ec.europa.eu/commission/commissioners/2014-2019/mimica/blog/force-good-changing-world-0_en
3 https://ec.europa.eu/research/iscp/pdf/policy/barcelona_declaration.pdf
4 The Barcelona Declaration was preceded by the Lisbon Summit (1992), where the European Council affirmed the pivotal role of Maghreb countries in the achievement of peace and development on both sides of the Mediterranean.

5 For a good review of regional integration theory and its potential static and dynamic effects which act as determinants for developed and developing countries in deciding to join an integration agreement, see Robson (1980), Baldwin and Venables (1995), Baldwin and Seghezza (1998), El-Agraa (1988), Jovanovic (2005), Acharya (2012), Hosny (2013).

6 The establishment of North–South fora around the Mediterranean as a means for dialogue and cooperation arose even before the creation of the European Community. For instance, French President Charles de Gaulle put into place the Union Française in the 1940s once it became clear that France was losing control over its African colonies (Turpin 1958). Then, as will be explained ahead in the chapter, the Global Mediterranean Policy set up by the European Community in the 1970s tried to create a common policy framework around the Basin. What all these initiatives have in common, though, is that they were all settled by northern countries, and therefore adapted primarily to their interests.

7 Far from being a regionally integrated area, the Mediterranean Basin holds the widest income gap in the world and its intra-regional flows of goods, capitals and people remain asymmetric, problematic and mainly defined by the consequences of colonialism, poverty, racism and armed conflicts.

8 Protocole relatif aux marchandises originaires et en provenance de certains pays bénéficiant d'un régime particulier à l'importation dans un des Etats Membres (Treaty of Rome, Annex 1957).

9 Article 227 of the Treaty of Rome.

10 The Evian Accords between newly independent Algeria and France, which affirmed their shared will to join compromises regarding their former and new relations, were in some parts incompatible with the rules of the Common Market (Evian Agreements 1962).

11 The independence of Algeria compelled France to protect its prominent place among the Six, whereas the UK's demand for accession entailed a less favourable treatment towards Morocco and Tunisia in order to avoid the eventual expansion of privileged exchanges to the UK and the Commonwealth under the same premises. Furthermore, the imminent entry into force of the CAP and the CET posed further risks for Maghreb trade with the region. In this context, both countries asked for the tabling of a new round of negotiations about their economic relations with the EEC. They did so by appealing to the 'déclarations d'intention en vue de l'association à la Communauté Economique Européenne des pays indépendants appartenant à la zone franc (Maroc, Tunisie) et du Royaume de Libye' and to Article 238 of the Treaty, whereby 'La Communauté peut conclure avec un Etat tiers, des accords créant une association caractérisée par des droits et obligations réciproques, des actions en commun et des procédures particulières.

12 On 8 December 1970, the so-called Rossi Report (1970) denounced in front of the Parliament the Mediterranean links 'noués dans le désordre' under a 'politique au fil de l'eau' (Berdat 2007). This statement pushed Parliament to work towards a comprehensive new framework 'et non un arrangement cosmétique des traités déjà conclus' (2007).

13 During the 1960s, the Six had signed a non-preferential trade agreement with Yugoslavia, two preferential trade agreements with Spain and Israel, two (provisional) Association Agreements with non-European countries (Morocco and Tunisia) and two other Association Agreements with countries from the continental area that aspired to Membership (Greece and Turkey).

14 Apart from Maghreb countries – including Algeria (1976) – bilateral trade and cooperation agreements were signed with Israel (1975), Egypt, Jordan, Lebanon and Syria (1977).

15 The Dialogue 5 + 5 was formed by five Mediterranean countries from the EU (Portugal, Spain, France, Italy and Malta) and the five components of the Arab Maghreb Union (Mauritania, Morocco, Algeria, Tunisia and Libya) as an informal sub-regional forum on economic and security issues.

16 The main originality of Association Agreements signed after 1995 lay in their humanitarian provisions and the liberalisation of trade, except for the agricultural sector. Since 2010, negotiations have been held between the EU and Mediterranean countries like Tunisia and Morocco for a Deeper and Complete FTA (ALECA for its French capital letters).
17 *Spaghetti bowl* calls for the wave of mixtured regional frameworks – mainly South–South ones – occurring since the 1980s. For further information about the concept, see Baldwin (2006).
18 Former French President Nicolas Sarkozy proposed the Union for the Mediterranean in 2008 precisely to create a narrower forum of stakeholders where only Mediterranean countries from the EU participated. However, the implementation of this project required the inclusion of the whole European area in order to avoid sub-regional divisions within the Common Market.
19 The Madrid Conference (1880) and that of Algeciras (1906) are illustrative in this respect. The former legitimized growing European ambitions on Morocco by enshrining the principle of freedom of appropriation by Europeans on real-estate assets and land holdings throughout Morocco. The latter, a meeting held by 12 European powers (Germany, Austria, Hungary, France, Italy, Russia, the United Kingdom, Spain, Portugal, Belgium, the Netherlands and Sweden) under the mediation of the USA, had to find a solution to the confrontation between France and Germany about such ambitions and ended up bringing forward the establishment of the French Protectorate in Morocco. Germany accepted in compensation for the concession by France of certain territories in Cameroons and Congo.
20 When the Treaty of Rome was signed in 1957 by the Six (Germany, France, Italy, Belgium, the Netherlands and Luxembourg), the principle of 'preferential' relations between Morocco and the EEC was established to give such relations a geo-historical basis.
21 Deduction of duties, tariff relief, exemptions or quotas for Moroccan products exported; exemptions from duties, tariff reductions, opening of quotas for imported European products.
22 The Common Agricultural Policy, the EU's cornerstone of protectionism, was originally conceived as a brake on the agricultural export potential of third countries on the Community market, particularly from Maghreb countries. This was especially the case for Morocco, whose agricultural exports lost any competitive advantage because of the obligation to sell at the same price as their European competitors.
23 Born to characterize the process of integration of the Asia Pacific region, it became a widespread concept in the 1990s, calling for the joint promotion of trade liberalization and regional frameworks. For more information, see Sutton (2007).
24 However, according to the WTO, the latter's implementation finished in 2015.
25 Since Tunisia is part of AMU and AGADIR, in order to eliminate the double counting of Morocco-Tunisia trade flows, Tunisia was considered separately from the rest of both integration regions (AMU-T and AGADIR-T, respectively) when showing Morocco's exports and imports with such areas.
26 https://es.scribd.com/document/367443857/Etude-d-Impact-Sur-Les-Implications-de-l-Adhesion-Du-Maroc-a-La-Cedeao#fullscreen&from_embed
27 Namely the Manufacturers Association of Nigeria (MAN), the Nigeria Labour Congress and the Organisation du commerce de l'union de l'Afrique de l'Ouest.

References

Acharya, A., 2012. Comparative Regionalism: A Field Whose Time has Come? *The International Spectator*, 41 (1), 3–15.
Achy, L., 2007. Le Commerce Intra-Régional: L'Afrique du Nord Est-elle Une Exception? *L'année du Maghreb*, 3, 501–520.

Achy, L., 2013. *Structural Transformation and Industrial Policy in Morocco*, Working Paper 796. Economic Research Forum.

African Development Bank, 2012. *Unlocking North Africa's Potential through Regional Integration: Challenges and Opportunities.* Tunis-Belvedere: AfDB Group.

Aït-Amara, H., 1995. Les échanges Europe-Maghreb à l'épreuve du GATT. *In*: M. Allaya, ed. *Les agricultures maghrébines à l'aube de l'an 2000: Options Méditerranéennes*, Série, B. Montpelier: CIHEAM, 5–12.

Akesbi, N., 2015. La question agricole dans les relations euro-marocaines. *Revue Marocaine des Sciences Politiques et Sociales, Cahiers Libres*, 3, 39–108.

Akesbi, N., 2017. Economie politique, et politiques économiques au Maroc. *Revue Marocaine des Sciences Politiques et Sociales*, XIV (4), 49–135.

Algeria: France-Algeria Independence Agreements (Evian agreements), 1962. *International Legal Materials*, 1 (2), 214–230. Available from: www.jstor.org/stable/20689578

Balassa, B., 1961. *The Theory of Economic Integration*. Routledge Revivals.

Baldwin, R., 2006. Multilateralising Regionalism: Spaghetti Bowls as Building Blocs on the Path to Global Free Trade. *The World Economy, Blackwell Publishing*, 29 (11), 1451–1518.

Baldwin, R., and Seghezza, E., 1998. Regional Integration and Growth in Developing Nations. *Journal of Economic Integration*, 13 (3), 367–399, September.

Baldwin, R., and Venables, A., 1995. Regional Economic Integration. *In*: G.M. Grossman and K. Rogoff, eds. *Handbook of International Economics*, Vol. III. Elsevier, 1597–1644.

Barbé, E., and Johansson-Nogués, E., 2008. The EU as a Modest 'force for good': The European Neighbourhood Policy. *International Affairs*, 84, 81–96, doi:10.1111/j.1468-2346.2008.00690.x

Bchir, M.H., Hammouda, H.B., Oulmane, N., and Jallab, M.S., 2006. *The Cost of non-Maghreb: Achieving the Gains from Economic Integration.* ATPC, No.44, Economic Commission for Africa.

Berdat, C. (2007). L'avènement de la politique méditerranéenne globale de la CEE. *Relations internationales*, 130 (2), 87–109. doi:10.3917/ri.130.0087.

Berrada, A., 1988. La marocanisation de 1973: éclairage rétrospectif. *Revue Juridique, Politique et Economique du Maroc (RJPEM)*, Faculté des sciences juridiques, économiques et sociales de Rabat, 28, 59–96.

Berrada, A., 2010. Les investissements directs étrangers au Maroc: Privatisation et perte d'influence de l'Etat sur les choix fondamentaux de politique économique (2ème partie). *Revue Marocaine d'Audit et de Développement*, 30, 66–86.

Berrada, A., 2016. *Les finances publiques du Maroc: quelques éléments d'analyse*. Rabat: Cahiers Libres-CRESS.

Berrada, A., 2017. La dette publique du Maroc: lecture critique d'écrits académiques. *Revue Marocaine des Sciences Politiques et Sociales*. Available from: www.sciencepo.ma/2017/06/?m=1

Biad, A., 2013. La construction du Maghreb au défi du partenariat euro- méditerranéen de l'Union européenne. *L'année du Maghreb*, IX, 103–124.

Bichara, K., 2013. *The European Union and the Arab World: From the Rome Treaty to the Arab Spring*. PapersIEMed. Barcelona: European Institute of the Mediterranean. Available from: www.iemed.org/publicacions-en/historic-de-publicacions/papersiemed-euromesco/the-european-union-and-the-arab-world-from-the-rome-treaty-to-the-arab-spring

Calandri, E., 2012. The United States, the EEC and the Mediterranean: Rivalry or Complementarity? *In*: E. Calandri, D. Caviglia, and A. Varsori, eds. *Détente in Cold War Europe: Politics and Diplomacy in the Mediterranean and the Middle East*. London: I.B. TAURIS, 33–48.

Darbot-Trupiano, S., 2007. Le Partenariat euroméditerranéen: une tentative d'intégration maladroite. *L'Espace Politique* [Online]. Available from: http://espacepolitique.revues. org/844, doi:10.4000/espacepolitique.844 [Accessed 9 May 2017]

De Ville, F., and Reynaert, V., 2010. The Euro-Mediterranean Free Trade Area: An Evaluation on the Eve of the (Missed) Deadline. *L'Europe en Formation*, 2 (356), 193–206.

Deblock, C., and Regnault, H., 2009. De la reconnexion Nord-Sud à la reconfiguration mondiale: nouvelles questions de recherche. *Colloque du GDRI-CNRS DREEM Istanbul*, 21–23, May.

Dkhissi, S., 2015. L'arrimage européen du Maroc à l'heure des mutations géostratégiques. *Revue Marocaine des Sciences Politiques et Sociales, Cahiers Libres*, 3, 11–38.

El-Agra, A., 1988. *International Economic Integration*. London: Palgrave Macmillan.

El Aoufi, N., 1990. *La marocanisation*. Casablanca: Les Editions Toubkal.

El Aoufi, N., Herzenni, A., and Bensaid, M., 2005. *Croissance économique et développement humain, en 50 ans de développement humain au Maroc et perspectives 2025*. Cinquantenaire de l'indépendance du Royaume du Maroc, Rabat.

El Ktiri, M., and Akesbi, N., 1987. *La réforme de la fiscalité marocaine à l'heure de l'ajustement structurel*. Casablanca: Les Editions Toubkal.

El-Malki, H., 2000. *La Méditerranée face à la Mondialisation*. Salé: Editions Toubkal.

El Mataoui, B., 2017. Politique de contraction budgétaire au Maroc (1993–2014): Bilan et perspectives d'avenir, *Economie politique du Maroc. Revue Marocaine des Sciences Politiques et Sociales*, XIV, 311–330, Avril.

Escribano, G., 2006. *Europeanisation without Europe? The Mediterranean and the Neighbourhood Policy*, EUI Working Paper RSCAS No. 2006/19. Firenze: European University Institute.

Essebbani, B., 2008. *La coopération entre le Maroc et l'Union Européenne: de l'association au partenariat*. THÈSE de Doctorat en Sciences Politiques, Université Nancy 2, Faculté de Droit, de Sciences Économiques et Gestion

Fernandez-Molina, I., 2016. *Moroccan Foreign Policy Under Mohammed VI, 1999–2014*. London: Routledge.

Guth, E., and Aeikens, H.O., 1980. *Implications of the Second Enlargement for the Mediterranean and ACP Policies of the European Community*. Annual Conference of the Association for Economic and Social Science of Agriculture, Hanover, October. Commission of the European Communities Spokesman's Group and Directorate-General for Information. X/235/80-EN.

Holgado, M., and Ostos, M., 2002. Los acuerdos de pesca marítima entre España y Marruecos: evolución histórica y perspectivas. *Estudios Agrosociales y Pesqueros*, 194, 189–214.

Hosny, A.S., 2013. Theories of Economic Integration: A Survey of the Economic and Political Literature. *International Journal of Economy, Management and Social Sciences*, 2 (5), 133–155.

Jaidi, L., and Martín, I., 2010. *Comment faire avancer le Statut Avancé UE-Maroc?* Documents IEMed.

Jovanovic, M., 2005. *International Economic Integration*. London: Routledge.

Lamodiere, J., 1977. *L'évolution du droit des investissements étrangers au Maroc*. Aix Marseille: Aix En Provence, CNRS.

Martin, M.V., 1988. The Spanish Accession to the EC and Its Likely Impacts on Agricultural Trade and Development in Morocco. *Journal of Agricultural Economics*, 39, 141–145, doi:10.1111/j.1477-9552.1988.tb00570.x

Martínez, L., et al., 2008. *Le Maroc, l'Union du Maghreb Arabe et l'intégration régionale*. Euro-MeSCo Paper, 67.

Oualalou, F., 1980. *Propos d'économie marocaine*. Rabat: SMER.

Oubenal, M., and Zeroual, A., 2017. Les transformations de la structure financière du capitalisme marocain, *Economie politique du Maroc. Revue Marocaine des Sciences Politiques et Sociales*, XIV, 137–159, Avril.

Remiro, A., and Martínez, C., 2012. *Unión Europea-Marruecos? una vecindad privilegiada?* Madrid: Academia Europea de Ciencias y Artes.

Robson, P., 1980. *The Economics of International Integration*. London: Allen & Unwin.

Sanchez, E., 2003. Les multiples dimensions de la coopération euro-méditerranéenne. *EIPASCOPE*, Numéro Spécial 25ème anniversaire, 81–85.

Santucci, J.C., 1972. L'unification maghrébine: réalisations institutionnelles et obstacles politiques. *In:* R. Le Tourneau, ed. *L'Unité Maghrébine: Dimensions et Perspectives*. Centre de Recherches et d'Etudes sur les Sociétés Méditerranéennes. Paris: CNRS, 135–162.

Schimmelfennig, F., 2007. Europeanization beyond Europe. *Living Reviews European Governance*, 2 (1). Available from: www.livingreviews.org/lreg-2007-1

Stora, B., 2011. Du Maghreb des États-nations au Maghreb des régions. *In:* K. Mohsen-Finan, ed. *Le Maghreb dans les relations internationales*. Paris: CNRS Éditions, 19–28.

Sutton, M., 2007. Open Regionalism and the Asia Pacific: Implications for the Rise of an East Asian Economic Community. *Ritsumeikan International Affairs*, 5, 133–152.

Tlemçani, M.B., 1991. Endettement et restructurations économiques et financières au Maghreb. *Revue Française d'Economie*, VI (3), 115–142.

Turpin, F., 2008. 1958 la Communauté franco-africaine: un projet de puissance entre héritage de la Ive République et conceptions gaulliennes. *Outre-mers*, 95 (1), 358–359. 1958 et l'outre-mer français, 45–58.

UNECA, 2013. *Regional Integration and Development of Intra-Regional Trade in North-Africa: What Potential Trade?* Rabat: ECA-NA.

Whitman, R.G., 2011. Norms, Power and Europe: A New Agenda for Study of the EU and International Relations. *In:* R.G. Whitman, ed. *Normative Power Europe*. Great Britain: Palgrave Macmillan, 1–22.

World Bank, 2006. *Is There a New Vision for Maghreb Economic Integration?* World Bank Report No. 38359. Washington, DC: World Bank.

World Bank, 2010. *Economic Integration in the Maghreb*. World Bank Report.

Zorob, A., 2008. Intraregional Economic Integration: The Cases of GAFTA and MAFTA. *In:* C. Harders and M. Legrenzi, eds. *Beyond Regionalism? Regional Cooperation, Regionalism and Regionalisation in the Middle East*. Aldershot/Burlington: Ashgate, 169–183.

Zouiri, H., 2010. *Le partenariat Euro-méditerranéen: Contribution au développement du Maghreb*. Paris: L'Harmattan.

Chapter 3

Demographic transitions and labour supply in Southern Mediterranean countries

Barbara Zagaglia

Introduction

In this chapter, we investigate the demographic changes underlying labour market transformations in Southern Mediterranean countries. It is not possible to understand the difficulties of, or opportunities in, labour markets without considering the dimensional and compositional changes in the population aspiring to participate therein.

We address the topic by considering the long- and medium-term changes in demographic regimes, which have led to long-lasting shifts in the size and composition of the working age population. We also analyze and discuss the changes that have taken place in the most recent years. With this approach, it is possible to fully understand how structural concerns are able to influence the current labour supply and how they can affect it in the near future.

The chapter is organized as follows. After a literature review, we analyze the characteristics of demographic transitions. Timing, pace and strengths and weaknesses of the transitional processes will be considered.

Next, we analyze overall population growth. Then, we examine the changes in the age structure and measure the growth and level of rejuvenation and ageing of the working age population during the transitions. In this respect, differences among countries are due to the different patterns of fertility and mortality decline and the different impact of migration flows during the demographic transitional process.

Following, we analyze labour supply perspectives. In particular, after looking at the prospects of the working age population, we apply derived projection techniques to trace reference scenarios for a workforce size up to the year 2030.

The chapter concludes by discussing policy implications. From the evaluation of demographic processes – the first drivers of change – and from the analysis of labour supply, we offer guidelines for interventions.

The countries under investigation are the those in North Africa (i.e. Algeria, Egypt, Libya, Morocco and Tunisia) and Mauritania. Albeit not on the shores of the Mediterranean and, ethnically speaking, in between Northern and sub-Saharan Africa (Tamburini and Vernassa 2010), Mauritania is part of the Greater Maghreb, a region with a well-defined cultural identity, and contributes to a political union, the Arab Maghreb Union.[1] Moreover, Mauritania has relations with the whole Euro-Mediterranean area, having stipulated the agreement for the Union for the Mediterranean.

By excluding from our analysis the countries on the southern-eastern shores of the Mediterranean, we interpret in a restrictive manner the 'Southern Mediterranean'. In doing so, we confine our analysis to a fairly homogeneous set of countries for which we can rely on a complete series of reliable statistical data. All the data we use in our analyses are official and sourced from international statistical institutions.

Background

Demographic transition is a classical topic in demographic research, and its characteristics, causes and implications have been extensively studied. Specific analyses have been conducted on well-defined geographical areas and countries. Regarding the geographical area of interest, in the 1980s and 1990s, studies were carried out on the salient characteristics of the transition in the countries of the Mediterranean Basin (e.g. Fargues 1986; Salvini 1990; Di Comite and Moretti 1992, 1999). In 2005, Tabutin and Schoumaker made a detailed demographic 'chronicle' of the whole Arab World and the Middle East from the 1950s to the 2000s. More recently, some of our studies have analyzed in detail the transitional paths in Southern Mediterranean countries, excluding Mauritania (Zagaglia and Moretti 2012; Moretti and Zagaglia 2015; Zagaglia and Moretti 2016) where the complexity and variety of the transitions have clearly emerged.

Among the components of demographic transition, fertility has been the most widely studied. Some studies have focussed on the aspects of fertility decline, examined in the broader context of Muslim or Arab countries (Fargues 2003; Tabutin and Schoumaker 2005; Casterline 2011; Aberstadt and Shah 2012; Abbasi-Shavazi and Torabi 2012). The delay and speed of decline compared with the other developing countries have been underlined and, for some countries, explanations have been put forward (for Algeria, see The World Bank 2010; for Egypt and Morocco, see Eltigani 2000). Different fertility models have also emerged for Southern Mediterranean countries and the postponement of childbearing has emerged as a key feature of this area, also leading to possible underestimation of fertility indicators (Zagaglia et al. 2012; Zagaglia and Moretti 2016).

The structure of populations has become a major concern in the literature in recent years.[2] It has been considered mainly in terms of changing ratios between the number of children and the number of elderly (dependent population) and the size of the working age population (potential supporters). According to this line of research, a favourable age structure, entailing low dependency ratios and a related high proportion of working age population, can provide opportunities to be captured and effectively addressed in order to promote social and economic development, an effect known as 'demographic dividend' (Gribble and Bremner 2012; Mason et al. 2017).

The exceptional period of historical maximum in the proportion of working age adults 'is a direct consequence of the demographic transition and its prominence varies according to the type of the demographic transition and the historical events that can interfere with the transition process' (Vallin 2005).

Dependency ratios were calculated and 'demographic windows' discussed for the Muslim countries by Jones (2012).[3] Some of 'our' countries were included in the analysis, while different possible demographic windows were calculated according to various indicators for the whole Mediterranean Basin by Carella and Parant (2016). In both studies, the peculiarities of the demographic transitions of the countries are neglected and the Southern Mediterranean area scantily analyzed.

The matter of population structure was also considered as regards the relation between the high proportion of young adults – the so-called youth bulge[4] – and political violence. Urdal (2012) to some extent forecasted the civil riots, which began in the area at the beginning of this decade, and were known as the 'Arab Spring'.[5] Indeed, he considered the Middle East and North Africa region, sub-Saharan Africa and Asia as the three world regions with the highest risk of conflict. Zagaglia (2013) located the explanation of those events in the context of the overall demographic changes that have taken place in recent decades in Southern Mediterranean countries.

The challenges of absorbing the growing numbers of youths in education and the labour force and ensuring their participation in public and political life were major concerns of Arab researchers Faour and Farah (2013) who also aimed to provide indications for public youth policy.

Demographic transitions in Southern Mediterranean countries

A demographic transition is a passage from one demographic regime to another. Different definitions have been provided[6] and scholars have formulated differing numbers of transitions.[7] However, demographers usually refer to and define demographic transition as the passage from the traditional regime of high mortality and fertility to the modern regime of low mortality and low fertility. It started in Western Europe in the eighteenth and nineteenth centuries and then spread, first through Europe, part of the Americas and other countries with European immigration and, later, to the rest of the world. That period heralded such extraordinary changes that it is possible to talk about a demographic revolution (Chesnais 1986).

Some parts of the world have entered the transition only recently. Among the countries which started the transition in recent decades, some of them have concluded or are close to concluding the transitional path, whereas others are late and the transition is still in progress.

In the Mediterranean region, in this respect, countries are experiencing very different situations. On the northern shore, in the European countries (France, Greece, Italy, Spain and the former Yugoslavian countries), the transition is over. It began in the eighteenth and nineteenth centuries and ended a few decades ago. Instead, on the southern shore, countries entered the transition at different times in the twentieth century and today they are at different stages of the transitional process.[8]

As regards the Southern Mediterranean countries, according to UN data,[9] the mortality decline seems to have already started in the area in the mid-1950s since the crude death rates and life expectancies assumed levels typical of the transitional stage. The crude death rate ranged between 20.2 per thousands in Morocco and 30.6 per thousands in Libya and life expectancy at birth between 36.67 in Libya and 45.67 in Morocco.[10] Instead, at that time, the fertility transition had not yet started because the crude birth rate was around 45.5–50 per thousands and the total fertility rate higher than six in all countries. These fertility levels are typical of the pre-transitional period.[11]

Figures 3.1 and 3.2 show the path of mortality and fertility as measured by female life expectancy at birth (females are more indicative of the progress made than males) and by the total fertility rate, respectively.[12]

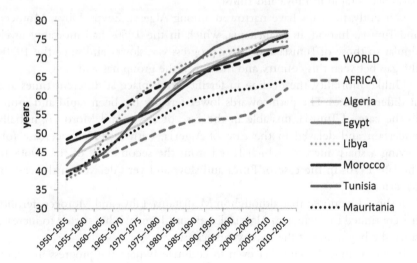

Figure 3.1 Life expectancy at birth, females, 1950–2015

Source: Our elaboration on UN data (United Nations, World Population Prospects: The 2017 Revision)

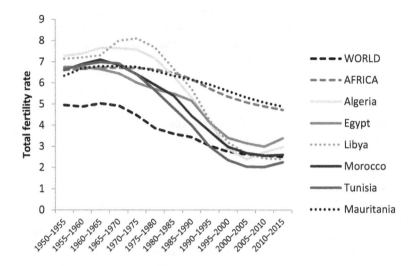

Figure 3.2 Total fertility rate, 1950–2015

Source: Our elaboration on UN data (United Nations, World Population Prospects: The 2017 Revision)

As regards female mortality, the progress in survivorship was continuous and particularly rapid in Libya and Tunisia.

Currently, the gaps have narrowed among Algeria, Egypt, Libya, Morocco and Tunisia. Instead, in Mauritania, which in the 1950s had mortality levels similar to those of Tunisia and Libya, progress was slower and since the 1970s, the gap between this country and the rest of the group has widened.

Unlike mortality, the decline in fertility took place at different times and at different rates. The path towards lower fertility has been rapid and sound in the case of Tunisia, unstable in the case of Egypt and Morocco, initially uncertain and delayed in the case of Algeria, with a sudden decrease following a sharp increase which lasted from the second half of the 1960s to the late 1970s in the case of Libya and slow and very delayed in the case of Mauritania.

It should be noted that although in Mauritania, Libya and Morocco, fertility has continued to decline, in Algeria, Egypt and Tunisia, it has started to increase since the beginning of the twenty-first century.

Finally, it must be said that even in countries where the progress in health transition has been greater, there are still some aspects that have fallen behind. For instance, in the aforementioned countries, infant mortality is still high or very high, and in Morocco, Egypt and especially in Mauritania, fertility among adolescents is high and represents a critical issue (Table 3.1).

Table 3.1 Principal mortality and fertility indicators, 2010–2015

	Fertility indicators			Mortality indicators		
	Crude birth rate (per thousands)	Total fertility rate	Adolescent fertility rate (births per 1,000 women ages 15–19)	Crude death rate (per thousands)	Life expectancy at birth	Infant mortality rate (per thousands)
Algeria	25.3	2.96	11.6	4.8	75.27 MF 76.49 F	28
Egypt	28.5	3.38	54.6	6.1	70.84 MF 73.05 F	19
Libya	21.3	2.4	6	5.2	71.46 MF 74.41 F	24
Mauritania	35.5	4.88	85.6	8.2	62.64 MF 64.08 F	68
Morocco	21.3	2.6	34	5.2	74.86 MF 75.97 F	28
Tunisia	19.1	2.25	7.6	6.4	75.05 MF 77.13 F	18
AFRICA	35.9	4.72	99.4	9.4	60.23 MF 61.90 F	57
WORLD	19.6	2.52	46.5	7.7	70.79 MF 73.11 F	35

Source: Our elaboration on UN data (United Nations, World Population Prospects: The 2017 Revision)

Population growth

At the beginning of the 1950s, the rate of natural increase, the difference between the crude birth rate and the crude death rate, was higher than 20 per thousands in all countries, except for Tunisia, which presented a slightly lower rate. Such high levels of growth are detectors of ongoing transition.[13]

In the following years, due to an uninterrupted mortality decline, the natural growth rate increased in all countries to more than 30 per thousands in Algeria, Morocco and Libya. In the period 1950–2015, peak population increase was reached by all countries in different moments in time: Morocco in 1959 (32.5 per thousands), Libya in 1971–1972 (38.1 per thousands) and Tunisia in 1979–1981 (26.2 per thousands), Algeria 1979–1981 (31.9 per thousands), and Egypt and Mauritania in 1985 (28.1 per thousands) and 1984–1987 (30.6 per thousands), respectively. In the case of Mauritania, the natural growth rate was more or less constant at a rate of around 30 per thousands for about 40 years, from the 1960s to the 1990s.

The countries in question now appear to have entered a new phase of more moderate natural growth. This phase consists of a natural growth rate of around 20 per thousands for Egypt, and a similar level for Algeria. Lower growth rates are recorded for Libya and Morocco (the rate is around 15 per thousands) and especially for Tunisia (around 11–12 per thousands).[14] In Mauritania, in spite of the decline, the rate of natural growth is still very high though it has just started to decline. The paths of fertility decline which, unlike mortality, did not change according to a clear-cut declining trend, primarily shaped such trends.

The pressure of a population which grew at such high levels, without an adequate level of social and economic development and with insufficient economic growth, made many of those living in these countries – with the exception of Libya – become emigrants. Algeria, Egypt, Morocco and Tunisia became sending countries towards Europe.[15] In the same period, a huge number of immigrants entered Libya, thanks to the economic possibilities offered by the country's natural resource endowment. As a result, the population growth rate rose to over 40 per thousands in 1966 and stayed at this high level for a whole decade. Since the second half of the 1990s, the situation has changed and also Libya has become a country of emigration. In more recent years, the severe political crises of the country ceased to attract foreign investment and labour, and net migration rates deteriorated. During the 1980s and 1990s, the situation also changed for Tunisia, which became an immigration country.[16] By contrast, the population of Mauritania, in spite of an extremely high and lasting rate of natural increase, did not have a similarly high population exodus, and in recent decades, net migration has even become positive.

The trends in natural population growth rates and net migration rates, from 1950 up to now, are shown in Figure 3.3.

Due to the demographic transition, since 1950, the population of the six countries has increased by over 146 million, without substantially affecting their demographic equilibria (with the exception of Morocco's population which, unlike today, in 1950 exceeded Algeria's). The largest increases were in Egypt (around 73 million people), Algeria (almost 31 million people) and Morocco (25.8 million people), followed by Tunisia, Libya and Mauritania. Libya and Mauritania, the smallest countries population-wise, are those that, in relative terms, have grown the most. The population of Libya has multiplied 5.54 times, due to the early and sudden reduction in mortality, the delay in fertility decline and a substantial stream of immigrants over time. The population of Mauritania has multiplied 6.33 times, due to the very slow decline in mortality and mostly in fertility (Table 3.2).

Changing age structure: the pivotal role of the working age population

For the purposes of our study, the population was divided into three major age classes: 0–14 years, 15–64 years and 65 years and over. This division corresponds to the ages when people are not yet able to enter the labour market and become employed because they are too young, the ages for entry and permanence in the labour market and, finally, the ages when people may retire because of declining physical capabilities.[17]

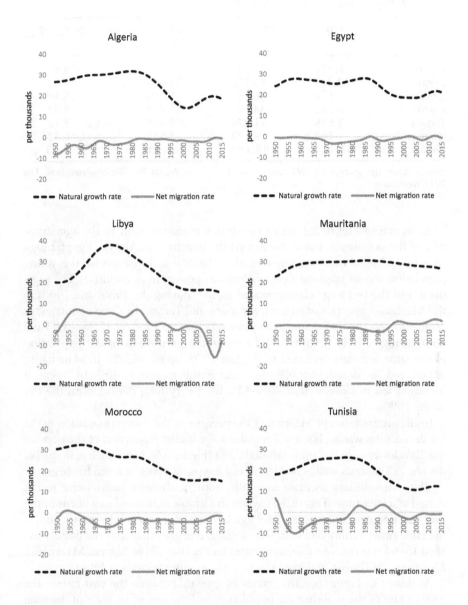

Figure 3.3 Natural growth rate and net migration rate, Southern Mediterranean countries, 1950–2015

Source: Our elaboration on UN data (United Nations, World Population Prospects: The 2017 Revision)

Table 3.2 Population size, 1950–2015, in thousands

Country	1950	2015	Absolute increase 1950–2015	P_{2015}/P_{1950}
Algeria	8,872	39,872	30,999	4.49
Egypt	20,713	93,778	73,065	4.53
Libya	1,125	6,235	5,110	5.54
Morocco	8,986	34,803	25,817	3.87
Tunisia	3,605	11,274	7,668	3.13
Mauritania	660	4,182	3,522	6.33
Total	**43,961**	**190,144**	**146,181**	**4.33**

Source: Our elaboration on UN data (United Nations, World Population Prospects: The 2017 Revision)

As shown in Figure 3.4, an extraordinary transformation in the age structure of the population has accompanied the transition in Algeria, Egypt, Libya, Morocco, Tunisia and, to a lesser extent, Mauritania. In particular, the young population was an important population component in all countries. The population of the 0–14 age class increased rapidly during the 1950s and 1960s in the Maghreb countries of Algeria, Morocco and Tunisia. In these countries, its proportion on the total population peaked in the late 1960s at 47.75, 48.03 and 46.37%, respectively (Figure 3.5). In Libya, the proportion of the population in the same age class increased in the late 1970s up to 48.22%. In Mauritania, it persisted for decades at 44%–46% and it still represents 40%. In Egypt, it increased less but persisted at 40%–42% for a very long period, until the eve of the 1990s.

In all countries except Mauritania, the pressure of the young population in the last decades has waned, but it still remains a significant proportion of the population. It is lower only in Tunisia (around 23%) (Figure 3.5). Nevertheless, in the last decade, in Tunisia as well as in Algeria and Egypt, an opposite trend has begun.

The extraordinary increase in adults, both in absolute and relative terms, started at a later time (Figure 3.5), when the sizable cohorts of newborns of the previous decades could reach older age because of increasing longevity and, at the same time, fertility had started to decline. The growth rate of the population aged 15–64 was considerable, sometimes higher than 3% in Algeria, Mauritania, Morocco and Tunisia, and even reached 4% in some periods in Libya.

As shown in Figure 3.6, the 'excess of growth' between the two rates – the growth rate of the working age population and the rate of increase of the total population – is similar in timing and duration for Algeria, Libya, Morocco and Tunisia.

The growth rate of the working age population far exceeded the growth rate of the total population from the late 1960s and late 1970s until the last decade. The excess was greater for Algeria and Libya due to both labour immigration that involved these countries, especially Libya, and the rapid fertility decline.

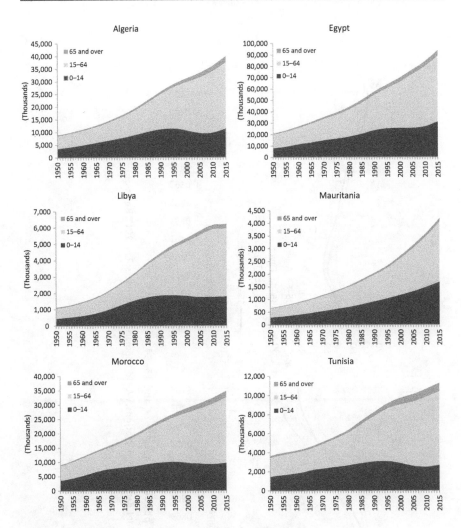

Figure 3.4 Population by major age classes, 1950–2015

Source: Our elaboration on UN data (United Nations, World Population Prospects: The 2017 Revision)

In Egypt, the growth rate of the working age population has been consistently above the total population growth rate only since the 1990s. Indeed, in Egypt, fluctuations in fertility decline, with periods of stalling and recovery (Moretti and Zagaglia 2015), caused phases of greater increase followed by phases of less increase in youth, who later passed into the adult population in different proportions.

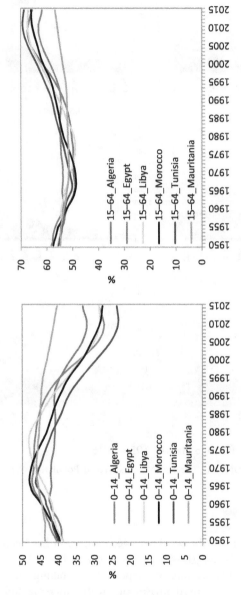

Figure 3.5 Proportions of population ages 0–14 and 15–64

Source: Our elaboration on UN data (United Nations, World Population Prospects: The 2017 Revision)

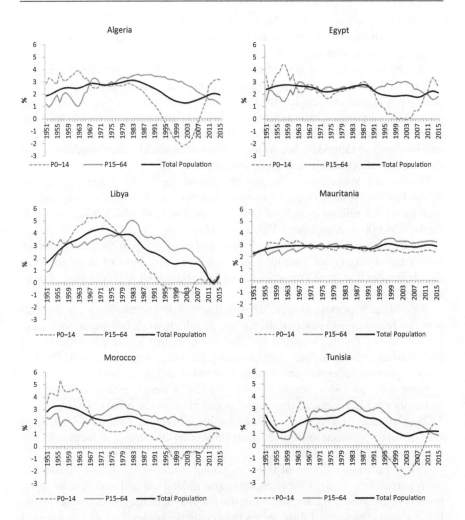

Figure 3.6 Rates of changes of total population, population aged 0–14 years and population aged 15–64

Source: Our calculation on UN data (United Nations, World Population Prospects: The 2017 Revision)

In Mauritania, where the decline in fertility and mortality is slow, the growth rate of the working age population has not undergone substantial changes, with values almost constant at around 3%.

This particular condition could have opened 'demographic windows of opportunities' for Algeria, Libya, Morocco and Tunisia and to a lesser extent for Egypt.[18]

If a positive challenge has become available for the Maghrebian countries and, at certain points, was exploited (Bloom et al. 2001), the high and prolonged growth rate levels were undoubtedly a critical structural concern for the weak economies of these countries unable to employ an increasing and progressively more educated labour supply.[19]

In very recent years, a new phase seems to have opened for Algeria, Egypt, Libya and Tunisia. The recent fertility recovery has caused an increase in the young population, which has overtaken the growth rate of the working age population. In Libya, emigration and loss of labour immigration has also occurred because political instability, which followed the fall and death of General Mu'ammar Gheddafi, has strongly influenced social safety conditions and the stability of economic and social institutions.

Despite the lowering of the growth rate of the working age population, in the last five years (2010–2015), there has been, in the area, on average, an increase of 1.8 million people of working age a year, of which 970,000 are in Egypt, 358,000 in Algeria and 353,000 in Morocco.

Finally, the structural dynamics of this population group in the period during which the demographic transition has unfolded contribute to show in detail the challenges that these countries have faced and which will continue to condition the near future.

We obtain important insights by splitting the whole working age interval into the following: 15–24 (youth, the age in which work competes with education), 25–44 (young working age, and the principal age of parenthood and childrearing), 45–54 (mature working age), 55–64 (last working age). The last age category includes workers, potential workers and the retired.[20]

Since the mid-1960s, young people ages 15–24 have increased considerably in number.[21] They became the largest population group of working age from 1975 to 1985 in Algeria, Morocco and Tunisia. Therefore, until the 1980s, there was an intense process of rejuvenation proven by the strong reduction in the median age, as shown in Table 3.3.

The population increase of those of young working age (25–44 years) has been particularly evident more recently and indeed exceptional. A slow aging process began which has intensified in the last two decades, and especially in the last few years (except in Libya), when the population older than 44 years started to increase considerably and, in Algeria, Libya, Morocco and Tunisia, the youth population started to decline. Despite the more recent dynamics, the working age population is, on the whole, still young, with the median age varying from 30.77 years in Mauritania to 35.85 in Tunisia.

Demographic perspectives of labour supply

Working age population prospects

Before making any reasoned hypothesis on the prospects of labour supply in Southern Mediterranean countries, we look at its maximum potential extent (theoretical maximum), which is represented by the size of the whole working age population.

Table 3.3 Median age of working age population

	1950	1960	1970	1980	1990
Algeria	31.18	30.84	30.25	28.25	28.8
Egypt	31.27	32.77	32	31.14	31.33
Libya	31.42	31.33	31.54	30.43	29.11
Mauritania	29.76	30.38	30.45	29.35	29.12
Morocco	29	30.92	31.95	28.51	29.44
Tunisia	31.98	32.41	31.85	29	30.69
	2000	2005	2010	2015	
Algeria	29.52	30.18	31.63	33.71	
Egypt	31.05	30.73	31.55	32.84	
Libya	29.34	30.13	31.75	30.77	
Mauritania	29.33	29.66	30.12	30.65	
Morocco	31.08	32.17	33.17	34.43	
Tunisia	32.11	32.87	34.09	35.85	

Source: Our calculation on UN data (United Nations, World Population Prospects: The 2017 Revision)

Note: Calculate on five-year age intervals

In demography, it is common to make projections on the future trends of a population and its subgroups. What is even more important is that it is possible to make reasonable predictions, especially for short and medium time periods. Indeed, underlying any population forecast, there are projections of its components of change (mortality, fertility and migration), which presume some hypothesis and prediction on future behaviours.

In modern societies, the demographic behaviours of fertility and mortality are not subject to extreme variations from one period to another, unless in exceptional circumstances, such that they are predictable with high reliability. The case of migrations is different, as they are more elastic and highly subject to economic circumstances and legal restrictions.

Furthermore, the historical paths of countries that have already concluded the demographic transition can be informative for the trends of populations in countries that undertook the fertility and mortality transitions at a later stage.

In this study, we draw on the latest revision of the UN population projections (World Population Prospects, the 2017 Revision). From the analysis of the speed and intensity of past decline in countries that have concluded their demographic transition, different models are created and applied by the UN statistical division to those countries that are currently undergoing the transition (for technical details, see UN 2017). We make use of the Zero Migration Variant, based on the assumption of the convergence of all countries in the world in terms of fertility and mortality behaviours by 2100.[22] The demographic transition is supposed to end for the majority of the world's countries by 2100, the last year of the projections. On that date, on the fertility side, the world total fertility rate would achieve the value of 1.97. The six Southern Mediterranean countries would converge to an end of the transition as well. All of them, with the exception of Mauritania, would reach and fall below replacement.

On the mortality side, the assumption consists of a normal decline, in line with the past trends and efforts in reducing the risk of dying and improving health conditions of progressive societies, both at world level and for Southern Mediterranean countries.

To assure a high degree of certitude to the future trends of the working age population, we restrict the time horizon to the next five decades, when the last of today's working age cohorts will be out of observation, and we focus on the period 2015–2030, for which reliable economic projections are available (see section ahead).

In the next 15 years, the number of people potentially able to get a paid job will increase substantially in all the Southern Mediterranean countries. The increase will be especially high in Egypt and Algeria, and the growth rates in these two countries will increase over time. The increase will be considerable in Morocco, where, although the growth rate will tend to decline, it will remain higher than 1%. Up to 2030, there will be over 19 million people more in Egypt, 6.3 million in Algeria and 4.5 in Morocco. In Mauritania, the pace of growth will be the most sustained and, in 2030, there will be 1.2 million more people of working age than in 2015. In Libya, the growth rate, positive albeit decreasing, will bring an absolute increase of 1.1 million in working age population. Tunisia will be the country with the lowest growth rate, total growth amounting to 0.8 million in the 15–64 age class.

Only after 2030 will the effects of the last 15 and subsequent years on fertility levels be evident. We expect different scenarios for the size of the working age population. The growth path will change direction first in Libya and Tunisia (from 2045), then in Algeria (from 2055) and, finally, in Morocco (from 2060), unlike Egypt and Mauritania, where the working age population will continue to grow, albeit at a slower pace (Table 3.4).

The labour force

Not all people of working age will enter the labour market. In order to estimate the number of those who would aspire to get a job and to whom employment must be guaranteed, we apply derived projection techniques in order to obtain estimates of the size of the future labour force. To the projected working age population by sex and five-year age intervals, we apply projected labour force participation rates by the same sex and age distribution.

Unlike the working age population, it is hard to make projections about labour indicators. Labour force participation rates are subject to great uncertainty, as their changes are the result of many different kinds of factors, some of a structural nature but others of a cyclical or accidental nature. For these reasons, they are usually carried out for short-term time intervals. Here, we

Table 3.4 Projected working age population size, 2015–2065

	2020	2025	2030	2035	2040	2045	2050	2055	2060	2065
Working age population (thousands)										
Algeria	27,547	29,708	32,382	34,515	35,960	36,564	36,587	36,583	36,942	37,909
Egypt	63,500	69,326	77,143	84,240	90,463	95,777	100,805	105,688	110,967	116,150
Libya	4,548	4,916	5,242	5,423	5,475	5,431	5,364	5,295	5,259	5,224
Mauritania	2,728	3,125	3,566	4,029	4,502	4,985	5,480	5,985	6,496	7,003
Morocco	24,556	25,946	27,442	28,800	29,905	30,641	30,921	31,052	31,032	31,088
Tunisia	7,996	8,229	8,546	8,789	8,964	8,961	8,809	8,633	8,569	8,605

	2015–2020	2020–2025	2025–2030	2030–2035	2035–2040	2040–2045	2045–2050	2050–2055	2055–2060	2060–2065
Average annual change (thousands, rounded values)										
Algeria	288	432	535	427	289	121	5	−1	72	193
Egypt	1,109	1,165	1,563	1,420	1,245	1,063	1,005	977	1,056	1,037
Libya	73	73	65	36	10	−9	−13	−14	−7	−7
Mauritania	72	79	88	92	95	97	99	101	102	101
Morocco	321	278	299	272	221	147	56	26	−4	11
Tunisia	50	47	63	49	35	0	−30	−35	−13	7

Average annual growth rate (%)										
Algeria	1.07	1.51	1.72	1.28	0.82	0.33	0.01	0	0.2	0.52
Egypt	1.83	1.76	2.14	1.76	1.43	1.14	1.02	0.95	0.97	0.91
Libya	1.68	1.55	1.29	0.68	0.19	−0.16	−0.25	−0.26	−0.14	−0.13
Mauritania	2.82	2.72	2.64	2.44	2.22	2.04	1.89	1.76	1.64	1.5
Morocco	1.35	1.1	1.12	0.97	0.75	0.49	0.18	0.08	−0.01	0.04
Tunisia	0.64	0.57	0.76	0.56	0.39	−0.01	−0.34	−0.4	−0.15	0.08

Source: Our calculation on UN data (United Nations, World Population Prospects: The 2017 Revision). Zero Migration Variant.

use the 2017 edition of the International Labour Organization (ILO) Labour Force Estimates and Projections produced by the ILO Department of Statistics. The projection period is 2017–2030 and projections are based on econometric methods (for technical details, see ILO 2017). Estimated labour force participation rates for 2015 (the base of the derived projection) are drawn from the same data source.

For evaluating the impact of population and economic changes, we consider three scenarios.

Scenario 1 (Expected labour supply)

It considers the population distribution by sex and age according to the UN Zero Migration Variant projection and the labour force participation rates by sex and age according to the ILO projections. It is the expected scenario of the labour force, determined by the dynamics of natural components of population and the forecast economic dynamics, which have been validated by experts.

Scenario 2 (Baseline labour supply scenario)

It considers the population distribution by sex and age as in Scenario 1 and the labour force participation rates by sex and age constant over time as in 2015 according to ILO estimates.

Scenario 3 (Feasible maximum labour supply)

It considers the population distribution by sex and age as in scenarios 1 and 2 and, for each Southern Mediterranean country, the labour force participation rates by sex and age of a reference country. It is assumed that the country under investigation could positively change the structure of its economy and its labour market in order to maintain labour force participation rates of the reference country as they were in 2015. In this case, the calculated labour force will represent a reasonable target for the country.

The country which in this analysis acts as 'reference' to the country analyzed is homogeneous according to the Human Development Index (it belongs to the same group, as defined in the Human Development Report 2016), culturally close and in a similar stage of demographic transition. Yet, from an economic point of view, it exhibits better performances in labour force participation rates by sex and age, higher employment rates and lower unemployment rates (overall and for young).

Algeria, Libya and Tunisia, which are high HDI countries, have Turkey as a reference, Egypt and Morocco, which are medium HDI counties, have Indonesia as a reference and Mauritania, a low HDI country, has Nigeria.

Our results show that the labour force will grow regardless of the scenario considered. However, the differences between Scenarios 1 and 2 are small, whereas significant increases are expected in Scenario 3 (Figure 3.7).

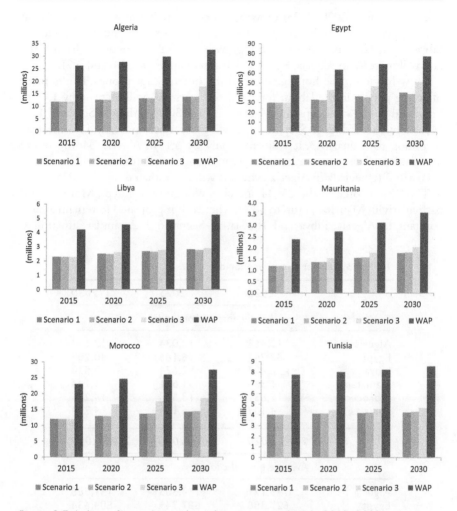

Figure 3.7 Labour force size and working age population, 2015–2030

In Scenario 1, the labour force will grow at a lower rate than the working age population in Algeria, Mauritania, Morocco and Tunisia, whereas it will outgrow the working age population growth rate in Egypt and Libya.

The effect of a strong economic transformation, as could be that simulated in Scenario 3, would lead to a substantial increase over time of the labour force. In this scenario, compared with Scenario 1, there would be an increase of an extra 3–4 million people every five years in Algeria and Morocco, an extra 10–13 million people in Egypt, an extra 300,000–400,000 in Tunisia, an extra 200,000–240,000 in Mauritania, and only an extra 120,000–130,000 people in Libya.

Moreover, whatever the scenario we consider, the greatest growth in the labour force will occur in the first five years (2015–2020). Indeed, in the second

Barbara Zagaglia

five-year period (2020–2025) growth will continue but at a lower rate. What will happen later (2025–2030) varies depending on the country. While for Libya, Mauritania and Morocco the growth rate will continue to decline, the rate will increase in Algeria, Egypt and Tunisia (Tables 3.5, 3.6 and 3.7).

Growth will not be homogeneous in the different age groups. The number of young people in the labour force (15–24 years old) will increase by 13% in Libya and by 27% in Egypt and Mauritania in 2030 according to Scenario 1. In Mauritania, according to Scenario 2, it will grow much more, by 43% whereas, according to Scenario 3, it will grow only by 6%. In Algeria, Morocco and Tunisia, it will decrease in both Scenario 1 and 2, whereas it will increase in Scenario 3 (especially in Algeria, where it will more than double).

The labour force in the 25–44 age class will grow in Egypt, Morocco and particularly in Mauritania (up to 48%), whereas it is projected to remain almost constant in Algeria, Libya and Tunisia, in Scenario 1. A similar situation is

Table 3.5 Labour force, Scenario 1

	2020	2025	2030
	Labour force (thousands)		
Algeria	12,463	13,034	13,694
Egypt	32,747	36,186	40,209
Libya	2,497	2,674	2,820
Mauritania	1,366	1,561	1,774
Morocco	12,851	13,568	14,299
Tunisia	4,109	4,164	4,224
	2015–2020	2020–2025	2025–2030
	Average annual change		
Algeria	149,171	114,305	131,988
Egypt	627,388	687,749	804,634
Libya	41,084	35,358	29,332
Mauritania	35,869	38,965	42,588
Morocco	172,464	143,330	146,324
Tunisia	22,782	10,942	11,886
	Average annual growth rate (%)		
Algeria	1.23	0.9	0.99
Egypt	2.01	2	2.11
Libya	1.72	1.37	1.07
Mauritania	2.81	2.67	2.56
Morocco	1.39	1.09	1.05
Tunisia	0.56	0.26	0.28

Table 3.6 Labour force, Scenario 2

	2020	2025	2030
	Labour force (thousands)		
Algeria	12,484	13,055	13,775
Egypt	32,424	35,261	38,578
Libya	2,482	2,642	2,771
Mauritania	1,373	1,577	1,802
Morocco	12,883	13,644	14,423
Tunisia	4,126	4,207	4,297
	2015–2020	*2020–2025*	*2025–2030*
	Average annual change		
Algeria	153,451	114,250	144,028
Egypt	562,728	567,290	663,423
Libya	38,125	32,081	25,718
Mauritania	37,311	40,754	44,873
Morocco	178,886	152,203	155,761
Tunisia	26,167	16,070	18,064
	Average annual growth rate (%)		
Algeria	1.27	0.89	1.07
Egypt	1.82	1.68	1.8
Libya	1.6	1.25	0.95
Mauritania	2.92	2.77	2.66
Morocco	1.44	1.15	1.11
Tunisia	0.64	0.39	0.42

Table 3.7 Labour force, Scenario 3

	2020	2025	2030
	Labour force (thousands)		
Algeria	15,833	16,679	17,762
Egypt	42,795	46,731	51,347
Libya	2,616	2,769	2,892
Mauritania	1,546	1,783	2,044
Morocco	16,584	17,594	18,601
Tunisia	4,465	4,554	4,658

(Continued)

Table 3.7 (Continued)

	2015–2020	2020–2025	2025–2030
Average annual change			
Algeria	823,339	169,052	216,689
Egypt	2,636,810	787,265	923,217
Libya	64,885	30,684	24,553
Mauritania	71,757	47,498	52,101
Morocco	919,143	201,878	201,459
Tunisia	93,809	17,807	20,874
Average annual growth rate (%)			
Algeria	6.02	1.04	1.26
Egypt	7.37	1.76	1.88
Libya	2.65	1.14	0.87
Mauritania	5.28	2.86	2.73
Morocco	6.49	1.18	1.11
Tunisia	2.22	0.39	0.45

expected in Scenario 2, whereas the growth in Egypt, Morocco and Mauritania is expected to be faster in Scenario 3.

Class 45–54 will increase rapidly in all three scenarios. In Scenario 1, it will grow up to 70% and beyond in Algeria, Libya and Mauritania. In general, unlike the other age classes, growth will be weaker in Scenario 2 than in Scenario 1. In Scenario 3, growth will be higher, doubling and more than doubling in Egypt and Mauritania, respectively.

The labour force in the 55–64 age class will expand the most. In Scenarios 1 and 2, it will grow especially in Libya, where in 2030, it will be 2.6 times the 2015 value, and in Mauritania, where it will increase by over 80%. In Scenario 3, it will grow the most in Egypt and Mauritania, where in 2030, it will be 2.6 and 2.7 times the 2015 value, respectively (Table 3.8).

Currently, the composition of the labour force by gender is unbalanced in favour of males in all countries. The situation is particularly disadvantageous for women in Algeria, where the sex ratio of labour forces is especially high and equal to 4.45, and less unfavourable for women in Mauritania, where the sex ratio is high but equal to 2.19.[23]

At each point in time, the imbalance decreases as it moves from Scenario 2 to Scenario 1 and particularly to Scenario 3.

Over time, the imbalance would worsen for all countries if the participation rates remained unchanged at the current level (Scenario 2), whereas in the ILO labour force participation rate forecast scenario (Scenario 1), the imbalance would

Table 3.8 Labour forces by broad age groups (index numbers, 2015 = 1)

	Scenario 1			Scenario 2			Scenario 3		
	2020	2025	2030	2020	2025	2030	2020	2025	2030
	15–24			15–24			15–24		
Algeria	0.83	0.81	0.99	0.86	0.9	1.15	1.49	1.6	2.04
Egypt	1.01	1.11	1.27	1.02	1.11	1.28	1.51	1.65	1.89
Libya	1	1.06	1.13	1	1.04	1.11	1.29	1.35	1.44
Mauritania	1.08	1.17	1.27	1.12	1.27	1.43	0.83	0.93	1.06
Morocco	0.95	0.94	0.95	0.97	0.98	1.02	1.35	1.38	1.46
Tunisia	0.89	0.85	0.91	0.9	0.88	0.96	1.16	1.15	1.29
	25–44			25–44			25–44		
Algeria	1.09	1.09	1.04	1.08	1.07	1.01	1.3	1.3	1.23
Egypt	1.11	1.19	1.26	1.1	1.16	1.22	1.34	1.42	1.48
Libya	1.02	1.01	1.01	1.02	1	0.99	1.06	1.04	1.03
Mauritania	1.15	1.31	1.48	1.15	1.3	1.46	1.31	1.49	1.67
Morocco	1.1	1.17	1.2	1.1	1.16	1.19	1.33	1.4	1.43
Tunisia	1.05	1.06	1.02	1.06	1.06	1.02	1.1	1.1	1.05
	45–54			45–54			45–54		
Algeria	1.16	1.41	1.71	1.16	1.39	1.66	1.34	1.61	1.92
Egypt	1.13	1.35	1.63	1.11	1.31	1.54	1.47	1.72	2.03
Libya	1.35	1.63	1.74	1.35	1.61	1.71	1.32	1.58	1.68
Mauritania	1.21	1.45	1.7	1.21	1.44	1.69	1.66	1.97	2.31
Morocco	1.05	1.17	1.38	1.05	1.17	1.36	1.34	1.48	1.71
Tunisia	1.02	1.1	1.26	1.02	1.1	1.26	1.05	1.13	1.29
	55–64			55–64			55–64		
Algeria	1.12	1.27	1.43	1.17	1.36	1.58	1.53	1.79	2.08
Egypt	1.21	1.43	1.68	1.17	1.32	1.48	2.03	2.31	2.6
Libya	1.34	1.97	2.64	1.33	1.95	2.6	1.16	1.69	2.26
Mauritania	1.24	1.51	1.83	1.23	1.49	1.8	1.89	2.29	2.76
Morocco	1.15	1.19	1.22	1.16	1.22	1.27	1.8	1.92	2.02
Tunisia	1.12	1.17	1.14	1.15	1.23	1.24	1.3	1.43	1.46

worsen for Morocco and Tunisia while it would improve for Algeria, Egypt and Mauritania. There would be no substantial changes for Libya.

In Scenario 3, the imbalance would improve considerably given that the sex ratio would halve in Algeria and would also significantly decline in Egypt and Morocco. Instead, in Mauritania, the greater participation in the labour market will occur with a slight disadvantage to the female components (Table 3.9).

Table 3.9 Sex ratio of labour forces

			Scenario 1	Scenario 2	Scenario 3
Algeria	2015	4.45			
	2020		4.36	4.56	2.23
	2025		4.29	4.76	2.25
	2030		4.21	4.92	2.26
Egypt	2015	3.29			
	2020		3.25	3.34	1.71
	2025		3.14	3.36	1.71
	2030		3.03	3.37	1.7
Libya	2015	3.05			
	2020		3.05	3.12	2.23
	2025		3.05	3.18	2.24
	2030		3.02	3.23	2.25
Mauritania	2015	2.19			
	2020		2.17	2.2	1.22
	2025		2.14	2.21	1.22
	2030		2.11	2.21	1.22
Morocco	2015	2.83			
	2020		2.87	2.88	1.61
	2025		2.91	2.93	1.62
	2030		2.95	2.98	1.63
Tunisia	2015	2.71			
	2020		2.77	2.79	2.16
	2025		2.81	2.85	2.19
	2030		2.84	2.91	2.21

Conclusions

In this study, we analyzed the extraordinary demographic changes in the last seven decades in Southern Mediterranean countries, namely Algeria, Egypt, Libya, Mauritania, Morocco and Tunisia, resulting from the transformation of their demographic regimes.

In particular, we showed that population growth, in general, and the working age population growth, in particular, are structural characteristics of these countries. In other words, they are long-lasting consequences of the unfolding demographic transition. Moreover, this evolution has not yet ended. This is the main demographic concern, and it certainly constitutes the challenge of governments in this area.

As we also showed, this geographical area should not be considered homogeneous: the countries are demographically differentiated due to their different transitional paths. On the one hand, there is Tunisia which, with its regular, continuous and rapid transition, is the country with the least critical demographic situation and the lowest growth in potential labour supply. On the other, there is Mauritania, the country that differs the most from the rest of the group and is more similar to Africa as a whole. Still in the midst of the transition, Mauritania has undergone a slow process of decline in both mortality and fertility, which has brought about, and will continue to bring about, a large increase in the total and in the working age population. In between lie the demographic transitions – and the demographic conditions – of Algeria, Libya, Morocco and Egypt.

Algeria and Egypt have completed the transition of mortality but not yet that of fertility. For these two countries, the demographic pressure is still strong and, after Mauritania, they will be the two countries in the region in which the growth of the working age population will be greater in the coming years. Such an increase will come to an end in Egypt while growth will be negative in Algeria only after 2065. As these are the two most populous countries in the region, the increase, in absolute terms, will be particularly significant. Up to 2030, the working age population will increase by around 1.3 million people a year on average in Egypt and 0.4 million people a year on average in Algeria.

In a somewhat similar demographic condition is Morocco which, despite some uncertainties in the fertility transition, is currently in a more advanced stage of the process of fertility decline than Algeria and Egypt. In this country, until 2030 the working age population will continue to grow at a positive but decreasing rate, higher than 1%, such that 0.3 million people a year on average will be added.

In Libya, mortality has declined rapidly but the beginning of fertility decline started late after a significant increase between the mid-1960s and mid-1970s. In the past, Libya was able to increase its working age population significantly thanks to strong immigration flows. Despite the current political, institutional, economic and social crisis, due to the dynamics of the sole natural components (fertility and mortality), the working age population will continue to grow, at decreasing but still sustained rates, until 2030. Moreover, these rates are expected to be higher than in Morocco.

Not all the growth in the working age population will turn into an effective labour supply. We considered three scenarios – a baseline scenario (Scenario 2), which assumes constant labour force participation rates at current levels such that all the labour force growth is determined by working age population growth, a scenario that emerges upon considering the ILO forecast activity rates (Scenario 1) and an ameliorative scenario that amounts to a maximum feasible increase of labour forces (Scenario 3).

Our results show that, whatever the scenario concerned, it will be necessary to guarantee employment to an increasing number of people. Availability of extra jobs must be greater in the first period, which in our periodization ends in 2020. The labour force will continue to grow but at a lower rate in the 2020–2025 period. In 2025–2030, the growth rate will continue to decline for Libya, Mauritania and Morocco, whereas it will resume in Algeria, Egypt and Tunisia.

Labour supply will not grow homogeneously by age. It will grow more in the mature age group and especially in the older class (45–54 and 55–64 years), but it will also be considerable in the 25–44 class.

In the young age class (15–24 years), trends will be different according to the scenario. In Algeria, Morocco and Tunisia, it will decrease according to Scenario 1 and 2, but grow according to Scenario 3 (in the latter case, especially in Algeria). In Mauritania, it will increase in Scenario 1 and even more in Scenario 2, whereas it would expand much less in Scenario 3. In Egypt and Libya, it will grow regardless of the scenario.

Moreover, the labour supply by gender, currently particularly unbalanced in favour of males, would improve towards a better representation of females only with a radical transformation of the labour market as in Scenario 3. If the current participation rates remained unchanged, the situation would even worsen over time for all countries, whereas if the labour market indicators fit the ILO forecasts, the imbalance would worsen over time for Morocco and Tunisia and would improve for Algeria, Egypt and Mauritania. There would be no substantial changes for Libya.

Therefore, different and well-structured policies for employment will be required that take into account the characteristics of the labour supply, which will be growing, heterogeneous and progressively aging.

Finally, in the next 15 years, the future reproductive behaviour of women in these countries will not modify the labour supply which, from a strictly demographic point of view, will be determined solely by mortality changes. Nevertheless, fertility levels will be able to influence indirectly the policies that will be implemented.

The fertility level, indeed, will influence the allocation of resources for carrying out policies in favour of the different population age groups, especially in favour of education, health care and prevention (where in these countries some critical issues still exist) and employment.

All this should be taken into consideration. Failing that, whatever the country, there will continue to be poor living conditions for much of the population, substantial emigration and social crises.

Notes

1 All the Greater Maghreb countries belong to the Arab Maghreb Union. They are Algeria, Libya, Mauritania, Morocco and Tunisia.
2 The structure of population is the distribution of the population by one or more salient characteristics – the principal being sex and age.
3 A demographic window is a time period of favourable levels of demographic dependency.
4 That is, 15–24-year-olds on the entire adult population or the total population.
5 A series of protests and demonstrations started in December 2010 in Tunisia and then spread to different extents to other northern and Middle Eastern countries.

6 For instance, Demeny (1968) and Chesnais (1986).

7 From a first (Thompson 1929; Notestein 1945) to a second (Lesthaeghe and van de Kaa 1986; van de Kaa 1987) and a third transition (Kohler et al. 2002).

8 In the discipline, there is no agreement about how to establish the end of the transition. Some scholars even deny that, in certain areas of the world, it has ever ended. We consider that a transition has ended when both life expectancy at birth for women has reached 73 years (following Chesnais 1986) and fertility has declined up to or below the replacement level.

9 In these countries, estimates of demographic events are inadequate for the period before the second half of the twentieth century, whereas starting from the Second World War, thanks to the estimates made by the United Nations, it is possible to calculate and analyze many indicators, which allow good measurements and significant comparisons. Moreover, increasingly numerous surveys allow important aspects to be highlighted in relation to the main demographic phenomena. We rely on the latest available version of the UN estimates of demographic indicators, the data series which starts with 1950. The 2017 Revision of the World Population Prospects updated the estimates for 2010–2015 and considers, for the Southern Mediterranean region, more favourable health conditions (lower mortality) than the previous 2015 Revision. In particular, a higher life expectancy at birth has been estimated for Tunisia, Morocco, Libya and Algeria (in the latter case, only for males). Unchanged is the estimate for Egypt, whereas for Mauritania, mortality has increased. As regards fertility, compared with the previous estimates, total fertility rate is higher for Algeria, Morocco and Tunisia and lower for Libya and Mauritania. The value for Egypt is confirmed.

10 Fargues (1986) confirms an earlier start of mortality decline, for Algeria and Morocco.

11 When one considers the pre-transitional levels in Europe and estimates for non-European countries at the end of the nineteenth and beginning of the twentieth centuries.

12 Both are pure measures of demographic behaviours. Unlike the crude birth and death rates, their values are not influenced by the population structure.

13 A natural growth higher than 20 per thousands means that – under the no-change hypothesis – the population doubles in fewer than 35 years.

14 It should be noted that a natural growth rate of 10 per thousands means a still short doubling time of the population, around 70 years.

15 Sending or emigration countries are countries where net migration (the number of immigrants minus than the number of emigrants) is negative while receiving or immigration countries are countries where net migration is positive. In the first case, the situation may also be consistent with substantial immigration whereas, in the second case, the situation may also be consistent with substantial emigration.

16 However, emigration continued. In Italy, for instance, one of its main destination countries, immigration from Tunisia has been substantial until now.

17 We consider the age of 15 as the minimum age of entry into the labour market, as 15 years old is the basic minimum age for working according to the ILO Convention (No. 138, 1973) and we set old age at 65. For the ratification dates of the minimum age for admission to employment see Normlex, Information System on International Labour Standards; for statutory ages at retirement, see note 20.

18 In a general way, it is the period when the proportions in the population between potential economic dependents and supporters change in favour of the latter, releasing resources for new and productive investments and increasing productivity.

19 Unemployment rates are high, especially among the young, women and the most educated (Eurostat 2016).

20 In Algeria, Egypt, Mauritania, Morocco and Tunisia, the statutory age at retirement is 60 years (55 for females in Algeria and Mauritania). In Libya, it is 65 years for males and 60 for females (UN, World Population Policy Database 2015).

21 Data available upon request. We do not show them so as not to overburden the presentation.
22 There are no migrations. This allows us to consider the changes in the size of the working age population as the mere effect of the changes in natural components and subsequently evaluate migration.
23 The sex ratio is the ratio of the number of males to the number of females.

References

Abbasi-Shavazi, M.J., and Torabi, F., 2012. Women's Education and Fertility in Islamic Countries. *In*: H. Groth and A. Souza-Poza, eds. *Population Dynamic in Muslim Countries: Assembling the Jigsaw*. Springer, 43–62.

Aberstadt, N., and Shah, A., 2012. Fertility Decline in the Muslim World, c. 1975- c. 2005: A Veritable Sea-Change, Still Curiously Unnoticed. *In*: H. Groth and A. Souza-Poza, eds. *Population Dynamic in Muslim Countries: Assembling the Jigsaw*. Springer, 11–27.

Bloom, D.E., Canning D., and Sevilla J., 2001. *Economic Growth and the Demographic Transition*, NBE Working Paper Series, Working Paper 8685. Cambridge: National Bureau of Economic Research.

Carella, M., and Parant, A., 2016. Age-Structural Transition and Demographic Windows Around the Mediterranean. *In*: R. Pace and R. Ham-Chande, eds. *Demographic Dividends: Emerging Challenges and Policy Implications*. Springer International, 83–113.

Casterline, J.B., 2011. Fertility Prospects in the Arab Region. *Expert Paper No. 2011/6, United Nations, Department of Economic and Social Affairs*. New York: United Nations.

Chesnais, J.C., 1986. La transition démographique: Etapes, formes, implications économiques. INED, *Travaux et documents*, Cahier No 113. Paris: Presses Universitaires de France.

Demeny, P., 1968. *Early Fertility Decline in Austria- Hungary: A Lesson in Demographic Transition*. Daedalus, Spring.

Di Comite, L., and Moretti, E., 1992. *Demografia e Flussi Migratori Nel Bacino Mediterraneo*. Rome: NIS.

Di Comite, L., and Moretti, E., 1999. *Geopolitica del Mediterraneo*. Rome: Carocci.

Eltigani, E.E., 2000. Changes in Family-Building Patterns in Egypt and Morocco: A Comparative Analysis. *International Perspective on Sexual and Reproductive Health*, 26 (2), 73–78.

Eurostat, 2016. *Labour Force Statistics for the Mediterranean Region. 2016 Edition*. Luxembourg: Eurostat.

Faour, T.A., and Farah, A-A., 2013. Arab Youth in the Context of Empowering Opportunities and Emerging Challenges. *Arab Family Health and Population: Researches and Studies*, VI (16), Pan Arab Project for Family Health.

Fargues, P., 1986. Un siècle of transition démographique en Afrique Méditerranéenne 1885–1985. *Population*, 41 (2), 205–232.

Fargues, P., 2003. Women in Arab Countries: Challenging the Patriarchal System. *Population & Societies*, 387.

Gribble, J., and Bremner, J., 2012. The Challenge of Attaining the Demographic Dividend. *Policy Brief*, September. Washington, DC: Population Reference Bureau.

International Labour Office (ILO), 2017. *ILO Labour Force Estimates and Projections: 1990–2030 (2017 Edition). Methodological Description*. Geneva: International Labour Office.

Jones, G.W., 2012. Where are all the Jobs? Capturing the Demographic Dividend in Islamic Countries. *In*: H. Groth and A. Souza-Poza, eds. *Population Dynamic in Muslim Countries: Assembling the Jigsaw*. Springer, 31–42.

Kohler, H-P., Billari, F.C., and Ortega, J.A., 2002. The Emergence of Lowest-low Fertility in Europe During the 1990s. *Population and Development Review*, 28 (4), 641–680.

Lesthaeghe, R., and van de Kaa, D.J., 1986. Twee demografische transities. *In*: R. Lesthaeghe and D.J. van de Kaa, eds. *Groei of krimp?* Deventer: Book Edition Mens en Maatshappij, Van Loghum Slaterus.

Mason, A., Lee, R., Abrigo, M., and Lee, S-H., 2017. *Support Ratios and Demographic Dividends: Estimates for the World*. Technical Paper No 2017/1. New York: United Nations, Department of Economic and Social Affairs, Population Division.

Moretti, E., and Zagaglia, B., 2015. Popolazione e migrazioni nell'Africa Mediterranea. *Il Politico*, LXXX (2–3), 141–171.

Notestein, E.W., 1945. Population: The Long View. *In*: T. Schultz, ed. *Food for the World*. Chicago: University of Chicago Press.

Salvini, S., 1990. La transizione demografica nei paesi del Mediterraneo sud-orientale. *Serie ricerche empiriche*. Florence: Dipartimento Statistico dell'Università di Firenze, 16.

Tabutin, D., and Schoumaker, B., 2005. La démographie du monde arabe et du Moyen-Orient des années 1950 aux années 2000. *Population*, 60 (5), 611–724.

Tamburini, F., and Vernassa, M., 2010. Introduzione al Grande Maghreb. *In*: F. Tamburini and M. Vernassa, eds. *I Paesi del Grande Maghreb. Storia, Istituzioni e geo-politica di una identità regionale*. Pisa: Plus – Pisa University Press, 5–17.

Thompson, W.S., 1929. Population. *American Journal of Sociology*, 34.

United Nations, Department of Economic and Social Affairs, 2017. *World Population Prospects: The 2017 Revision, Methodology of the United Nations Population Estimates and Projections*, Working Paper No. ESA/P/WP.250. New York: United Nations.

United Nations Development Programme, 2016. *Human Development Report 2016: Human Development for Everyone*. New York: United Nations Development Programme.

Urdal, H., 2012. A Clash of Generations? Youth Bulges and Political Violence. *Expert Paper No. 2012/1, United Nations, Department of Economic and Social Affairs*. New York: United Nations.

Vallin, J., 2005. The Demographic Window: An Opportunity to Be Seized. *Asian Population Studies*, 1 (2), 149–167.

van de Kaa, D.J., 1987. Europe's Second Demographic Transition. *Population Bulletin*, 42 (1), Washington.

World Bank, 2010. *Fertility Decline in Algeria 1980–2006: A Case Study. Report 63073*. Washington, DC: World Bank.

Zagaglia, B., 2013. Demographic Transitions and Social Changes in the Mediterranean Region. *IEMed: Mediterranean Yearbook 2013*, 285–287.

Zagaglia, B., and Moretti, E., 2012. *Demographic Transitions and Social Changes in Mediterranean Countries*. Conference Paper Series, No MDT2012–0024. Athens: ATINER's.

Zagaglia, B., and Moretti, E., 2016. Discussing Demographic Transitions in Southern Mediterranean Countries. *In*: B. Koch, F. Soumakis, and T. Cierco Gomes, eds. *Selected Topics in Social Sciences*. Athens: Athens Institute for Education and Research, 41–53.

Zagaglia, B., Moretti, E., and Cela, E., 2012. Convergenze e divergenze riproduttive nella riva sud del Mediterraneo. *Rivista Italiana di Economia, Demografia e Statistica*, LXVI (3/4), 159–166.

Chapter 4

Measuring women's empowerment in the Southern Mediterranean

An opportunity to address the key development challenges

Marco Zupi

Introduction: defining women's empowerment

Based on literature review (Zupi 2015), and especially in reference to certain classic contributions on the right-based approach and multidimensional views such as those proposed by Kabeer (2002, 2005), Dijkstra (2006) and Ibrahim and Alkire (2007), we can define women's empowerment as women being able to decide and act, which means the transfer to women of control, competences and responsibility for resources and decision-making, as well as strengthening their ability to make choices. This means a combination of immediate improvements in women's material living standards (personal dimension) and a psycho-social and political dimension (collective) (Degnbol-Martinussen and Engberg-Pedersen 2003).

Consequently, the promotion of women's empowerment can be structured into five components related to rights, capacities and opportunities:

*   women's sense of self-worth
*   women's right to have and to make choices
*   women's right to have access to opportunities and resources
*   women's right to the power to control their own lives, both within and outside their homes
*   women's ability to influence the direction of social change to create a more just social and economic order and institutional arrangements, nationally and internationally (Ibrahim and Alkire 2007).

This indicates that women's empowerment is multidimensional, not only economic (including the monetary component). Another important point arising from these preliminary considerations is that women's empowerment may be defined as an end in itself and instrumental to development.

Development means change in terms of enlarging the range of people's choices, resilience of complex adaptive eco- and social systems; as a result, promoting development means expanding opportunities and capabilities, promoting freedom in terms of human rights for everyone. Certainly these goals mean empowerment, that is, transfer of control, competences and responsibility over decision-making and resources to people; in other words, a combination of personal, relational and collective dimensions.

In this context, women's empowerment redresses the imbalance of power in the household and community decision-making processes. Investment in women is an excellent development policy because changes in relationships of power and control between women and men depend on greater self-reliance, self-confidence and the capacity for collective action on the part of women and awareness on the part of all men.

The combination of gender mainstreaming strategies across policies and priorities of goals at national and international levels from above and women's empowerment practices, which incorporate social, political, institutional, economic and cultural relations (Mikkelsen 2005), translates into operative terms development goals, including the gender equality goal as stated by the Beijing Plan of Action (1995). Therefore, women's empowerment is an instrument for gender equality.

A consensus at global level has emerged in recent decades on the importance of gender-mainstreaming strategies across policies and priorities of goals at national and international level, complementary to women's empowerment practices. Gender mainstreaming, based on the women's empowerment framework, embodies strategies for addressing gender equality.

In this chapter, after a preliminary definition of women's empowerment, a corresponding conceptualization based on the capabilities approach is proposed. The next two sections explore how women's empowerment should be measured, and then how practical proposals have been developed, underlining the relevance of some UN solutions towards which national and international policies are invited to orient their strategies. These solutions appear particularly relevant for their potential political impact because, as clarified in the fourth section, the new Sustainable Development Goals framework and process under implementation emphasizes policy-oriented monitoring and evaluation. The fifth section identifies countries in Southern Mediterranean as cases that should be better studied, given the lack of detailed information, their relevance in the context of a redefinition of regional and international political equilibria and dramatic social changes that have occurred in the last decade with uncertain developments. A brief description of some available data follows, inspired by the recommendation to follow the ten-step process experienced in the recent Senegalese experience implemented by UN Women and CeSPI with the *Indice de l'autonomisation des femmes*. The concluding section draws attention to some issues recognized as problematic in women's empowerment in Southern Mediterranean countries which need attention.

Conceptualization of women's empowerment

In conceptualizing women's empowerment, we suggest adopting the capabilities approach proposed by Amartya Sen (Morris 2009) to clarify the relationship between women's empowerment and other key developmental terms, which is the implicit mechanism or theory of change on the basis of which policy initiatives can be evaluated. This suggestion is due to the fact that, rather than just focussing on economic resources, the explicit focus on opportunities or freedoms to achieve what an individual reflectively considers valuable (i.e. capabilities) can be directly applicable to the concept women's empowerment and it is evaluative in nature, as it implies normative aspects and is relevant for policy evaluation (as difficult as it is to measure it).

The capability approach is not a theory to explain women's empowerment, but it provides concepts and normative frameworks within which to conceptualize, measure and evaluate women's empowerment as well as the institutions and policies that affect them.

The well-being of a woman (or group of women) can be seen in terms of the quality (the 'wellness') of the woman's being and doing. Her being and doing may be the outcome of her own or other people's decisions and actions. Sen uses the term 'functionings' to designate well-being, wellness, advantage or personal welfare achievements: they are the state of a woman, especially the various things she manages to do or be in leading her life (Sen 1993). The relevant functionings can vary from elementary achievements, such as being adequately nourished or in good health, to more complex ones such as being happy, having self-respect, taking part in the life of the community and so on (Sen 1992).

Such actual achievements – the functionings – are different from the freedom to achieve them, which is the real opportunity that a woman has to accomplish what she values. This freedom is termed 'capabilities' by Sen, meaning the alternative combinations of things a person is free to choose, do or be (Sen 1993).

In theory, from a developmental perspective, the focus can be on both the well-being achievements (functionings) and the well-being freedoms (capabilities). Consequently, strategies and policies can be evaluated according to their impact on women's capabilities as well as their actual functionings.

According to Sen, freedom is crucial. Therefore, what is ultimately important is that people have the freedoms or valuable opportunities (capabilities) for the functionings, that is freedom to choose from which results are obtained in terms of final achievement. The focus lies in the range of possible ways of life from which each person can choose, rather than in the final account of good lives. Women should have the freedom to lead the kind of lives they want to lead, to do what they want to do and to be the person they want to be.

In a broader way, a theory of change that can be derived from the capabilities approach should imply that financial resources and economic production, as well as political practices and institutions (such as effective guarantees and protections of freedom of thought, political participation; social structures, institutions and norms; social practices; traditions and habits) are the main inputs for various capabilities.

The capability approach pays great attention to the linkages among:

- economic, social, political, institutional and cultural inputs or resources available
- capabilities
- material, mental and social well-being (achieved functionings, results or ends).

The relation between an input and the achievement of certain beings and doings is influenced by conversion factors. Conversion factors influence how a person can be or is free to convert the characteristics of the input into a functioning, and they are categorized into three groups:

- internal to the person (such as physical condition)
- social, that is from the society in which one lives (such as public policies, social norms and correlated institutions – such as the household and interfamilial relations – in which they work, practices that unfairly discriminate)
- environmental, that is emerging from the physical or manmade environment in which a person lives (such as means of transportation).

Capabilities do not to refer exclusively to a woman's abilities or other internal powers, but refer to an opportunity made feasible, and constrained by, both internal and external conversion factors.

Social constraints, institutions and policies are important factors that influence, promote, protect and restrict well-being. The attention paid to conversion factors that make possible the conversion of physical inputs into functionings, and to the social, institutional and environmental context means that social institutions broadly defined are considered as specific factors in the expansion of capabilities.

Sen and Nussbaum have paid much attention to the social norms and traditions that form women's preferences and that influence their aspirations and their effective choices (Nussbaum 2000; Sen 1999, 1995).

Summing up, following the capabilities approach, the emphasis is on individual goals, values and capabilities, as well as on social institutions. Amartya Sen underlines the importance of people as agents of change, that is, of agency. Agency is the ability of a person to choose and act to modify reality in order to make choices and control their own lives, playing a pro-active role in development terms. The idea of agency is a practical implementation of the empowerment concept. Unlike a person's well-being (freedom and achievements), which concerns only the person's 'wellness', a person may also pursue goals that reduce her well-being and even end her life, such that a person's agency concerns the totality of her considered goals and objectives, everything she has reasons to pursue, whether or not they are connected with her own well-being (Sen 1999).

Following the emphasis on agency and voice, it is important to ask not only what it means for an individual's life or for a group to be doing well, and which capabilities and functionings are most important, but also who should decide these questions, how they should do so and who should act to effect change. Such a focus on agency becomes crucial in solving the problem of the selection and weighting of capabilities.

Similar to well-being, a person's agency position in a social arrangement can be judged from two different perspectives: the actual achievement of agency, and the freedom to achieve agency, that is, to decide what she should achieve. Similar to well-being, agency is qualified and constrained by the available social, political and economic opportunities.

Moreover, rather than being confined to a narrow and Western-centric notion of independent individual agency, it is important to consider the option to broaden the understanding of agency in a more collective sense, that is, attributed to the community as a whole, shared between all members of a community as defined by reciprocal relationships that give them a community identity, beyond an individual-centred socio-cultural perspective (Pearce et al. 2017).

The approach to measure women's empowerment

Facts and statistics on resources, capabilities and achievements, as well as individual and collective agency across countries, are abundant, but data availability and reliability in terms of consistency of the collected data, precision of measurement and information directly related to the phenomenon under investigation is a huge problem. Data of this sort do not provide either a complete characterization of women's empowerment, which is place based, or a comprehensive description of the economic, social and political dimensions of it. Not only do existing numbers and indices fail to capture the concrete meaning of women's empowerment, but they can also be questioned by many who perceive them as misleading, inaccurate and false measures. Measurement problems are universal, but there are particular problems in developing countries, not only because their capacity for data collection and financial resources is limited, but also because they do not prioritize these issues (Tayyib et al. 2012).

Given the conceptualization of women's empowerment, indicators of its relevant dimensions and their measurement should follow. This is no easy task: it may be said that the value of the empowerment concept lies precisely in its 'fuzziness', its openness (and dependence on the agents' views), and therefore a precise measurement is very difficult or even impossible. In the same way as development, the focus of empowerment measurement could be on:

- material and social resources (pre-conditions, such as asset ownership)
- agency and voice (the intervening process of change, with women as the main protagonists, such as women's participation in domestic decision-making)
- the achievements in terms of ability to make transformative choices catalyze change (outcomes, such as the improvement in women's nutrition).

Alternatively, other methodological implications are that the measurement could focus on three different categories of composite indicators:

- direct evidence of empowerment (such as the improvement in women's nutrition)
- source of empowerment (such as asset ownership)
- setting or indirect source indicators (such as a wife and husband who are about the same age) (Kabeer 2002).

In Roy Bhaskar (Bhaskar 1978), Tony Lawson (Lawson 1997; Lawson 2003) and Jesper Jespersen (Jespersen 2009)'s realist perspective, 'reality' neither merely consists of a puzzle where the pieces are known in advance nor exists independently of observations and interpretations. The nature of social reality (its ontology) is both open and indeterminate, it is mediated by our perceptions and beliefs and it determines the type of knowledge that can be acquired.

Institutions are crucial and intertwined parts of our complex social reality in the form of formal power relations (legislative action), formal/informal agreements (e.g. negotiations) and the organization of the social arena (such as markets).

Our knowledge of reality can be depicted in stratified form, by considering three different levels of cognitive data. At the analytical level, the epistemological approach we propose (Zupi 2019) to tackle the complexity of effectiveness and aid measurement is as follows:

- the constitutional discourse of the Rule of Law (*de jure* reality)
- empirical 'objective' facts and practices (*de facto* reality)
- subjective perceptions, opinions and attitudes (*de habitu* reality).

These three different levels of reality are all important; they interact but are not the same (Zupi 2011) as graphically represented in Figure 4.1. Each of them can be translated into numerical 'facts' or products, always embedded in the social and political structure of the time and place where they are made. There is no strict and regular causal sequence among the three levels of reality, through which one level under certain conditions systematically causes the

Figure 4.1 Ontological dimensions or levels of observable reality

other two. Therefore, a permanent combination of information on narratives (the Rule of Law discourse), stylized facts ('objective' facts) and perceptions (opinions and attitudes) is recommended.

In practice, we propose to collect data simultaneously on the three aforementioned levels of information, drawing on:

- national constitutions, statutes, laws, regulations, decrees and codes; international conventions, agreements and treaties; private contracts (i.e. the system of rules that are enforced through social institutions to govern behaviour)
- regular population census, administrative factual data (i.e. data regularly collected by the government for its day-to-day operations to support its functioning of hospitals, schools, police stations, civil statistics, etc.) and survey data (whenever possible standardized) on the implementation of formal and informal norms[1]
- surveys, focus groups, interviews (whenever possible on a regular basis and embedded into census and administrative data) about opinions and attitudes.[2]

We propose a collection, dynamic analysis and evaluation of laws, facts and opinions, all of them being the key sources of information on women's empowerment in a given context, as a practical way to plan, monitor and evaluate policies' and institutions' impact on the change of power distribution within society. Clearly, the difficulty of an effective triangulation among data of different nature, size, frequency and reliability cannot be underestimated and is a very important challenge.

Broadly speaking, priority should definitely be given to administrative data sources, such as hospital and court registers, as they should be the core components of national statistical systems. However, poor countries, under-funded and dependent on donor support, are typically oriented to promote ad hoc household surveys. Sources of micro-data are essential due to the place-based nature of empowerment, and they should be used and strengthened to reach capacity (ownership principle), with additional primary ad hoc sources of information – such as extra modules of existing household surveys – when necessary.

Literature and practice of measuring women's empowerment

Women's empowerment processes and achievements are closely tied to contextual specific realities at national and local (i.e. sub-national) level. Such localized development or a place-based approach (Barca 2009) is the proper way to measure change, by addressing all the place-based features of countries, in terms of cultural, social and institutional specificities, which are regarded as relevant dimensions to define appropriate policies. It implies the need to reconsider and re-elaborate the real meaning of women's empowerment processes as country-specific or locally embedded dynamics.

Based on the definition and conceptualization of women's empowerment and the relevance of national specificities, the measurement of women's empowerment can follow. But the reality is that statistical indicators and measures are just imperfect attempts to translate into operative terms definitions and correlated conceptualizations, and both measures and definitions contribute to confusion (Lister 2015).

Sen (1992) argued that it is often easier to observe and measure functionings than capabilities. If Sen rejects any predetermined list of capabilities and emphasizes the idea of agency to say that each group should select its own capabilities and prioritize them, Nussbaum (2000) proposed a list of ten capabilities, conceived as the moral entitlements of every human being, that is universal and general, and its highly abstract level is criticized precisely because it risks violating the basic tenets of capabilities and approach to agency. Sabine Alkaike proposed different ways in which individual and group agency might be measured (Alkire 2009), and Ingrid Robeyns proposes her list of capabilities for the study of gender inequality in Western societies based on a four-step methodology, based on unconstrained brainstorming, literature review, existing indicators mapping and comparisons and final discussions (Robeyns 2003).

Many other possible measurements and frameworks have been proposed in the last decade, even if not necessarily implemented empirically. Kabeer (2005) defined female education, women's participation in paid employment and their political representation as key components of women's empowerment; Beteta (2006) proposed the Gender Empowerment Enabling Environment, combining:

- responses to the World Value Survey
- the number of women's organizations in a country
- the country's legal framework ([a] ratification and signature of the Convention on the Elimination of All Forms of Discrimination Against Women [CEDAW]; [b] respect for women's rights; [c] the tolerance of government for discrimination against women).

In 2006, the World Economic Forum introduced the Global Gender Gap Index to measure the gaps in terms of outcome variables rather than input variables, focussing on five dimensions of women's empowerment:

- economic participation
- economic opportunity
- political empowerment
- education attainment
- health and well-being, with a net prevalence of the economic dimensions implying rich economies' bias and a process of 'Othering' poor economies and those in poverty, established and maintained as different.

In 2013, the Women's Empowerment in Agriculture Index was developed for the International Food Policy Research Institute (Alkire et al. 2013), including two sub-indices:

- the percentage of women who are empowered in five domains of in agriculture (the so-called 5DE: [a] the decisions about agricultural production, [b] access to and decision-making power about productive resources, [c] control of use of income, [d] leadership in the community and [e] time allocation)
- the Gender Parity Index focussed on the percentage of women who are empowered or whose empowered score meets or exceeds that of the men in their households.

Phan (2016) proposed a measurement of women's empowerment using microdata from the Demographic and Health Surveys (DHS) to capture the level of empowerment of individual women depending on their current status on four aspects:

- labour-force participation
- household decision-making

- contraceptives use
- education.

These and other indices are proposed to measure women's empowerment at country level or at individual and family level, mainly focussing on economic dimensions.

In theory, the requirements for these kinds of measures are simple (Dijkstra 2006):

- proper measurement should cover a limited number of indicators
- these indicators together should cover as many dimensions of women's empowerment as possible
- data should be available for many countries and at sub-national level
- data should be simple to calculate and to understand
- data should allow comparisons between countries and territories but also over time.

However, the proposed indicators always face the practical obstacle of severely limited data availability. Whenever possible, they are operationalized by using Demographic and Health Survey (DHS), that is, large sample sizes and nationally representative surveys carried out by the US Agency for International Development and the World Bank, data and qualitative interviews to be made available on a regular basis or administrative information at aggregate national level, as well as demographic census data and aggregate accounts data provided by national institutes of statistics and Systems of National Accounts. The main limitation to making comparisons possible is always data coverage at both cross-sectional (i.e. disaggregated at local level) and time series levels.

In terms of correspondence with conceptualization and the approach to measure empowerment, most existing indicators of women's empowerment focus on multidimensional preconditions (economic and social in particular, institutional and political a little less) or, even more, on achievements (almost all the indicators, combining economic, social and political dimensions). On the contrary, the agency is less monitored and translated into active participation in decision-making processes (at the micro-data level of political, economic and social dimensions).

Because the aim is not to present a significant amount of literature developed on women's empowerment measurement during the last 20 years in a comparative perspective, which is beyond the scope of this chapter, what can be highlighted here is its indirect relevance to a parallel process of political attention paid to the issue.

In particular, a major political stimulus came from the 1995 UN Beijing Platform for Action when it identified a specific strategic objective aiming to '*generate and disseminate gender aggregated data and information for planning and evaluation*', which was a milestone in promoting political attention to it. The importance of the collection, analysis and dissemination of sex-disaggregated data and gender-sensitive variables is starting to be widely recognized by governments at both the national and sub-national level, by international statistical institutes and units and other key policy advisory bodies, because adequate data are essential to impact on development decision-making. However, so far many countries have failed to measure gender equality indicators properly, because of capacity limitation and lack of political will.

In practice, together with the still on-going debates on conceptualizing women's empowerment, a series of indices have been proposed on the broader theme and on measurement of women's empowerment by national institutes of statistics and international organizations, such as the UN entities (Zupi 2015).

Relevant examples are the Gender-Related Development Index and the Gender Empowerment Measure were developed by the UN Development Programme (UNDP) in 1995 and replaced by the Gender Inequality Index (GII) in 2010 as an interesting new indicator of women's disadvantages in comparison to men in reproductive health, education, political empowerment and labour market achievements, but still lacking information on women's participation in local government, participation and income from informal sectors, asset ownership, gender-based violence and participation in community decision-making.

Since 2013, the Organisation for Economic Co-operation and Development (OECD) Development Centre has proposed the Social Institution and Gender Index (SIGI) as an assessment of discriminatory social institutions at both country and sub-national levels (Nowacka 2015). The OECD SIGI, introduced in 2007 only at national level, focuses on gender and institutions: a crucial aspect in the attempt to deal with gender inequalities from a transformative perspective. In this sense, SIGI measures social institutions as reflected by societal practices and legal norms perpetuating inequalities between women and men, thus paying attention to the root causes of women inequality based on the assessment of institutions, particularly the household and interfamilial relations (Harper et al. 2014).

Instead of measuring gender inequalities in outputs related to education, health, economic or political participation (all core human development indicators developed by UNDP), SIGI measures important inputs – social institutions – to which the inequalities can be ascribed, and that are conceived as long-lasting codes of conduct, norms, traditions, informal and formal laws (Branisa, Klasen and Ziegler 2009).

SIGI is composed of five sub-indices which make disaggregated information available. Each of the five sub-indices measures a different dimension of social institutions related to gender inequality:

- family code (legal age of marriage, early marriage, parental authority in marriage, parental authority in divorce, inheritance rights of widows, inheritance rights of daughters)

- physical integrity (violence against women, laws on domestic violence, laws on rape, laws on sexual harassment, attitudes towards violence, prevalence of violence in the lifetime, female genital mutilation prevalence, unmet need for family planning)
- son preference (missing women, fertility preferences)
- ownership rights (secure access to land, secure access to non-land assets, access to financial services)
- civil liberties (access to public space, political quotas, political representation).

As SIGI indicators primarily measure social institutions that raise problems in the developing world, SIGI covers only non-OECD countries (Branisa, Klasen, Ziegler, Drechsler and Jütting 2009), which can be considered a limitation in terms of the 'Othering' process of differentiation between 'the rich' and 'the poor'. This means that, rather than adopting a genuine place-based and culture-specific approach, in adapting a general frame to all contexts, there is an implied assumption of a legitimate distinction between the OECD and the rest of the world.

In November 2016, UN Women and the *Centro Studi di Politica Internazionale* together with the Italian Ministry of Foreign Affairs and International Cooperation, presented the preliminary results of an innovative initiative implemented in Senegal to provide technical expertise to the Ministry of Family, Women and Childhood in developing a system of indicators for measuring women's empowerment. This ambitious initiative is relevant because it was the first aimed at combining the two key concepts of agency and capabilities, as well as the economic, political, social and cultural dimensions of empowerment, measuring change across the legal-normative framework (*de jure* level), factual variables (*de facto* level) and attitudes towards women's empowerment (*de habitu* level) in parallel, recognizing their relevance as three different, if mutually interdependent, layers of reality (Zupi 2016a). Built on the experiences and lessons learnt from the previous national indicators, the ambitious aim of this new index (*Indice de l'autonomisation des femmes*, IAF) is to measure women's empowerment in all its four dimensions and to realize the full spectrum of the three layers of reality in parallel, if feasible. The IAF is composed of four domains and each of them is the combination of various sub-components:

- social (family code, social relations, security and violence, reproductive healthcare, health and bodily integrity and safety, nutrition, education)
- economic (resources, employment and social protection, economic poverty)
- political/human rights (political freedom, agency and voice in public arena and in decision-making, equal justice, freedom of movement)
- cultural (technology and media, education, participation in and control of cultural life, time-autonomy and leisure activity, freedom of choice).

For each sub-component, there are many variables to be considered in order to monitor the dynamics of empowerment processes (preconditions,

processes and outcomes). The particular attention paid to agency is con-
verted into a focus on the discriminatory practices occurring in five key
institutions to be constantly addressed. These institutions are the household and interfamilial relations, the market, the nearest social community
(e.g. the village), the state and the rest of the world. The process of setting
and assessing variables to be included into the indicators was empowering in itself, in accordance with the principle of a place-based, context-
and culture-specific definition, and was based on the direct involvement of
representatives of the Senegalese society (women's associations, academic
experts, public administration officers, governmental bodies, etc.), without
an a priori list to be approved. At the end of the pilot run, through a long
participatory process, the Senegalese application identified 210 *de facto* variables and 102 *de habitu* variables, together with those of the *de jure* level
(whose numbers depend on the laws correlated to the de facto variables),
and looked at data from existing population census data, administrative data
and household surveys as key sources.

UN goal, targets and indicators to measure women's empowerment

In the framework of the expansion and progress of the global development
agenda, established following the Millennium Summit of the United Nations
in 2000 with the adoption of eight Millennium Development Goals (MDG),
the UN General Assembly adopted the new Sustainable Development Agenda
in September 2015. By 2015, the world was only partially and slowly meeting
the key targets of the MDG-3 directly aiming 'to promote gender equality and
empower women', with only one specific target to reach (eliminate gender
disparity in primary and secondary education by 2005, and in all levels of education by 2015).

The new SDG-5 enhances and tries to complete the effort of MDG-3 as
it aims 'to achieve gender equality and empowerment of all women and girls'
(Table 4.1). In March 2016, the Inter-Agency and Expert Group on SDG Indicators (IAEG-SDGs) proposed six plus three specific targets, together with the
idea that all the SDGs indicators should be disaggregated, where relevant, by
sex, so as to provide women and girls with equal human rights and access to
education, health care, decent work, information and representation in political
and economic decision-making processes (UN–ECOSOC 2016).

The current situation in women's empowerment indicators within the SDG
framework is that there is a directly dedicated SDG, with six plus three specific
targets and 14 correlated indicators intended to monitor the targets, together
with other 39 explicitly women's referred indicators among the total of 232
SDG indicators spread among the 17 SDGs and 169 correlated targets.

Among all the parties involved in the SDG agenda implementation, the EU
is fully committed to implementing the SDG-5 agenda. The Council adopted

Table 4.1 Targets related to Goal 5: achieve gender equality and empower all women and girls

5.1 End all forms of discrimination against all women and girls everywhere

5.2 Eliminate all forms of violence against all women and girls in the public and private spheres, including trafficking and sexual and other types of exploitation

5.3 Eliminate all harmful practices, such as child, early and forced marriage and female genital mutilation

5.4 Recognize and value unpaid care and domestic work through the provision of public services, infrastructure and social protection policies and the promotion of shared responsibility within the household and the family as nationally appropriate

5.5 Ensure women's full and effective participation and equal opportunities for leadership at all levels of decision-making in political, economic and public life

5.6 Ensure universal access to sexual and reproductive health and reproductive rights as agreed in accordance with the Programme of Action of the International Conference on Population and Development and the Beijing Platform for Action and the outcome documents of their review conferences

5a. Undertake reforms to give women equal rights to economic resources, as well as access to ownership and control over land and other forms of property, financial services, inheritance and natural resources, in accordance with national laws

5b. Enhance the use of enabling technology, in particular information and communications technology, to promote the empowerment of women

5c. Adopt and strengthen sound policies and enforceable legislation for the promotion of gender equality and the empowerment of all women and girls at all levels

the conclusions on the Gender Action Plan 2016–2020 on 26 October 2015 (Council of the European Union 2015) as focussing on:

- ensuring girls' and women's physical and psychological integrity
- promoting the social and economic rights/empowerment of women and girls
- strengthening girls' and women's voice and participation.

In July 2017, the UN General Assembly adopted the global indicator framework (UN General Assembly 2017) and the Secretary-General submitted the report on progress towards the Sustainable Development Goals (UN Secretary-General 2017), based on a UN High-level Political Forum for Sustainable Development thematic review of SDG-5, led by UN Women and UN-DESA (UN High-level Political Forum for Sustainable Development 2017).

In the framework of the current implementation of the SDG agenda, it is important to stress that placing a strong and explicit focus on gender necessarily requires a twin-track approach, with gender equality as a specific goal (SDG-5) mainstreamed in targets and indicators across other goals, acting to address the structural inequalities which persist for women and girls and to foster the necessary political will, resources and national ownership to create sustainable and effective action on gender equality.

Applying women's empowerment measurement in Southern Mediterranean countries

In the UNDP Human Development Report 2010, Tunisia, Algeria and Morocco were celebrated as developmental success stories for their unprecedented performances in human development over 40 years (UNDP 2010).

During the so-called Arab Spring, which exploded in a strong demand for democracy, jobs, dignity and liberty, both national governments and international organizations showed a weak disposition and insufficient ability to grasp the more profound and structural phenomena across Southern Mediterranean countries and which are related to women.

Due to the lack of detailed information, the relevance of those countries in the context of a redefinition of regional and international political equilibria, and dramatic social changes occurring in the last decade – with the civil war in Syria, destabilization in Libya and refugee camps in the neighbouring countries, mainly victimizing women and girls – here the aim is to present just a few data to describe women's empowerment dynamics in Algeria, Egypt, Libya, Morocco and Tunisia. This will indicate the direction of analysis to be conducted in detail and potentially in a comparative perspective. In particular, following the ten-step process experienced in the recent Senegalese case implemented by UN Women and CeSPI, the recommendation is:

- to describe the state-of-the-art and networking of relevant stakeholders
- to guarantee local and national ownership, with the active participation of coordinating bodies oriented to gender mainstreaming, from the identification of variables to the review of design and findings
- to identify place-based, context- and culture-specific lists of variables as referred to *de facto*, *de habitu* and *de jure* levels of reality
- to map and finally validate existing data and eligible sources for the given list of variables
- to collect data and create a data matrix
- to test the quality of data and integrate them with a pilot survey
- to develop preliminary synthetic indicators for each dimension (and sub-component) and for each level of reality
- to improve the dataset with missing key data and mainstream women's empowerment across the regular collection of data at the national level
- to develop the final indexes (such as the IAF, one for each level of reality based on the feasibility, complementarity, accountability and parsimony criteria) and visualize them
- to use the final index to influence and evaluate policies.

On the basis of such a ten-step process, what follows merely describes some very basic data of interest and takes cautious steps to present and analyze them. The legitimacy of a proper design and selection of variables, data and correlated sources cannot come from external experts but is intimately connected to an empowering, locally controlled process.

De jure *reality*

A first level of reality to be addressed is the constitutional discourse of the Rule of Law (*de jure* reality).

Across Southern Mediterranean countries, a key obstacle facing women continues to be the personal status law: the law varies from country to country but, with the exception of Tunisia and Morocco, it is not gender friendly (i.e. based, for example, on the CEDAW).

In practice, due to the importance of the dynamics of empowerment processes (preconditions, process and outcomes) and following the applied process to develop IAF in Senegal, the *de jure* reality is a composite discourse including international rules and norms (such as CEDAW), constitution, customary laws, conventions, statutory laws (including general codes such as civil or criminal law) and judge-made laws, rules and statutes. Again, it is crucial and preliminary to understand the hierarchy and coherence of laws to properly understand the composite *de jure* reality. And for each specific law, it would be necessary to monitor the entire process (discussion, approval, implementation, campaigning to enforce it if needed).

If we look at the official discourse of the Constitution at a very preliminary stage in the analysis, the narrative is not discriminatory:

- According to the Algerian Constitution (amended in 2008), women enjoy the same civil and political rights as men and have the status of full citizens (Arts. 29 and 31).
- In Egypt, the 2014 Constitution established equality for all citizens and that the State shall ensure the achievement of equality between women and men in all civil, political, economic, social, and cultural rights (Arts. 9, 11 and 180).
- Libya has no constitution as such, but the 1997 Charter on the Rights and Duties of Women in Jamahiriya Society guarantees the equal rights of men and women.
- In Morocco, the 2011 Constitution establishes that men and women should enjoy equal rights and freedoms in all civil, political, economic, social, cultural and environmental matters (Art. 19).
- In Tunisia, the 2014 Constitution reaffirms equal rights and freedoms in all civil, political, economic, social, cultural dimensions and the equality of opportunities between women and men to have access to all levels of responsibility in all domains (Arts. 21, 34, 46).

In practice, however, a better proxy of the *de jure* narrative is given by laws such as the family code, which addresses women's rights in marriage, divorce, succession, repudiation and issues such as polygamy, but also the labour code, legislation on gender-based violence and relations with customary and religious traditions (and practices).

As a reference, the data collected by OECD SIGI and covering just the year 2014 on the five sub-indices give us a national proxy of the state of gender inequality and discrimination of some formal and informal social institutions and norms, focussing on the underlying factors that drive gender inequality in education, employment, income and political participation (see Table 4.2).

Although the data show heterogeneous profiles in the region, the situation is generally critical. The index value of Egypt and Morocco or Tunisia appear very different; in particular, Egypt scores 0.67 on the family code sub-index, whereas Morocco scores 0.46 and Tunisia 0.43.

Behind these data there is a reality of discrimination. In the case of Egypt, there is no unified Family Code and religion governs women's rights within the family. In the case of Islamic law, recognition of parental authority, as well as inheritance rights and the right to initiate divorce, discriminates against women; early marriage is frequent (particularly in rural areas) and only men can be the head of the household.

As a general comment that applies to many countries, including Senegal (studied in more detail), it is important to underline the fact that personal status laws have come later and are less secularized than other laws; reforms have not removed

Table.4.2 Comparison of North African countries' SIGI by sub-indices of discrimination, 2014

	Discriminatory family code – sub-index	Restricted physical integrity – sub-index	Son bias – sub-index	Restricted resources and assets – sub-index	Restricted civil liberties – sub-index	Social Institutions and Gender Index (SIGI)
Algeria	0.43	0.336	...	0.591	0.255	...
Egypt	0.666	0.737	0.374	0.591	0.814	0.428
Libya	0.434	0.355	...	0.591	0.609	...
Morocco	0.461	0.316	0.157	0.388	0.195	0.105
Tunisia	0.431	0.16	0.478	0.591	0.45	0.199

Source: OECD-SIGI online dataset

Note: The sub-index ranges from 0 for no discrimination to 1 for very high levels of discrimination. The technical annex to the 2014 edition of the OECD-SIGI Report provides details on how its sub-indices are constructed. In practice: 0 = Women and men enjoy the same rights in law and in practice; 0.25 = The legislation is not well implemented; 0.5 = The customary laws and practices discriminate against women; 0.75 = The legislation is contradictory, non-specific or limited in scope and definition; 1 = Women and men do not enjoy the same rights in the legal framework. See OECD-SIGI 2014.

the Islamic inspiration of law in many countries. Notwithstanding the difference between the Personal Status Code and the Islamic Law and despite the attention paid to women's empowerment, the caution shown by many governments with regard to the questioning of traditional legacy should not be underestimated.

Moreover, in general terms, some customary practices are discriminatory and female genital mutilation is widespread. The official criminal code does not criminalize domestic violence as such and violence within marriage is considered socially acceptable because a wife should obey her husband, as explicitly stated by the previous Constitution.

Therefore, the Constitution, but also laws, religious laws and customary practices and various degrees of law application, have to be analyzed in detail as potential discriminatory, limiting women's freedom, and define the complex map of the *de jure* layer of reality.

De facto *reality*

A second level of reality to be addressed is the factual reality that should be focussed on inputs, capabilities and achievements.

Focussing just on achievements, it is clear that the concept is much wider and richer than what can be caught in any index or set of indicators. There are sufficient arguments for the incorporation of measures of education, health, job and political power dimensions among others to measure a more comprehensive level of achievements, reflecting inequality in achievement between women and men. A participatory multi-stakeholder process at the national level is the best solution to select and validate the list of variables for inclusion and to move from the ideal full list of variables to the final selection based on the feasibility, complementarity and parsimony criteria.

The UNDP GII introduced in 2010 is only one example. This index comprises five variables:

* maternal mortality ratio: number of deaths due to pregnancy-related causes per 100,000 live births.
* adolescent birth rate: number of births to women ages 15–19 per 1,000 women ages 15–19.
* share of seats in parliament: proportion of seats held by women in the national parliament expressed as a percentage of total seats; for countries with a bicameral legislative system, the share of seats is calculated based on both houses
* population with at least some secondary education: percentage of the population age 25 and older that has reached (but not necessarily completed) a secondary level of education
* labour force participation rate: proportion of the working age population (age 15 and older) that engages in the labour market, either by working or actively looking for work, expressed as a percentage of the working age population.

Although information in its current form is absolutely preliminary and insufficient to describe the complex reality of women's empowerment, these factual data confirm the heterogeneous profiles in the region (see Table 4.3). This situation may be viewed as generally critical. The GII value of Egypt and Tunisia (or Libya) appears very different; Egypt scores 0.56, whereas Tunisia scores 0.29 and Libya 0.17. In particular:

- on the number of deaths due to pregnancy-related causes per 100,000 live births, Algeria is at the opposite extreme to Libya (140 vs. nine)
- on the births to women ages 15–19 per 1,000 women of the same age, Egypt is opposite to Libya (51.9 vs. 6.2)
- on the proportion of seats held by women in the national parliament Egypt is markedly different from Tunisia (2.2% vs. 31.3%)
- on the ratio of female to male proportion of the adult population that reach a secondary level of education, Tunisia is the opposite of Libya (75.2% vs. 148.5%)
- on the ratio of female to male proportion of the working age population that engages in the labour market, Algeria lags far behind Libya (23.9% vs. 35.3%).

As the five component variables are moderately but not perfectly correlated, additional inspection is needed – through regression or principal component analysis for example – to better detect the relationships.

Table 4.3 Comparison of North African countries' facts by five UNDP-GII dimensions of achievements, 2016

	Maternal mortality ratio	Adolescent birth rate	Share of seats in parliament	Ratio of female to male population with at least some secondary education	Ratio of female to male labour force participation rate	Gender Inequality Index
Algeria	140	10.6	25.7	95.5	23.9	0.429
Egypt	33	51.9	2.2	80	29.9	0.565
Libya	9	6.2	16	148.5	35.3	0.167
Morocco	121	31.7	15.7	77.4	34.1	0.494
Tunisia	62	6.8	31.3	75.2	35.2	0.289

Source: UNDP online dataset

Note: Maternal mortality rate and adolescent birth rate are the variables, among the five considered, that are indicator of the burden (of maternal deaths and of fertility on teen mothers, respectively), so that the higher the value, the more serious the problem. The meaning of the signs is reversed for the other three variables. The Gender Equality Index ranges from 0, where women and men fare equally, to 1, where one gender fares as poorly as possible in all measured dimensions.

Moreover, the proxies of achievements merely represent the results, without providing any specific information on the causal factors and mechanisms in the explanation of those results. Therefore, understanding of the root causes and processes, as well as identification of appropriate policies and interventions to change the situation, requires diagnostic and investigation of theories of change to achieve the empowerment of women and girls.

Last, many other factual data must be taken into account, in order to integrate them and the *de jure* level of reality (e.g. variables on violence against women) but also to explore other dimensions of empowerment. An example is the low percentage of women who hold a bank account at a formal financial institution compared with the percentage of men all over Southern Mediterranean countries, the gender divide and gender differences in land tenure and access to productive resources. Another example is the importance of a proxy of time deficits that girls and women are unable to compensate for, due to the gendered distribution of care responsibilities within families: a very important dimension that is generally neglected in the literature and in policy making (Antonopoulos et al. 2017).

De habitu *reality*

A third level of reality to consider is subjective perceptions, opinions and attitudes (*de habitu* reality).

A UN Women comparative study of Southern Mediterranean men, women and their views and experiences about gender equality is an example of data collection through surveys as a way to gain better understanding from different perspectives of women's empowerment in order to cross-validate data on the other levels of reality, but also to look at different dimensions of the same phenomenon (El Feki et al. 2017).

Information on men's and women's perspectives, perceptions and attitudes, stereotypes and norms that fight or perpetuate discrimination are complementary to stylized facts and legislative discourse.

A recent UN Women study, the International Men and Gender Equality Survey, conducted together with *Promundo* and in accordance with confidentiality procedures due to the sensitive nature of the questions, confirms the differences also in terms of views between Egypt and Morocco, the only two Southern Mediterranean countries included in the research, together with Lebanon and Palestine (see Table 4.4).

In general, many men and fewer women surveyed in both Egypt and Morocco support a wide array of inequitable attitudes on some important dimensions of women's empowerment, such as women's rights and roles as caregiver and organizer of domestic life, the priority of men's access to jobs over women's, resistance to women's political leadership positions and violence against women. Attitudes are very important because they frequently translate into actions and behavioural changes affect *de facto* reality. This means that the three layers of reality – *de facto*, *de habitu* and *de jure* – are distinct, yet intrinsically

Table 4.4 Comparison of men's and women's attitudes on key dimensions of women's empowerment in Egypt and Morocco (%[**], 2016–2017)

	Egypt		Morocco	
	Men	Women	Men	Women
A woman's most important role is to take care of the home and cook for the family	86.8	76.7	71.5	48.7
A man should have the final word about decisions in the home	90.3	58.5	70.7	46.8
There are times when a woman deserves to be beaten	53.4	32.8	38.2	20.6
A woman should tolerate violence to keep the family together	90	70.9	62.2	45.9
Unmarried women should have the same right to live on their own as unmarried men	8.3	33.4	53.3	80.4
More rights for women mean that men lose out	35	17	41	19
A married woman should have the same right to work outside the home as her husband	31	75	55	89
Willing to work with female boss	55	88	70	87
There should be more women in positions of political authority	29	68	67	91
There should be a law on allowing safe abortion on demand	9	14	27	48
We have already achieved equality between women and men in society	70	52	58	49
I would approve of my son marrying more than one wife[*]	43.4	8.2	68.5	16.9
Women should have the right to end a marriage through divorce	35	76	52	90
If a woman is raped, she should marry her rapist	64	60	60	48

Source: Based on El Feki et al. 2017.

Note: [*] Question asked of Muslim respondents only.
[**] Response rates were generally very high: around 90% or more.

linked, levels, which must be addressed together, because they enter into mutual and reciprocal dependence and may reinforce a common trend without a one-sided causal relation.

Moreover, a mixture of equitable and inequitable attitudes (and practices, not considered in the table) appear across the countries and the sexes, without substantial differences between younger and older men's views on women's empowerment, which is quite unexpected based on the assumption of more equitable attitudes among younger men.

A traditional patriarchal view is much more prevalent in Egypt than in Morocco and among men than among women. However, the gap between men's and women's attitudes, controlling for nationality, is not constant.

In particular, the gap is very large between the two countries and within the same sex group in the case of the attitude to the statement that 'Unmarried women should have the same right to live on their own as unmarried men'. Egyptians are much more resistant to equality of rights than Moroccans; the gap is even wider if we compare males and males, females and females.

In other cases, the nationality gap prevails, such as in the attitudes on the assertions that 'A married woman should have the same right to work outside the home as her husband', 'I would approve of my son marrying more than one wife' or 'Women should have the right to end a marriage through divorce'. In these cases, the differences between men and women within the same country are much wider. There are also some unexpected results: a higher proportion of Moroccans than Egyptians think that 'More rights for women mean that men lose out', even if Egyptians appear more resistant to equality of rights and tend more often to say that 'We have already achieved equality between women and men in society'.

Conclusions

In Southern Mediterranean countries, the vast majority of people live in middle-income countries but, despite the fact that the level of per capita GNI is relatively high, women continue to suffer from higher rates of unemployment (the gender gap is 12%, much higher than in the rest of the world) and lower rates of employment (around 50%). They are less likely to participate in the labour force and face higher risks of vulnerable employment, that is, being self-employed or a contributing family worker. In addition to the discrimination suffered by women and the youth, these gender gaps also represent a substantial and serious waste of the development potential of women and young people in terms of their skills, talent and motivation (ILO 2017; ILO and IFAD 2017).

Socio-cultural factors influence the participation of women in political life, but also the persistence of the harmful practice of female genital mutilation/cutting, and institutions such as the family are key determinants of a change in attitudes and actions.

The lack of institutions guaranteeing full social, economic and political citizenship of women, particularly in rural areas, and the lack of the administrative and institutional capacity to effectively implement respect for their agency act against the prospects of bringing about transformative change in the region. Institutions must be intended in the broad sense: law, codes and social norms, poor governance, land tenure, access to credit, market and informal market functioning (Angel-Urdinola and Tanabe 2012) are to some degree responsible for the failure of women's empowerment.

Education rates are relatively high in the region and have improved remarkably in the last decade, particularly among girls. This phenomenon raised hopes and expectations of employment and social mobility, but such expectations have to date been disappointed. The automatism imagined by the human capital theory on the relationship between education and average salary level has not been achieved, and hence the result has created widespread frustration (Zupi 2016b).

It makes sense to talk of the uprisings and dissatisfaction under the heading of 'Bread and Roses': democracy, human rights and dignity (roses) cannot be regarded separately from the demand for decent jobs (to be a breadwinner).

The risk of the revival of outdated patriarchal and tribal models of social relations (Mir-Hosseini 2011), the lack of gender mainstreaming among the priorities of Southern Mediterranean governments, the big issue of migration facing the Mediterranean Basin today and over the near future, the 'clash of civilizations' hoped for by tiny minorities in the name of a regressive 'Return to Sharia' (Tausch and Heshmati 2016) and unrealistic calls for pure national (or sub-national) culture and identity are all real phenomena.

This is why our recommendation is to start and conduct a detailed investigation, such as that based on the ten-step process implemented in Senegal, to understand women's empowerment in the region across the three layers of reality and to improve knowledge and datasets. The importance of context is indissolubly linked to the relevant phenomena of our time, and some of them force us to think rapidly beyond and across national borders. This is, for instance, the case of international migration. In this context, the so-called feminization of migration, with the migration of women independently from men, represents a new frontier of discrimination, violence and abuse against girls and women, forcing us to look beyond the idea of empowerment as just context specific. In analytical terms, women's migration from and to Southern Mediterranean countries should be addressed on the same three fronts proposed here: (a) the discourse of the Rule of Law, (b) empirical facts and practices and (c) subjective perceptions, opinions and attitudes.

As migration leads to an overlapping of structural processes with emergencies affecting the endogenous processes of progress in women's empowerment, institutions are crucial. They are fundamental and intertwined parts of our complex social reality, comprising formal power relations (legislative action), formal/informal agreements (negotiations), the organization of the social arena (such as markets) and transnational spaces (such as migration dynamics), attitudes and value systems. There is no question that a deep compression of the institutions is a prerequisite to tackle the challenge of women's empowerment. In the new stage of globalization, women's empowerment has to do with local, national, cross-border and international attitudes, laws and practices, and an appropriate magnifying glass is needed to see and orient them.

Notes

1 The most commonly used standardized surveys are the following: Living Standards Measurement Study – LSMS, Demographic and Health Surveys – DHS, Core Welfare Indicator

Questionnaire – CWIQ, and Multiple Indicator Cluster Surveys – MICS. See M. Jerven (2014), Benefits and Costs of the Data for Development Targets for the Post-2015 Development Agenda Post-2015 Consensus, Data for Development Assessment Paper, Copenhagen Consensus Centre, Copenhagen, September.

2 One of the objectives of a post-2015 'data revolution', to use the term coined and used in the UN system to emphasize the need to ensure high-quality information and evidence on the premise that no one gets left behind as development occurs, should be to shift the balance in data collection from survey to administrative data. This means investing in the stronger capacity in state administration.

References

Alkire, S., 2009. Concepts and Measures of Agency. *In*: K. Basu and R. Kanbur, eds. *Arguments for a Better World*. Oxford: Oxford University Press.

Alkire, S., Meinzen-Dick, R., Peterman, A., Quisumbing, A., Seymour, G., and Vaz, A., 2013. The Women's Empowerment in Agriculture Index. *World Development*, 52.

Angel-Urdinola, D.F., and Tanabe, K., 2012. *Micro-Determinants of Informal Employment in The Middle East and North Africa Region*, World Bank SP Discussion Paper, 1201.

Antonopoulos, R., Esquivel, V., Masterson, T., and Zacharias, A., 2017. Time and Income Poverty in the City of Buenos Aires. *In*: R. Connelly and E. Kongar, eds. *Gender and Time Use in a Global Context: The Economics of Employment and Unpaid Labor*. Palgrave Macmillan.

Barca, F., 2009. *An Agenda for A Reformed Cohesion Policy: A Place-Based Approach to Meeting European Union Challenges and Expectations*. Independent Report prepared at the request of Danuta Hübner, Commissioner for Regional Policy, Bruxelles.

Beteta, H.C., 2006. What Is Missing in Measures of Women's Empowerment? *Journal of Human Development*, 7 (2).

Bhaskar, R., 1978. *A Realist Theory of Science* (2nd ed.). Hassocks Sussex: Harvester Press.

Branisa, B., Klasen, S., and Ziegler, M., 2009. *Background Paper: The Construction of the Social Institutions and Gender Index (SIGI)*. Paris: OECD-DC.

Branisa, B., Klasen, S., Ziegler, M., Drechsler, D., and Jütting, J, 2009. *The Social Institutions and Gender Index (SIGI)*, Technical note. Paris: OECD-DC.

Council of the European Union, 2015. *Council Conclusions on the Gender Action Plan 2016–2020*. Brussels: Council of the European Union, 26 October.

Degnbol-Martinussen, J., and Engberg-Pedersen, P., 2003. *Aid: Understanding International Development Cooperation*. London: Zed Books.

Dijkstra, G., 2006. Towards a Fresh Start in Measuring Gender Equality: A Contribution to the Debate. *Journal of Human Development*, 7 (2).

El Feki, S., Heilman, B., and Barker, G., eds., 2017. *Understanding Masculinities: Results from the International Men and Gender Equality Survey: Middle East and North Africa*. Cairo and Washington, DC: UN Women and Promundo-US.

Harper, C., Nowacka, K., Alder, H., and Ferrant, G., 2014. *Measuring Women's Empowerment and Social Transformation in the Post-2015 Agenda*. London: ODI-OECD.

Ibrahim, S., and Alkire, S., 2007. *Agency & Empowerment: A Proposal for Internationally Comparable Indicators*, OPHI Working Paper Series.

IFAD, 2017. Promoting Women's Empowerment in the Middle East and North Africa: A Rapid Evidence Assessment of Labour Market Interventions. *Impact Brief*, (9), Geneva.

ILO, 2017. *World Employment and Social Outlook: Trends 2017*. Geneva: International Labour Office.

Jerven, M., 2014. *Benefits and Costs of the Data for Development Targets for the Post-2015 Development Agenda Post-2015 Consensus*. Data for Development Assessment Paper, Copenhagen: Copenhagen Consensus Centre, September.

Jespersen, J., 2009. *Macroeconomic Methodology: A Post-Keynesian Perspective*. Cheltenham: Edward Elgar Publishing.

Kabeer, N., 2002. *Discussing Women's Empowerment: Theory and Practice*. 3, Stockholm: Sida Studies.

Kabeer, N., 2005. Gender Equality and Women's Empowerment: A Critical Analysis of the Third Millennium Development Goal. *Gender & Development*, 13 (1).

Lawson, T., 1997. *Economics and Reality*. London: Routledge.

Lawson, T., 2003. *Reorienting Economics*. London: Routledge.

Lister, R., 2015. To Count for Nothing: Poverty Beyond the Statistics. *Journal of the British Academy*, 3, 139–165.

Mikkelsen, B., 2005. *Methods for Development Work and Research* (2nd ed.). London: Sage.

Mir-Hosseini, Z., 2011. Beyond 'Islam' vs 'feminism'. *IDS Bulletin*, 42 (1), 67–77.

Morris, W., 2009. *Amartya Sen: Contemporary Philosophy in Focus*. Cambridge: Cambridge University Press.

Nowacka, K., 2015. *SIGI Country Studies: Building Evidence on Discriminatory Social Institutions at the Sub-National Level*. Paris: OECD-DC.

Nussbaum, M., 2000. *Women and Human Development: The Capabilities Approach*. Cambridge: Cambridge University Press.

OECD-SIGI, 2014. *SIGI Synthesis Report*. Paris: OECD Development Centre.

Pearce, E., McMurray, K., Walsh, C.A., and Malek, L., 2017. Searching for Tomorrow: South Sudanese Women Reconstructing Resilience Through Photovoice. *International Migration & Integration*, 18, 369–389.

Phan, L., 2016. Measuring Women's Empowerment at Household Level Using DHS Data of Four Southeast Asian Countries. *Social Indicators Research*, January, 126 (1), 359–378.

Robeyns, I., 2003. Sen's Capability Approach and Gender Inequality: Selecting Relevant Capabilities. *Feminist Economics*, 9 (2–3), 61–92.

Sen, A.K., 1992. *Inequality Re-Examined*. Oxford: Clarendon Press.

Sen, A.K., 1993. Capability and Well-being. *In*: M. Nussbaum and A.K. Sen, eds. *The Quality of Life*. Oxford: Clarendon Press.

Sen, A.K., 1995. Gender Inequality and Theories of Justice. *In*: M. Nussbaum and Glover, eds. *Women, Culture and Development: A Study of Human Capabilities*. Oxford: Clarendon Press.

Sen, A.K., 1999. *Development as Freedom*. New York: Knopf.

Tausch, A., and Heshmati, A., 2016. *Islamism and Gender Relations in the Muslim World as Reflected in Recent World Values Survey Data*, Discussion Paper No. 9672. Bonn: IZA World of Labor.

Tayyib, S., Rocca, V., and Bossanyi, Z., 2012. *Core Gender Indicators for Assessing the Socio-Economic Status of the Agricultural and Rural Population*. FAO Regional Office for Europe and Central Asia.

UN General Assembly, 2017. *Work of the Statistical Commission Pertaining to the 2030 Agenda for Sustainable Development*, Resolution adopted, A/RES/71/313. New York, 10 July.

UN High-level Political Forum for Sustainable Development, 2017. *HLPF Thematic Review of SDG 5: Achieve Gender Equality and Empower all Women and Girls*. New York: United Nations, 7 July.

UN Secretary-General, 2017. Progress towards the Sustainable Development Goals. E/2017/66, New York, 7 July.

UNDP, 2010. *The Human Development Report 2010.* New York: United Nations.

UN-ECOSOC, 2016. Report of the Inter-Agency and Expert Group on Sustainable Development Goal Indicators. Note by the Secretary-General, E/CN.3/2016/2/Rev.1, New York, 19 February.

Zupi, M., 2011. *Una proposta teorico-metodologica per la valutazione strategica delle iniziative di sviluppo.* Rome: CeSPI, mimeo.

Zupi, M., 2015. *Measuring Rural Women's Empowerment: Issues & Challenges.* Issues Paper for the 2015. UNWOMEN – CeSPI – DGCS/MAECI Seminar. Milan, May.

Zupi, M., ed., 2016a. *Manuel méthodologique sur la mesure de l'autonomisation des femmes. Le cas du Sénégal.* Dakar: UNWomen and CeSPI, December.

Zupi, M., 2016b. Women and Young Rural People in North Africa and Middle East: The Great Challenge for Development. *Afkar/Ideas*, 49.

Zupi, M., 2019. The Political Economy of Aid: Foreign Aid Effectiveness, Theories, Methods and the Challenges that Lie Ahead. *In:* A. La Chimia and P. Trepte, eds. *Public Procurement and Aid Effectiveness: A Roadmap Under Construction.* Oxford: Bloomsbury – Hart Publishing, in Print.

Chapter 5

Spatial agglomeration, innovation clustering and firm performances in Turkey[1]

*Anna M. Ferragina, Giulia Nunziante,
and Erol Taymaz*

Introduction

The aim of the proposed study is to investigate how firms' productivity in Turkey is affected at spatial level by agglomeration of firms, clustering of innovation and localization of foreign direct investment (FDI). The choice of Turkey is based on the importance that economies of agglomeration play in the Turkish economy. Turkey is a very interesting case study also due to the emerging role over the last decade of science parks, innovation clusters, incubators and an increasing presence of foreign multinational corporations. Besides, Turkey is among the countries of the Southern Mediterranean region most integrated into global manufacturing markets, with a strong human capital base, a large number of engineers and skilled workers. However, the country is also marked by a very high regional unemployment and strong provincial inequalities. The regional inequality in Turkey has become more persistent since liberalization in the 1980s. Filiztekin (1998), Dogruel et al. (2003), Gezici and Hewings (2007), Yadira and Öcal (2006), Kılıçaslan and Özatağan (2007) and Filiztekin and Çelik (2010) all focus on the way regional income gaps evolved, concluding that even though there are small signs of convergence, they are far from successful and the East–West duality is an ongoing problem for the Turkish economy.

Given this background, several questions are worth investigating. Do firms localized in production clusters exhibit higher productivity? How far is the concentration of innovation of firms in the same cluster likely to increase productivity? To what extent does the concentration of foreign multinationals in such clusters have a stronger productivity spillover? How are firms able to benefit from spillovers and enjoy agglomeration effects depending on their size, technology and ownership? Is there a difference in firms' absorptive capacity? Hence, we interact the main variables of agglomeration and innovation at region-sector level with firm size (measured by the number of employees) and with innovation investment. These interaction variables reveal whether large firms and innovation performers benefit more from agglomeration effects and spillovers.

Our analysis aims to provide a measure of spillovers on productivity from geographical and sectoral clustering of firms and from their innovation. To this purpose, we build specific indices of agglomeration and innovation activity at territorial level. We also use indicators of innovation performed by domestic and by foreign multinationals at the spatial level of analysis adopted.

The specific additional insights of this analysis are the focus on agglomeration economies and innovation spillovers taking into account a multidimensional approach, both at spatial and firm levels, in the effort to capture at the same time regional characteristics of the economic systems and firm heterogeneity. Analysis at firm level is crucial to detect agglomeration economies, as some factors are firm specific and driven by factors related to the individual skills of owners, workers and managers, to different sizes, specific approaches to production and different innovation strategies (Bloom and van Reenen 2010). Hence, we control for the impact of firm characteristics (specifically the role of size, ownership and firm innovation). Furthermore, we also check whether the regional endowment of territories where firms are located and in particular their R&D and location of foreign multinationals exert a positive effect on firm productivity.

By focussing on the agglomeration economies in the local context within which firms operate, and at the same time concentrating on firm-specific determinants of productivity, our research fills a gap in the literature. There is an almost complete lack of studies addressing such issues for Turkey at micro level: most of the studies are carried out at industry level (Coulibaly et al. 2007; Onder et al. 2003; Öztürk and Kılıç 2016) or at province level (Çetin and Kalayci 2016).

We adopt panel estimates of output by the Generalized Method of Moments (GMM) system methodology controlling for time-fixed effects. Using system GMM dynamic panel estimation techniques, we try to address simultaneity and endogeneity on inputs and also the possible endogeneity between agglomeration and productivity. We use unbalanced panel data including all private establishments employing 25 or more people for 2006–2013. Spatial unit of analyses are the provinces.

The chapter is organized as follows. After a literature review of the main strands of analysis on spatial agglomeration, innovation and firm performance and on the specific studies carried out on localization economies in Turkey on the topics of interest, we describe in the third section the data and in the fourth section some stylized facts on firm clustering, spatial innovation and productivity in Turkey, showing the features in terms of spatial concentration of firms, employment, FDI, innovation and relationships between these variables. Further, we develop the country-specific analysis and describe our methodology in the fifth section and our results in the sixth section by considering the specific empirical model and the econometric specification carried out to capture regional innovation, productivity spillovers and productivity dynamics and differentials deriving from the geographical and sector clustering of firms, innovation spillovers and performances. Conclusions and policy implications follow.

We find support that in an open economy, agglomeration leads to higher efficiency. In particular, our results confirm the outcome that firms in the same industry benefit more from each other as they are more technologically similar. Hence, sector distance matters, as this may facilitate the flow and absorption of knowledge among firms. We also found that FDI impact is positive, albeit limited, the territorial and social redistribution depending on the firm level of technology.[2] Technology plays a critical role due to lower absorptive capacity of less technologically sophisticated firms.

The results from the overall empirical analysis emphasise the policy recommendations in this context regarding promotion of agglomeration, localized innovation and foreign investment, which may support the structural transformation of the economy.

Literature review

Spatial agglomeration, innovation and firm performance

Clustering of economic activities has been traditionally seen as a crucial mechanism for employment, firm growth and resilience. The clustering of industries in specific areas has improved industrial productivity in a number of countries. According to the Marshall theory, specialization economies increase the interaction between firms and workers, and speed up the process of innovation and growth, as firm agglomeration in the same sector produces positive externalities and facilitates the growth of all manufacturing units within it. These advantages are mainly based on information sharing and intra-industry communication. On the other hand, according to the Jacobs theory (1969), knowledge externalities are associated with the diversity of neighbour industries (urbanization economies). Clustering can also be an important driver of R&D via a broad range of processes like learning-by-doing, externalities on inputs, labour market pooling and R&D cooperation between firms (Baltagi et al. 2012). Porter (1998) also emphasized cluster's significant role in a firm's ongoing ability to innovate and further enhance firm's productivity. Besides, an extensive literature shows that firms' behaviour depends on the spatial availability of territorial resources devoted to innovation and growth (Henderson et al. 2002).

The literature on the effects of agglomeration economies is extensive and dates back to a few seminal papers (Marshall 1890; Glaeser et al. 1992; Porter 1998; Jacobs 1969; Audretsch and Feldman 1996) which describe the positive effects related to technology transfers and to pro-competitive forces (increased competition, reallocation of resources towards more productive firms, productivity improvements of incumbent firms).

The theory surrounding agglomeration economies and spillover effects mainly identifies two types of externalities: localization (or specialization) economies and diversification economies. Localization economies may arise from industrial specialization available to the local firms within the same sector (Marshall-Arrow-Romer or MAR externalities) and from the emergence of the intra-industry transmission of knowledge (Glaeser et al. 1992) as firms learn from other firms in the same industry (Porter 1998). These economies explain the development of industrial districts (ID). Unlike localization economies, however, Jacobs's (1969) economies indicate that the diversity of industries and knowledge spillovers across geographically close industries promote innovation and growth via inter-industry knowledge spillovers (Acs et al. 2007). The latter reflects external economies passed on to enterprises as a result of the large-scale operation of the agglomeration, independent of the industry structure. For instance, more densely populated areas are more likely to house universities, industry research laboratories and other knowledge-generating facilities.

It is recognized that clustering is especially important as a driver of R&D via a broad range of processes like learning-by-doing, externalities on inputs, labour market and knowledge and R&D cooperation between firms (Rosenthal and Strange 2001; Paci and Usai, 2006; Ellison et al. 2010; Martin et al,. 2011; Baltagi et al. 2012). The theory on agglomeration economies also argues that positive knowledge spillovers are more likely to occur if firms are located in the same area, as geographical proximity encourages the diffusion of ideas and technology due to the concentration of customers and suppliers, labour market pooling, worker mobility and informal contacts (Greenstone et al. 2010). Technology transfers (intra- and inter-industry knowledge spillovers) may occur via vertical linkages (along the supply chain and the creation of specialized suppliers) and horizontal linkages (collaboration among firms, imitation, concentration of customers and suppliers; labour market pooling and worker mobility; informal contacts).

The nexus between spatial agglomeration and knowledge spillovers has been largely investigated within the 'geography of innovation' literature, which concentrates on measuring localized spillovers from R&D spending (Griliches 1979; Breschi and Malerba 2001; Bottazzi and Peri 2003; Audretsch and Feldman 2004). Within this literature, the private technology of individual firms spills over to other firms and becomes public knowledge, thereby increasing the productivity of all firms. Rosenthal and Strange (2001) and Ellison et al. (2010) consider the importance of input sharing, matching and knowledge spillovers for manufacturing firms at various levels of geographic disaggregation, and other studies have found that knowledge spillovers tend to vanish rapidly as distance increases (Audretsch and Feldman 1996; Keller 2002). The concentration generates dynamic processes of knowledge creation, learning, innovation and knowledge transfer (diffusion and synergies). As a result, the cluster becomes a centre of accumulated competence across a range of related industries and across various stages of production (De Propris and Driffield 2006).

Another important strand of research related to these topics of analysis is the large body of literature which has focussed on detecting spillovers from the presence of multinational enterprises (MNEs), where horizontal and vertical spillovers can be inferred indirectly through estimation of their effects on firms' total factor productivity. The location choice of foreign MNEs as a source of potential spillovers from FDI is stressed by a large amount of research through a range of different channels including the creation of forward and backward linkages, competitive and demonstration effects, transfer of skilled workforce and transfer of (pecuniary and non-pecuniary) externalities to local firms (Aitken and Harrison 1999; Gorg and Greenaway 2004; Haskel et al. 2002; Javorcik 2004; Ferragina and Mazzotta 2014). These spillover effects from MNEs, whether intra- or inter-industry, are more likely to materialize when firms are geographically closer.

Studies on localization economies in Turkey

The limited number of studies on productivity for Turkish manufacturing generally focus on productivity and export relationships, FDI, trade or technical efficiency (see Taymaz and Saatçi 1997; Taymaz and Yılmaz 2007; Lenger and Taymaz 2006). FDI is found to be an important channel for transfer of technology and the modern, advanced technologies introduced by multinational firms can diffuse to domestic firms through spillovers.

One of the first attempts to identify the effects of regional agglomeration was made by Taymaz and Saatçi (1997). They estimated stochastic production frontiers with efficiency effects and found that regional agglomeration of firms enhances technical efficiency.

Onder et al. (2003) analyzed spatial characteristics of total-factor productivity (TFP) in Turkish manufacturing. They investigated technical efficiency, technical change and TFP changes by estimating a trans-log Cobb-Douglas production function employing SFA methodology using regions' share in production, population density and a specialization index based on the value added to represent regional characteristics. Their findings suggest that average firm size and regional characteristics are the main determinants of technical efficiency. They also indicate that firms operating with a larger scale are more efficient than small-scale ones, and that industries located in metropolitan areas are more technically efficient than their counterparts in the peripheries.

Coulibaly et al. (2007) attempt to capture the relationship between productivity and agglomeration using two-digit Turkish manufacturing data for 1980–2000 period and several proxies such as accessibility, localization and urbanization. The estimation results suggest that both localization and urbanization economies, as well as market accessibility, are productivity-enhancing factors in Turkey.

Karacuka and Catik (2011) examine productivity spillovers from foreign and domestic companies based in Turkey and also report spillover effects from neighbouring companies. Öztürk and Kılıç's (2016) analysis of the link between productivity and agglomeration was quite different, employing the Ellison and Glaeser index and total factor productivity to represent agglomeration economies and productivity levels in Turkish manufacturing industries in the period 1980–2001. Their results indicate that Turkish manufacturing industries stand as an example of negative externalities.

Çetin (2016) employs spatial econometric methods to analyze intra- and inter-industry knowledge spillovers in industrial zones and concludes that there are spillover effects in the industrial zone of Ankara, and that more than half of the spillovers are due to geographical factors.

Çetin and Kalayci (2016) investigate the effects of R&D spillovers at province level also using spatial econometrics. Their results suggest the presence of R&D knowledge spillovers at provincial level in Turkey, shown by spatial spillover effects in nearly one third of the total effects.

Since the literature is based only on regional, industrial or provincial analyses, the novelty we propose is investigation at firm level of the impact of localization economies on co-located firm performances based on the emphasis on complementarity between the micro- and the macro-dimension.

Data description

We use an unbalanced panel dataset for all enterprises that either employed at least 20 people or had at least three local units during the period 2006–2013.[3] The spatial unit of analysis is the 'region' defined at the NUTS 2 level (a typical NUTS 2 region covers three or four provinces). The data source is the Turkish Statistics Institute (TurkStat) Longitudinal Database. The database is unbalanced because of exit from and entry into the industry and/or the database.

Table 5.1 contains the number of all firms, domestic firms and foreign firms from 2003 to 2013 and the share and the number of R&D performers among all three groups.[4] Foreign firms are more likely to conduct R&D. About 4%–5% of domestic firms perform R&D, whereas about 18%–19% of foreign firms perform R&D. However, there was a decline in the share of domestic R&D performers after the 2009 crisis in spite of an increase in the number of firms doing R&D.

Table 5.2 shows the share of foreign firms out of the total number of firms, employment and value added, and their relative size and labour productivity. The share of foreign firms both in terms of number and employment and value added decreased after the 2009 crisis mainly because of the increase in the number of domestic firms (the entry rate for domestic firms was higher than for foreign firms after 2009). Foreign firms are about four times larger than domestic firms (in terms of the number of employees per firm) and twice as productive (in terms of value added per employee). However, sectoral distribution mainly explains this asymmetry.

In Table 5.3, where the sectoral distribution of foreign firms is described for the 2011–2013 average, it appears that foreign firms have larger shares in tobacco products, chemicals, pharmaceuticals and motor vehicles. Foreign firms

Table 5.1 Number of firms in Turkey sample

	Number of firms			Share of R&D performers		
	All	Domestic	Foreign	All	Domestic	Foreign
2003	13,936	13,499	437	3.4	2.9	18.1
2004	16,869	16,318	551	3.1	2.7	15.1
2005	20,060	19,442	618	3.8	3.4	17.6
2006	21,215	20,428	787	3.3	2.9	14.9
2007	20,556	19,780	776	4	3.4	17.3
2008	22,533	21,772	761	4.2	3.7	17.5
2009	19,526	18,812	714	5.4	4.9	18.2
2010	23,735	22,896	839	5.4	5	16.9
2011	28,657	27,691	966	4.9	4.5	17.5
2012	30,867	29,927	940	5	4.5	19.3
2013	33,630	32,634	996	4.5	4.1	18.5

Table 5.2 Share of foreign firms, 2003–2013

	# of firms	Employment	Value added	Relative	Relative labor
	%	%	%	size	productivity
2003	3.1	11.7	24.1	3.7	2.1
2004	3.3	12	25.8	3.7	2.2
2005	3.1	11.2	24.1	3.6	2.2
2006	3.7	13.4	28.6	3.6	2.1
2007	3.8	13.5	28.5	3.6	2.1
2008	3.4	13.1	25.9	3.9	2
2009	3.7	13.1	27	3.6	2.1
2010	3.5	11.7	23.8	3.3	2
2011	3.4	12.2	23.4	3.6	1.9
2012	3	11.6	23	3.8	2
2013	3	11.1	22.2	3.8	2

Table 5.3 Sectoral distribution of foreign firms, 2011–2013 average

		%	%	%	Size	Productivity
10	Food	3.34	12.35	20.35	3.7	1.65
11	Beverages	6.57	30.86	48.98	4.7	1.59
12	Tobacco products	34.21	59.54	99.49	1.74	1.67
13	Textiles	1.77	3.02	3.62	1.71	1.2
14	Wearing apparel	0.85	4.36	7.82	5.13	1.79
15	Leather products	0.78	1.76	1.98	2.24	1.13
16	Wood products					
17	Paper products	5.69	15.13	23.52	2.66	1.55
18	Printing					

		%	%	%	Size	Productivity
19	Coke and refined pet					
20	Chemicals	12.47	24.22	33.76	1.94	1.39
21	Pharmaceuticals	19.05	37.46	43.08	1.97	1.15
22	Rubber and plastics	4.08	13.41	25.94	3.29	1.93
23	Non-metallic mineral	2.31	8.39	22.22	3.63	2.65
24	Basic metals	3.16	10.09	10.49	3.19	1.04
25	Fabricated metal	2.65	6.69	14.32	2.52	2.14
26	Computers, electronics	5.65	17.73	15.89	3.14	0.9
27	Electrical equipment	4.97	17.39	28.34	3.5	1.63
28	Machinery	3.54	15.91	30.25	4.49	1.9
29	Motor vehicles	11.53	47.9	64.38	4.16	1.34
30	Other transport equipment	6.95	14.16	15.45	2.04	1.09
31	Furniture	0.76	1.83	3.32	2.42	1.81
32	Other manufacturing	3.62	9.51	17.6	2.62	1.85
33	Repair and installation	2.93	4.23	8.44	1.44	1.99
Total		3.12	11.61	22.8	3.73	1.96

are two to five times larger, on average, than domestic firms. Foreign firms' labour productivity is almost equal to that of domestic firms in pharmaceuticals, basic metals, computers and other transportation equipment industries. The productivity differential (the productivity of foreign firms relative to the productivity of domestic firms) is higher than two in non-metallic mineral and fabricated metal industries. There is a weak positive correlation between relative size and productivity of foreign firms across industries, that is, productivity differential between domestic and foreign firms is explained partly by differences in firm size.

Stylized facts on firm clustering, spatial productivity and innovation in Turkey

We provide a preliminary descriptive part as a background for our econometric analysis. We illustrate the pattern of clustering using maps that exploit information on the exact location of firms (also considering the location of foreign firms). The maps depict at province level the concentration of value added, foreign firms' shares, relative labour and TFP productivity, suggesting high firm clustering and the unique nature of Turkish economy in terms of strong regional imbalances. The number of foreign and domestic R&D performers give us a hint on spatial innovation spillover.

Furthermore, Figures 5.1–5.3 help investigate in a preliminary unconditional way the benefits of regional agglomeration using the correlations between some of the variables mapped earlier. TFP growth and employment growth maps give

Value added share (log)

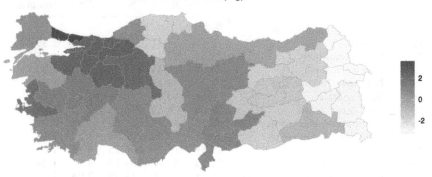

Map 5.1 Value added share (log)

Foreign firm share

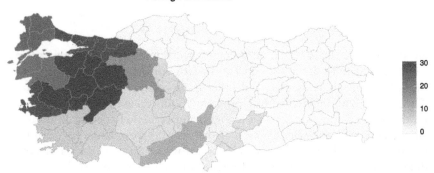

Map 5.2 Foreign firm share

Number of foreign R&D performers

Map 5.3 Number of foreign R&D performers

Number of domestic R&D performers

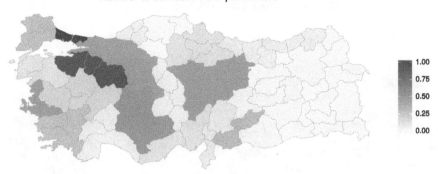

Map 5.4 Number of domestic R&D performers

Relative labour productivity

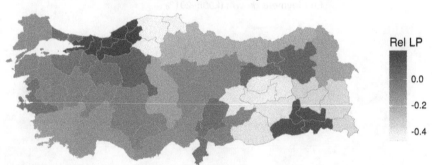

Map 5.5 Relative labour productivity

Relative productivity (TFP)

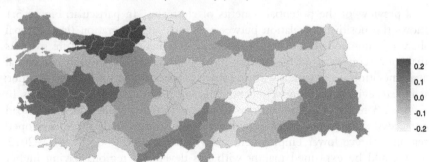

Map 5.6 Relative productivity (TFP)

TFP growth rate (2006–2013, annual)

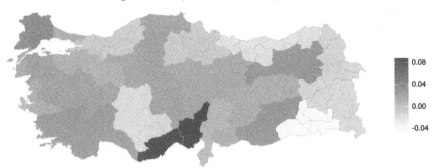

Map 5.7 TFP growth rate, 2006–2013, annual

Employment growth (2006–2013)

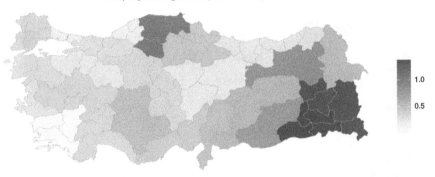

Map 5.8 Employment growth, 2006–2013

us a preview of the potential benefits of clustering. In particular, Figure 5.1 shows the positive correlation between regional agglomeration (log regional share of value added) and regional relative productivity. The picture suggests that more concentrated regions are more productive. In Figure 5.2, regional agglomeration is compared with the share of foreign firms in regional output: it appears evident that more concentrated regions attract more foreign firms. In Figure 5.3, regional agglomeration (log regional share of value added) is instead correlated with employment growth: here quite surprisingly more developed regions achieve lower employment growth from 2006–2007 to 2011–2012. This could be explained mainly with less developed regions having higher population growth, but it could also be because concentration enhances productivity but not employment.

Figure 5.1 Geographical concentration and productivity in Turkey

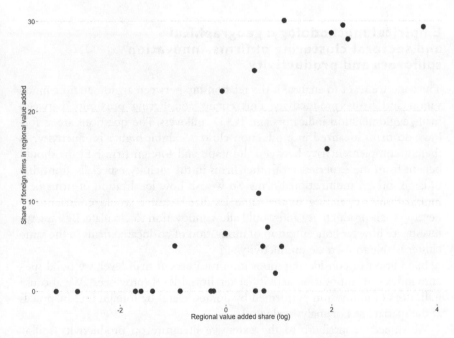

Figure 5.2 Geographical concentration and foreign investment in Turkey

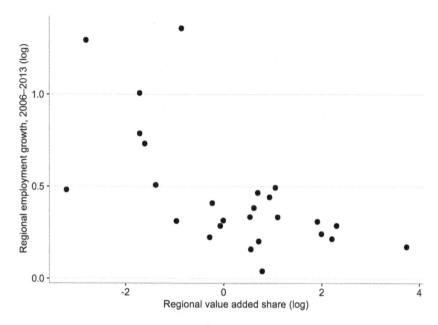

Figure 5.3 Geographical concentration and employment growth in Turkey

Empirical methodology: geographical and sectoral clustering of firms, innovation spillovers and productivity

The issue we want to analyze is the relationship between agglomeration, innovation and firms' productivity. This entails considering proximity between firms, agglomeration indicators and R&D spillovers. The questions are as follows: do firms localized in production clusters exhibit higher productivity? Is there a complementarity between domestic and foreign firms? Firms should benefit from the experience of other firms in the vicinity, especially from that of large foreign multinational firms. So we ask how localization of firms near multinationals operating in the same localized cluster would contribute to develop their productivity and would allow innovation to circulate. Besides, we investigate how far concentration of innovation of co-located firms in the same cluster is able to increase productivity.

In addition to considering innovation measures at firm level, we build specific indexes of innovation activity at territorial level (provinces). We also use indicators of innovation performed by domestic and by foreign multinationals at the spatial level of analysis adopted.

We directly contribute to the extensive literature on productivity spillovers from agglomeration economies, as well as to the literature on localized knowledge spillovers from innovation, checking for spillovers between firms taking place within regions and controlling for regional features being more conducive to productivity growth. In order to distinguish between the two effects, we used a proxy for regional attractiveness, that is, value added per head. This controls for initial regional factors. We also include time dummies.[5]

We use panel estimates for output (by GMM-system), controlling for time-fixed effects. Simultaneity and endogeneity is hence addressed using GMM dynamic panel estimation techniques. This methodology allows us to distinguish the direction of the nexus clustering and productivity and to focus on whether more regional clustering leads to higher productivity, ruling out the other direction of causality, that is, that higher productivity leads to more regional clustering.

We consider different externality transmission channels, and which variable available in the data might best capture that. The first, most important, channel is to capture the spillovers between firms in the same industry (horizontal spillovers). Three variables are adopted for this purpose: the regional share variables by sector, that is, the output share of the region in the sector output, the number of firms by sector-region and the output of firms by sector-region.

We then look at the R&D/innovation performed by domestic and by foreign firms which can be considered as an innovation spillover channel. The share of output of R&D performing domestic and foreign firms in the region/sector and the number of R&D performing domestic and foreign firms in the region/sector are the two proxies considered.

The third important issue is related to the presence of spillovers by foreign firms. We consider for this purpose the shares of foreign firms in the region and in the sector. As not all firms are able to benefit from spillovers and enjoy agglomeration effects, it is important also to control for the role of firms' absorptive capacity. Hence, we interact agglomeration and spillover variables with firm size (measured by the number of employees) and with innovation variables. Such interaction variables will reveal whether large firms and innovation performers benefit more from agglomeration effects and spillovers. For example, if large firms benefit more, the coefficient of firm size-agglomeration effect interaction variable will be positive.

Model and descriptive statistics

In order to test the effects of agglomeration economies and spillovers, a Cobb-Douglas production function is estimated:

$$q_{i,t} = \alpha_i + \alpha_{Lq}q_{i,t-1} + \alpha_K K_{i,t} + \alpha_{LK}K_{i,t-1} + \alpha_L L_{i,t} + \alpha_{LL}L_{i,t-1}$$
$$+ \alpha_M M_{i,t} + \alpha_{Lm}M_{i,t-1} + D_t + \Sigma\beta_j X_{i,j,t} + e_{it}$$

where q is real output, K capital, L labour, M inputs, D time dummies, and e the error term. Subscripts i and t denote firm and time, respectively. α_i's account for unobserved, time-invariant firm-specific effects. X is a vector of variables that explains total factor productivity, and it includes the variables that measure agglomeration effects and spillovers.

The *output variable* of the production function is the value of production (sales adjusted by changes in final product inventories). It is deflated by sectoral price indices at the NACE 4-digit level to find real output.

Inputs of the production function are capital, labour and other inputs (raw materials, parts and components). Capital is measured by depreciation allowances, labour by the average number of employees and inputs by the value of all inputs adjusted by changes in raw materials and work-in-process inventories. The capital variable is deflated by the investment price index, whereas the input variable is deflated by sectoral price indices.

We use the GMM-system method to estimate the production function that controls for the endogeneity of inputs, autocorrelation and heteroscedasticity. The methodology we use, GMM system, takes care of endogeneity of input by creating instrumental variables from existing variables. In the case of the GMM-system, two equations are estimated jointly, the differenced equation and the level equation where first differences are used as instruments.

The GMM-system model is defined as a dynamic model: it includes the lagged values of the dependent variable (output) and all inputs. This specification allows for a flexible functional form and incorporates various adjustments.

The output and all input variables are used in log form. Therefore, the coefficients of input variables give us short-term factor elasticities. The long-run factor elasticities are defined by $\varepsilon_i = (\alpha_i + \alpha_{Li})/(1 - \alpha_{Lq})$, where ε is the long-term elasticity of factor i, α_i the coefficient of factor i, α_{Li} the coefficient of the lagged value of factor i, and α_{Lq} the coefficient of the lagged value of output.

The returns to scale parameter is defined by $\kappa = \varepsilon_K + \varepsilon_L + \varepsilon_M$, where κ is the returns to scale parameter, and the subscripts $_K$, $_L$ and $_M$ denote capital, labour and inputs, respectively. There are constant returns to scale when $\kappa = 1$, increasing (decreasing) returns when $\kappa > 1$ ($\kappa < 1$).

In order to capture the effects of all shocks and exogenous technological change, all models include time dummies, that is, a dummy variable for each year. A dummy variable for foreign ownership is included in the model to capture the effects of foreign ownership on productivity. Foreign firms are, by definition, multinational firms, and are able to transfer technology from abroad, mainly from the parent firm. Therefore, foreign firms are likely to be more productive than domestic firms.

Technological activities of firms are captured by a dummy variable that is equal to 1 if the firm performs R&D activities, and 0 otherwise. Since the firm can generate new products and/or processes as a result of R&D activities, the R&D dummy variable is expected to have a positive coefficient, that is, R&D performers would be more productive.

Since the main purpose of our study is to analyze the effects of agglomeration and spillovers, especially from foreign firms, we use a number of proxy variables that are expected to capture the effects of such factors. Note that there are a number of alternative proxy variables. For example, agglomeration can be measured by the density of firms (the number of firms), or by the density of production activities (output). Therefore, we experimented with a number of alternative variables, and replaced one set of explanatory variables by another.

The first set of proxy variables for agglomeration effects includes the (log) numbers of domestic and foreign firms in the same sector (defined at the NACE 4-digit level) and region (defined at NUTS 2 level). These variables will have positive coefficients if agglomeration of firms leads to higher productivity. We use the number of domestic and foreign firms separately because the extent of spillovers could differ between domestic and foreign firms.

We use two additional variables, the number of domestic and foreign R&D performers in the same sector and region to test whether R&D performers are more likely to spillover knowledge and technology to other firms that operate in the same sector and region.

The second set includes the (log) output of domestic and foreign R&D performers in a given sector and region. This set defines agglomeration in terms of output instead of the number of firms as defined in the first set. The number of firm variables would be meaningful if spillovers take the form of imitation, whereas the output variable could reflect spillovers in the form of externalities and labour turnover.

The third set includes a number of variables about output shares. 'Regional share (sector)' is the share of the region in total output of the sector in which the firm operates. The 'Foreign share (sector)' and 'Foreign share (region)' variables are defined similarly for foreign firms. If there are agglomeration economies in a sector, the firms located in a region where that sector is concentrated would be more productive. If there are spillovers from foreign firms within a sector, then the 'Foreign share (sector)' variable will have a positive coefficient. However, if spillovers from foreign firms have a geographical dimension, then the coefficient of the 'Foreign share (region)' variable will be positive.

Benefiting from spillovers is not a passive process, and firms cannot enjoy agglomeration effects to the same extent. To control for the role of the absorptive capacity, we interact agglomeration and spillover variables with firm size (measured by the number of employees) and R&D dummy variable. These interaction variables will reveal whether large firms and R&D performers benefit more from agglomeration effects and spillovers. For example, if large firms benefit more, the coefficient of firm size-agglomeration effect interaction variable will be positive. Finally, we also include in the model the output share of large firms in the same sector and region to test whether spillovers originate only from large firms.

Descriptive statistics for all the variables for the period analyzed are presented in Table 5.4. Note that with the exception of dummy variables (FDI and R&D performer) and share variables (Regional output share, Foreign share sector and Foreign share region), all variables are in log form. As shown in the table, the share of foreign firms was 3.2% and the share of R&D performers 4.6%. The average

Table 5.4 Descriptive statistics on Turkey sample

Variable	Mean	Std dev	Min	Max
Output	14.634	1.79	−1.265	23.018
Number of employees	3.664	1.153	0	9.663
Capital stock	11.074	1.983	−0.604	20.111
Inputs	14.4	1.97	−1.295	22.968
FDI	0.032	0.175	0	1
R&D performer	0.046	0.21	0	1
Number of domestic firms (region/sector)	3.608	1.756	0	7.416
Number of foreign firms (region/sector)	0.74	0.869	0	3.497
Number of R&D performing domestic firms (region/sector)	0.7	0.784	0	3.332
Number of R&D performing foreign firms (region/sector)	0.148	0.372	0	2.398
Regional output share	0.291	0.281	0	1
Foreign share (sector)	0.114	0.156	0	1
Foreign share (region)	0.197	0.106	0	0.534
Output of domestic firms (region/sector)	16.385	4.848	0	21.364
Output of foreign firms (region/sector)	0.351	2.435	0	21.81
Output of R&D performing domestic firms (region/sector)	3.052	6.975	0	24.097
Output of R&D performing foreign firms (region/sector)	9.994	9.233	0	24.395

Notes: All variables are in log form.
FDI and R&D performer are dummy variables.
Regional output share, Foreign share (sector) and Foreign share (region) are in percentage.

number of domestic firms in the same sector and region is 36.9 ($e^{3.608}$). In the most concentrated case of the agglomeration of domestic firms, it reaches 1,663. In other words, 1,663 firms operating in a sector are located in the same region.

The average number of foreign firms in the same sector-region is much smaller (only 2.1) and its maximum value becomes 33. The average number of R&D performing domestic (foreign) firms in the same region/sector is 2.01 and 1.16, respectively. Although the number of foreign firms is small, the average sectoral share of foreign firms is 11.4%, and the average regional share of foreign firms is 19.7%. The significant difference between the number and output of foreign firms shows that these two measures could reflect different aspects of agglomeration effects and spillovers emanating from foreign firms.

Estimation results

Estimation results are presented in Table 5.5a (without interaction effects) and Table 5.5b (with interaction effects). We included agglomeration and spillover variables in blocks of variables to ascertain the effects of correlations between explanatory variables.

Estimation results for the production functions are quite robust and sensible. The returns to scale parameter is around 1.05 for almost all models that indicates that there are mild increasing returns to scale in Turkish manufacturing. The (long-run) elasticities of capital, labour and inputs are around 0.055, 0.356 and 0.635, respectively, which is reasonable. The coefficient of the lagged output variable is small (around 0.2), that is, output adjusts quickly.

The coefficients of foreign ownership and R&D variables are statistically significant.[6] in all models. Foreign firms in Turkish manufacturing are around 13% more productive than domestic firms. As may be expected, R&D performers are more productive than non-R&D performers, and the average productivity differential between R&D performers and non-performers is around 5%–6%. Hence, FDI is found to be an important channel for transfer of technology, which confirms previous studies on Turkey on the productivity–FDI relationship (Taymaz and Saatçi 1997; Taymaz and Yılmaz 2007; Lenger and Taymaz 2006).

Estimation results suggest that there are productivity spillovers from foreign firms operating in the same sector-region. The coefficient of the number of foreign firms operating in the same sector-region is positive and statistically significant. If the number of foreign firms increases by 1%, productivity of all firms operating in that sector and region increases by 0.04% (Model 4, Table 5.5a). That is, these effects are economically significant as well.

We also find that the number of domestic firms operating in the same sector-region seems to have a negative effect on productivity when the model includes the variable on foreign firms (compare Models 3 and 4, Table 5.5a). There could be congestion or negative competition effects due to agglomeration of domestic and, most probably, technologically inferior firms. This confirms another study which examined productivity spillovers from foreign and domestic companies based in Turkey and also reports negative spillover effects from neighbouring companies (Öztürk and Kılıç 2016). However, our analysis does not confirm the results of Saatçi and Taymaz (1997), Karacuka and Catik (2011), or Çetin and Kalayci (2016), which suggests the presence of R&D knowledge spillovers at provincial level in Turkey.

In order to check whether agglomeration and spillover effects differ by firm characteristics, we use the number of R&D performing domestic and foreign firms in the same sector-region instead of total number of firms (Model 5, Table 5.5a). In that case, the coefficients of both domestic and foreign firms become positive and statistically significant. The coefficient of the number of R&D performing foreign firms is almost equal to the coefficient of the number of foreign firms (around 0.04), but the coefficient of the number of domestic R&D performers is somewhat smaller (0.008). These results reveal that the extent of spillovers from R&D performing and non-performing firms is quite similar. Domestic R&D performers generate positive spillovers, but they are weaker compared with those generated by foreign firms.

In another group of regressions, we used proxy variables defined in terms of total output instead of total number of firms produced by domestic and

Table 5.5a Production function estimation results for Turkey, 2006–2013, GMM-System results

	(1)	(2)	(3)	(4)	(5)	(6)	(7)	(8)
VARIABLES	GMM	GMM	GMM	GMM	GMM	GMM	GMM	GMM
Returns to scale	1.051	1.046	1.044	1.045	1.046	1.046	1.048	1.047
Lag output	0.217**	0.217**	0.216**	0.214**	0.217**	0.213**	0.218**	0.216**
	(0.0207)	(0.0208)	(0.0207)	(0.0207)	(0.0207)	(0.0208)	(0.0208)	(0.0207)
Labor	0.485**	0.488**	0.479**	0.485**	0.501**	0.500**	0.497**	0.497**
	(0.0555)	(0.0556)	(0.0544)	(0.0546)	(0.0563)	(0.0558)	(0.0559)	(0.0560)
Lag labor	-0.208**	-0.211**	-0.207**	-0.209**	-0.218**	-0.215**	-0.216**	-0.215**
	(0.0331)	(0.0333)	(0.0327)	(0.0328)	(0.0336)	(0.0333)	(0.0335)	(0.0335)
Capital	0.0370**	0.0374**	0.0369**	0.0370**	0.0380**	0.0378**	0.0379**	0.0379**
	(0.0044)	(0.0044)	(0.0044)	(0.0044)	(0.0045)	(0.0044)	(0.0045)	(0.0044)
Lag capital	0.00586**	0.00592**	0.00587**	0.00598**	0.00608**	0.00615**	0.00608**	0.00607**
	(0.0021)	(0.0021)	(0.0020)	(0.0020)	(0.0021)	(0.0021)	(0.0021)	(0.0021)
Inputs	0.485**	0.479**	0.487**	0.482**	0.466**	0.468**	0.472**	0.471**
	(0.0556)	(0.0560)	(0.0551)	(0.0553)	(0.0567)	(0.0563)	(0.0564)	(0.0564)
Lag inputs	0.0184	0.0198	0.0166	0.02	0.026	0.0261	0.0229	0.024
	(0.0278)	(0.0279)	(0.0276)	(0.0276)	(0.0282)	(0.0280)	(0.0281)	(0.0281)
Foreign (dummy)		0.133**	0.130**	0.115**	0.130**	0.109**	0.138**	0.130**
		(0.0188)	(0.0182)	(0.0171)	(0.0186)	(0.0173)	(0.0199)	(0.0187)
R&D performer (dummy)		0.0602**	0.0590**	0.0539**	0.0576**	0.0509**	0.0617**	0.0545**
		(0.0095)	(0.0092)	(0.0089)	(0.0093)	(0.0091)	(0.0096)	(0.0091)
N domestic firms (sector-region)			-0.00099	-0.0161**				
			(0.0015)	(0.0026)				
N foreign firms (sector-region)				0.0427**				
				(0.0039)				
N domestic R&D performers (sect-reg)					0.00771**			
					(0.0018)			
N foreign R&D performers (sect-reg)					0.0416**			
					(0.0040)			
Regional share (sector)						0.0663**		
						(0.0081)		
Foreign share (sector)						0.198**		
						(0.0179)		
Foreign share (region)						0.0614**		

	(1)	(2)	(3)	(4)	(5)	(6)	(7)	(8)
Q domestic firms (sect-reg)							0.00255** (0.0004)	
Q foreign firms (sect-reg)							0.00359** (0.0009)	
Q domestic R&D performers (sect-reg)								0.000750** (0.0002)
Q foreign R&D performers (sect-reg)								0.00169** (0.0002)
Firm size * Regional output share								
Firm size * Foreign share (sector)								
Firm size * Foreign share (region)								
R&D performer * Regional output share								
R&D performer * Foreign share (sector)								
R&D performer * Foreign share (region)								
Firm size * Q domestic R&D performers (sect-reg)								
Firm size * Q foreign R&D performers (sect-reg)								
R&D performer * Q domestic R&D performers (sect-reg)								
R&D performer * Q foreign R&D performers (sect-reg)								
Q share of large firms (sect-reg)								(0.0150)
Constant	2.795** (0.2450)	2.837** (0.2480)	2.802** (0.2490)	2.886** (0.2550)	2.904** (0.2510)	2.889** (0.2510)	2.824** (0.2500)	2.876** (0.2490)
Observations	123947	123947	123947	123947	123947	123947	123947	123947
Number of ID	32739	32739	32739	32739	32739	32739	32739	32739
AR1	-20.33	-20.11	-20.53	-20.31	-19.61	-19.73	-19.85	-19.79
AR2	2.964	2.961	2.953	2.843	2.924	2.827	2.982	2.937
AR3	2.015	1.993	1.981	2.003	1.991	1.954	1.988	1.999
Hansen J	37.05	35.75	36.26	35.78	33.74	34.74	34.16	34.13
Jdf	22	22	22	22	22	22	22	22
Jp	0.0234	0.0323	0.0285	0.032	0.0522	0.0413	0.0473	0.0477

foreign firms in the same region. Model 7 shows that when the outputs of both domestic and foreign firms are higher in a sector-region, firms operating in that sector-region are likely to be more productive. These results, when compared with those of Model 4, support the congestion and competition arguments for domestic firms. If there are more domestic firms in a sector-region, it creates negative effects, but if total output produced by domestic firms increases in a sector-region, then firms become more productive. Note that, in this case too, the coefficient of output of foreign firms is higher than the coefficient for domestic firms. In other words, foreign firms' output generates more spillovers.

When the output variables are replaced by the output of R&D performers, the results are the same: there are strong spillovers from the output of both domestic and foreign R&D performers, and the spillovers from foreign firms are stronger that those from domestic firms.

Finally, we redefined agglomeration and spillover variables separately at the sectoral and regional level instead of narrower sector-region level. In this case (Model 6) the 'Regional share (sector)' variable shows the share of that region in the sectors' total output, the 'Foreign share (sector)' the share of foreign firms in the sectors' total output, and the 'Foreign share (region)' the share of foreign firms in the regions' total output. Therefore, for example, the 'Foreign share (region)' variable shows if there are regional spillovers from foreign firms that benefit firms operating in the same region but in different sectors, whereas the 'Foreign share (sector)' variable shows if there are spillovers from foreign firms that are beneficial to all firms operating in the same sector irrespective of its location.

Estimation results show that there are pure agglomeration effects ('Regional share (sector))', that is, if a region's share in a sector's total output is higher, the firms operating in that region and sector are more productive. Moreover, there are additional spillovers from foreign firms to all firms operating in the same sector, and to all firms operating in the same region, that is, there are spillovers at the sectoral and regional level independent of each other.

In Models 9 and 10 (Table 5.5b), different variables used to capture agglomeration and spillover effects are included in the model to check the robustness of estimation results. There is no significant change in estimation results. The only exception is that the coefficient of the output of foreign R&D performers becomes insignificant when the model also includes other variables about spillovers from foreign firms.

Finally, Models 11–14 (Table 5.5b) include interaction variables that are used to understand whether absorptive capacity is important in benefiting from agglomeration effects and spillovers. Most of the variables interacting with firm size have statistically insignificant coefficients at the 5% level, that is, firm size does not matter in benefiting from spillovers. The only exception is the interaction with 'Foreign share (sector)' variable that has a negative and statistically significant coefficient. It seems spillovers from foreign firms operating in the same sector are more important for small firms than large firms. This result does

Table 5.5b Production function estimation results for Turkey, 2006–2013, GMM-System results

	(9)	(10)	(11)	(12)	(13)	(14)	(15)	(16)
VARIABLES	GMM	GMM	GMM	GMM	GMM	GMM	GMM	GMM
Returns to scale	1.041	1.04	1.085	1.046	1.043	1.047	1.047	1.046
Lag output	0.210**	0.210**	0.204**	0.213**	0.207**	0.216**	0.220**	0.216**
	(0.0207)	(0.0207)	(0.0205)	(0.0208)	(0.0203)	(0.0207)	(0.0210)	(0.0210)
Labor	0.482**	0.483**	0.521**	0.500**	0.451**	0.499**	0.487**	0.488**
	(0.0549)	(0.0548)	(0.0737)	(0.0558)	(0.0531)	(0.0560)	(0.0563)	(0.0559)
Lag labor	-0.207**	-0.208**	-0.208**	-0.215**	-0.189**	-0.216**	-0.208**	-0.205**
	(0.0329)	(0.0328)	(0.0344)	(0.0333)	(0.0314)	(0.0335)	(0.0336)	(0.0332)
Capital	0.0366**	0.0367**	0.0364**	0.0378**	0.0353**	0.0380**	0.0374**	0.0372**
	(0.0044)	(0.0044)	(0.0044)	(0.0044)	(0.0042)	(0.0044)	(0.0045)	(0.0045)
Lag capital	0.00606**	0.00607**	0.00559**	0.00615**	0.00516**	0.00608**	0.00522*	0.00536*
	(0.0020)	(0.0020)	(0.0020)	(0.0021)	(0.0020)	(0.0021)	(0.0021)	(0.0021)
Inputs	0.485**	0.483**	0.487**	0.468**	0.518**	0.469**	0.477**	0.475**
	(0.0558)	(0.0557)	(0.0575)	(0.0563)	(0.0528)	(0.0564)	(0.0569)	(0.0567)
Lag inputs	0.0201	0.0207	0.0213	0.0262	0.00679	0.025	0.0179	0.0197
	(0.0278)	(0.0278)	(0.0284)	(0.0281)	(0.0267)	(0.0281)	(0.0282)	(0.0280)
Foreign (dummy)	0.0974**	0.0985**	0.119**	0.109**	0.127**	0.137**	0.134**	0.108**
	(0.0162)	(0.0164)	(0.0190)	(0.0173)	(0.0187)	(0.0193)	(0.0194)	(0.0177)
R&D performer (dummy)	0.0445**	0.0426**	0.0595**	0.0481**	0.0648**	-0.0125	0.0603**	0.0497**
	(0.0083)	(0.0080)	(0.0079)	(0.0117)	(0.0077)	(0.0153)	(0.0096)	(0.0091)
N domestic firms (sector-region)	-0.0181**	-0.0187**						
	(0.0036)	(0.0036)						
N foreign firms (sector-region)	0.0199**	0.0217**						
	(0.0026)	(0.0027)						
N domestic R&D performers (sect-reg)	0.00225							
	(0.0026)							
N foreign R&D performers (sect-reg)	0.00702*							
	(0.0035)							
Regional share (sector)	0.0906**	0.0906**	0.135**	0.0656**				0.0659**

(Continued)

Table 5.5b (Continued)

VARIABLES	(9) GMM	(10) GMM	(11) GMM	(12) GMM	(13) GMM	(14) GMM	(15) GMM	(16) GMM
	(0.0144)	(0.0143)	(0.0517)	(0.0081)				(0.0079)
Foreign share (sector)	0.136** (0.0126)	0.141** (0.0129)	0.124 (0.0857)	0.205** (0.0186)				0.205** (0.0183)
Foreign share (region)	0.0613** (0.0146)	0.0611** (0.0146)	0.848* (0.3970)	0.0587** (0.0155)				0.0550** (0.0154)
Q domestic firms (sect-reg)								
Q foreign firms (sect-reg)								
Q domestic R&D performers (sect-reg)		0.000408* (0.0002)			0.00438 (0.0023)	0.000678** (0.0002)		
Q foreign R&D performers (sect-reg)		-8.80E-05 (0.0002)			0.00296** (0.0011)	0.00177** (0.0002)		
Firm size * Regional output share			-0.0173 (0.0126)					
Firm size * Foreign share (sector)			0.0192 (0.0193)					
Firm size * Foreign share (region)			-0.198* (0.0995)					
R&D performer * Regional output share				0.0179 (0.0185)				
R&D performer * Foreign share (sector)				-0.0627** (0.0209)				
R&D performer * Foreign share (region)				0.0463 (0.0394)				
Firm size * Q domestic R&D performers (sect-reg)					-0.00033 (0.0003)			
Firm size * Q foreign R&D performers (sect-reg)					-0.00092 (0.0006)			
R&D performer * Q domestic R&D performers (sect-reg)						-0.00013 (0.0005)		

	(1)	(2)	(3)	(4)	(5)	(6)	(7)	(8)
R&D performer * Q foreign R&D performers (sect-reg)						0.00392** (0.0008)		
Q share of large firms (sect-reg)							0.0331** (0.0070)	-0.00601 (0.0064)
Constant	2.881** (0.2610)	2.886** (0.2600)	2.728** (0.2500)	2.891** (0.2510)	2.690*** (0.2440)	2.887*** (0.2500)	2.848** (0.2540)	2.854** (0.2540)
Observations	123.947	123.947	123.947	123.947	123.947	123.947	121.218	121.218
Number of ID	32.739	32.739	32.739	32.739	32.739	32.739	32.403	32.403
AR1	-20.3	-20.28	-20.08	-19.71	-21.69	-19.72	-20.1	-20.08
AR2	2.793	2.792	2.686	2.82	2.829	2.931	2.989	2.877
AR3	1.952	1.957	1.887	1.956	1.935	1.998	1.996	1.925
Hansen J	37.76	37.78	39.71	34.51	41.78	33.97	35.04	34.6
Jdf	22	22	22	22	22	22	22	22
Jp	0.0195	0.0194	0.0117	0.0436	0.00665	0.0495	0.0383	0.0426

Standard errors in parentheses

** $p < 0.01$

Notes: Standard errors in parentheses (** $p < 0.01$, * $p < 0.05$).
All variables are in log form. There are 123,947 observations (32,739 firms) in the sample.
FDI and R&D performer are dummy variables.
Regional output share, Foreign share (sector) and Foreign share (region) are in percentage.
All model includes time dummies.
GMM instruments: From the 2nd lag for output, labour, and inputs, and from the 1st lag for capital.

not confirm the study by Onder et al. (2003) which also analyzed spatial characteristics of technical efficiency, technical change and TFP changes by estimating a trans-log Cobb-Douglas production function employing stochastic frontier analysis (SFA) methodology using regions' share in production, population density and a specialization index based on the value added to represent regional characteristics. Their findings suggest that firms operating on a larger scale are more efficient than small scale ones.

As regards interactions with R&D performer variables, the estimation results show that R&D does not matter much for benefiting from spillovers. It seems that R&D non-performers benefit more from spillovers from foreign firms operating in the same sector (Model 12), but when we look at spillovers from foreign R&D performing firms in the same sector-region, R&D activity enhances absorptive capacity, that is, absorptive capacity created by R&D activity matters for spillovers from other (foreign) R&D performers. These results may indicate that there could be spillovers specific to technologically sophisticated firms.

Models 15 and 16 are estimated to check whether only large firms generate spillovers. When the output share of large firms in the same sector-region is the only spillover variable (Model 15), the estimation results suggest that there are spillovers from large firms to others operating in the same sector-region. However, when three aggregate spillover variables are included in the model (Model 16), the coefficient of the output of large firms in the same sector-region becomes insignificant, that is, the existence of large firms does not create more spillovers.

Productivity dynamics and differentials

The previous section summarized the results of production function estimates that reveal which factors contribute to total factor productivity. In this section, we will look at the dynamics of productivity by region and firm size.

By using the estimated coefficients of the production function, the (log) level of total factor productivity for each firm-year is calculated as follows:

$$TFP_{i,t} = q_{i,t} - \alpha^*_{Lq} q_{i,t-1} + \alpha^*_K K_{i,t} + \alpha^*_{LK} K_{i,t-1} + \alpha^*_L L_{i,t}$$
$$+ \alpha^*_{LL} L_{i,t-1} + \alpha^*_M M_{i,t} + \alpha^*_{Lm} M_{i,t-1}$$

where $TFP_{i,t}$ is the (log) TFP level of firm i at time t. α^*'s are estimated values of production function coefficients.

We estimated TFP levels from coefficients estimated for all models, and checked whether there are significant differences between TFP levels calculated for each model. The coefficients of correlation between TFP levels are above 0.99 for all models. In other words, all models give similar TFP estimates at the firm level. We use the coefficients of Model 9 (Table 5.5b) in the following analysis.

We ranked all regions by gross domestic product (GDP) per capita and formed five regions on the basis of their ranking. Region 1 has the highest and Region 5 the lowest GDP per capita. Figure 5.4 presents the mean

TFP levels for those five regional groups for the period 2006–2013. It seems that Regions 1 and 2 have similar TFP levels, whereas Regions 3, 4 and 5 lag behind the more developed regions. Interestingly, the economic crisis in 2009 had a stronger negative effect on less developed regions (especially the least developed one) in terms of productivity level whereas the developed regions (1 and 2) were able to increase their productivity throughout the period. The less developed regions, after stagnation until 2011, achieved a rapid increase in productivity in 2012 and 2013 (Table 5.6).

Figure 5.5 presents similar data grouped by firm size. All firms are classified into three groups, large (employing 250 or more people), medium (50–249 employees) and small (20–49) categories. There are significant productivity differentials between large firms on the one hand, and small and medium-sized firms on the other. Small and medium-sized firms have, on average, similar productivity levels. The effect of the economic crisis on productivity across size categories is similar to that for regions. Less productive categories (small and medium-sized firms) felt the effect of the economic crisis more than large firms did. Although the TFP level for small and medium-sized firms stagnated before and during the crisis, it increased almost continuously for large firms throughout the period (Table 5.7).

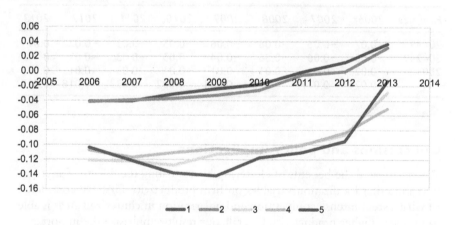

Figure 5.4 Mean TFP by region (weighted)

Table 5.6 Mean TFP by region (weighted)

Region	2006	2007	2008	2009	2010	2011	2012	2013
1	−0.04086	−0.04054	−0.03106	−0.02401	−0.01794	−0.00118	0.01215	0.03699
2	−0.04157	−0.0393	−0.03714	−0.0327	−0.02575	−0.00529	−0.00036	0.03215
3	−0.12111	−0.12248	−0.12766	−0.11292	−0.11044	−0.09968	−0.08667	−0.02886
4	−0.10743	−0.11709	−0.11065	−0.10562	−0.10815	−0.10078	−0.08362	−0.05089
5	−0.10373	−0.12133	−0.13838	−0.14214	−0.11753	−0.11041	−0.09518	−0.01332
Stdev	0.038637	0.044074	0.051108	0.052233	0.0496	0.055162	0.052058	0.038365

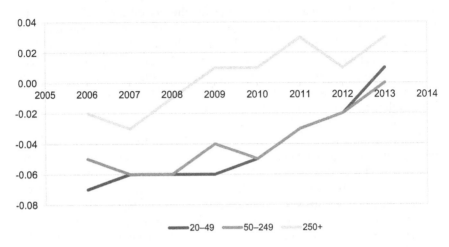

Figure 5.5 Mean TFP by firm size (weighted)

Table 5.7 Mean TFP by firm size (weighted)

Firm size	2006	2007	2008	2009	2010	2011	2012	2013
20–49	−0.07	−0.06	−0.06	−0.06	−0.05	−0.03	−0.02	0.01
50–249	−0.05	−0.06	−0.06	−0.04	−0.05	−0.03	−0.02	0
250+	−0.02	−0.03	−0.01	0.01	0.01	0.03	0.01	0.03
	0.021	0.017	0.028	0.034	0.032	0.033	0.018	0.017

Conclusions and policy implications

We investigated the benefits of clustering by estimating the effects of aggregation and other localization variables on firm productivity. First, we considered to what extent intense competition and polarization in clusterized areas is able to promote higher productivity. Overall, our results emphasize the importance of agglomeration economies in Turkey: there are positive externalities from foreign firm agglomerations; by contrast, the externalities from agglomeration of domestic firms are negative, suggesting congestion effects.

Important localized innovation spillovers are also found. Besides, there is evidence on the usual outcome that firms in the same industry benefit more from each other as they are more technologically similar and that sector closeness also matters as this may facilitate the flow and absorption of knowledge among firms. We also found that the territorial and social redistribution of spillovers may be limited in particular from foreign multinationals. This might also occur because firms open to foreign markets are in general subcontractors which do not have total autonomy to conduct technological innovation.

We also considered innovation spillovers by type of firm (small and medium-sized enterprises/large, high/low innovating and hence with high/low absorptive capacity). Hence, we interacted agglomeration and spillover variables with firm size (measured by the number of employees) and innovation variables. These interaction variables revealed that innovation performers benefit more from agglomeration effects and spillovers, as in most of our estimations the coefficient of the firm innovation–agglomeration effect interaction variable is positive.

Polarization of activities was confirmed to be an enhancing factor of firm performance. A model of development based on strong polarization is confirmed to be enhancing in most cases firm performance and growth.

However, recent decades have witnessed an increasingly unbalanced process of regional growth in Turkey which has led to large income and employment gaps across regions, consequent massive migration, concentration of the population in large cities and along the coast, degradation and isolation of inland areas, environmental impoverishment and abandonment.

Recommendations to address crucial policy questions arise from this analysis:

- Unbalanced process of regional growth in most Mediterranean countries has to be avoided as it can lead only to large income and employment gaps across regions, consequent massive migration, concentration of population in large cities and along the coast, degradation and isolation of internal areas, environmental impoverishment and abandonment, which all have witnessed in recent decades.
- While a reallocation of resources to less developed regions could be costly and counterproductive given that regional tax incentives to poor regions may shift jobs away from areas that do not receive the subsidy, rather than create new ones, the policy target for the government should rather be to invest in transportation infrastructure, ease access to housing and develop regional complementarities. Such policies would expand job opportunities for those outside coastal regions and lead in the long term to a more sustainable convergence of standards of living among regions.
- The experience drawn from this analysis may also lend support to identify key drivers and patterns of localized production and provide a benchmark to analyze the issue of efficiency of clusters of small and medium-sized enterprises in Southern Mediterranean countries. In particular, the results may be useful within the Euro-Med cluster cooperation on industry and innovation framework. The emerging innovation clusters based in Tunisia, Morocco and Lebanon, the Central Business Districts (CBDs) in Tunisia, the Special Economic Zones and the role of multinational corporations are key elements in this context.
- These results also represent the economic underpinning of policy analysis aimed at fostering innovation at regional level. In spite of the challenges of globalization, places still make the difference and can emerge as laboratories of new local-global, private-public partnerships.

Notes

1 Part of the project entitled 'Spatial proximity and firm performances: how can location-based economies help the transition process in the Mediterranean region? Empirical evidence from Turkey, Italy and Tunisia', funded by the EU Commission (euro 10,000) under the 2015 Internal Competition for the FEMISE project on '*Support to economic research, studies and dialogue of the Euro-Mediterranean Partnership*' as per the Contract signed between the Commission and the FEMISE association no. ENPI/2014/354–494 ('Commission-FEMISE contract'). The purpose of this agreement is to provide an original research work in the fields of social and economic analysis by the Team Leader Anna M. Ferragina. Members of the team: Erol Taymaz, Ünal Töngür, Sofiane Ghali, Habib Zitouna, Giulia Nunziante, Fernanda Mazzotta, and Anna Ferragina.
2 This might also occur because firms open to foreign markets are in general subcontractors which have no autonomy to conduct either technological or non-technological innovation.
3 We use the terms 'firm' and 'enterprise' interchangeably.
4 A firm is 'foreign' if at least 10% of its shares are held by foreign agents. Note that most of the foreign firms are majority owned, that is, foreign agents own more than 50% of shares.
5 However, we do not include regional dummies, as controlling on average across the years for regional fixed effects might absorb some of the regional and sector externalities we are trying to estimate.
6 Unless otherwise noted, 'statistically significant' means statistically significant at the 1% level.

References

Acs, Z., Armington, C., and Zhang, T., 2007. The Determinants of New-Firm Survival Across Regional Economies: The Role of Human Capital Stock and Knowledge Spillovers. *Papers in Regional Science*, 86 (3), 367–391.

Aitken, B.J., and Harrison, A.E., 1999. Do Domestic Firms Benefit from Direct Foreign Investment? Evidence from Venezuela. *American Economic Review*, 89 (3), 605–618.

Audretsch, D.B., and Feldman, M.P., 1996. Knowledge Spillovers and the Geography of Innovation and Production. *American Economic Review*, 86 (3), 630–640.

Audretsch, D.B., and Feldmann, M.P., 2004. Knowledge Spillovers and the Geography of Innovation. *Handbook of Regional and Urban Economics*, 4, 2713–2739.

Baltagi, B.H., Egger, P.H., and Kesina, M., 2012. *Firm-level Productivity Spillovers in China's Chemical Industry: A Spatial Hausman-Taylor Approach*. Mimeo.

Bloom, N., and van Reenen, J., 2010. Why Do Management Practices Differ across Firms and Countries? *Journal of Economic Perspectives*, 24 (1), 203–224, Winter.

Bottazzi, L., and Peri, G., 2003. Innovation and Spillovers in Regions: Evidence from European Patent Data. *European Economic Review*, 47, 687–710.

Breschi, S., and Malerba, F., 2001. Geography of Innovation and Economic Clustering. *Industrial and Corporate Change*, 10 (4), 817–833.

Çetin, D., 2016. *Knowledge Spillovers and Clusters: A Spatial Econometric Analysis on Ankara and Istanbul OIZs*. Germany: LAP Lambert Academic Publishing.

Çetin, D., and Kalaycı, E., 2016. Spatial Econometric Analysis of R&D Spillovers in Turkey. *Journal of Applied Economics and Business Research*, 6 (1), 55–72.

Coulibaly, S., Deichmann, U., and Lall, S., 2007. *Urbanization and Productivity: Evidence from Turkish Provinces Over the Period 1980–2000*, Policy Research Working Paper Series 4327. The World Bank.

De Propris, L., and Driffield, N., 2006. The Importance of Clusters for Spillovers from Foreign Direct Investment and Technology Sourcing. *Cambridge Journal of Economics*, 30 (2), 277–291.

Dogruel, F., Dogruel, A., Enric, S., and Enric, Y., 2003. Macroeconomics of Turkey's Agricultural Reforms: An Intertemporal Computable General Equilibrium Analysis. *Journal of Policy Modeling*, 25 (6–7), 617–637, September.

Ellison, G., Glaeser, E.L., and Kerr, W.R., 2010. What Causes Industry Agglomeration? Evidence from Coagglomeration Patterns. *American Economic Review*, 100, 1195–1213, June.

Ferragina, A.M., and Mazzotta, F., 2014. FDI Spillovers on Firms' Survival in Italy: Absorptive Capacity Matters! *The Journal of Technology Transfer*, 39 (6), 859–897.

Filiztekin, A., 1998. *Convergence Across Provinces and Industries in Turkey*, Working Paper, No. 08. Koc University.

Filiztekin, A., and Çelik, M.A., 2010. Regional Income Inequality in Turkey. *Megaron*, 5, 116–127.

Gezici, F., and Hewings, G.J.D., 2007. Spatial Analysis of Regional Inequalities in Turkey. *European Planning Studies*, 15 (3), 383–403.

Glaeser, E., Kallal, H., Scheinkman, J., and Shleifer, A., 1992. Growth of Cities. *Journal of Political Economy*, 100, 1126–1152.

Gorg, H., and Greenaway, D., 2004. Much Ado about Nothing? Do Domestic Firms Really Benefit from Foreign Direct Investment? *World Bank Research Observer*, 19 (2), 171–197.

Greenstone, M., Hornbeck, R., and Moretti, E., 2010. Identifying Agglomeration Spillovers: Evidence from Winners and Losers of Large Plant Openings. *Journal of Political Economy*, 118 (3), 536–598.

Griliches, Z., 1979. Issues in Assessing the Contribution of Research and Development to Productivity Growth, *Bell Journal of Economics*, 10 (1), 92–116, Spring.

Haskel, J., Pereira, S., and Slaughter, M., 2002. *Does Inward Foreign Direct Investment Boost the Productivity of Domestic Firms?* NBER Working Paper 8724.

Henderson, J.V., Dicken, P., Hess, M., Coe, N., and Yeung, H.W.C., 2002. Global Production Networks and the Analysis of Economic Development. *Review of International Political Economy*, 9, 436–464.

Jacobs, J., 1969. *The Economies of Cities*. New York: Random House.

Javorcik, B.S., 2004. Does Foreign Direct Investment Increase the Productivity of Domestic Firms? In Search of Spillovers Through Backward Linkages. *American Economic Review*, 94 (3), 605–627.

Karacuka, M., and Catik, A.N., 2011. *A Spatial Approach to Measure Productivity Spillovers of Foreign Affiliated Firms in Turkish Manufacturing Industries*. DICE Discussion Paper 21. Avai lable from: http://hdl.handle.net/10419/45793

Keller, W., 2002. Geographic Localization of International Technology Diffusion, American Economic Review. *American Economic Association*, 92 (1), 120–142, March.

Kılıçaslan, Y., and Özatağan, G., 2007. Impact of Relative Population Change on Regional Income Convergence: Evidence from Turkey. Review of Urban & Regional Development Studies, 19 (3), 210–223.

Lenger, A., and Taymaz, E., 2006. To Innovate or to Transfer? *Journal of Evolutionary Economics*, Springer, 16 (1), 137–153, April.

Marshall, A., 1890. *Principles of Economics*. London: Palgrave Macmillan.

Martin, P., Mayer, T., and Mayneris, F., 2011. Spatial Concentration and Plant-Level Productivity in France. *Journal of Urban Economics*, 69 (2), 182–195.

Onder, Ã.O., Deliktas, E.R., and Lenger, A., 2003. Efficiency in the Manufacturing Industry of Selected Provinces in Turkey: A Stochastic Frontier Analysis. *Emerging Markets Finance and Trade, Taylor & Francis Journals*, 39 (2), 98–113, March.

Öztürk, S., and Kılıç, D., 2016. Do Firms Benefit from Agglomeration? A Productivity Analysis for Turkish Manufacturing Industry. *Ekonomik Yaklasim*, 27 (98), 115–140.

Paci, R., and Usai, S., 2006. *Agglomeration Economies and Growth: The Case of Italian Local Labour Systems, 1991–2001*, Working Paper CRENoS 200612. Sardinia: Centre for North South Economic Research, University of Cagliari and Sassari.

Porter, M.E., 1998. Location, Clusters and the 'new' Microeconomics of Competition. *Business Economics*, 33 (1), 7–17.

Rosenthal, S.S., and Strange, W.C., 2001. The Determinants of Agglomeration. *Journal of Urban Economics*, 50.

Saatci, G., and Taymaz, E.,1997. Technical Change and Efficiency in Turkish Manufacturing Industries. *Journal of Productivity Analysis*, 8, 461–475.

Taymaz, E., and Yilmaz, K., 2007. Productivity and Trade Orientation: Turkish Manufacturing Industry Before and After Customs Union. *The Journal of International Trade and Diplomacy*, 1, 127–154.

Yıldırım, J., and Öcal, N., 2006. Income Inequality and Economic Convergence in Turkey. *Transition Studies Review*, 13 (3), 559–568.

Chapter 6

Youth unemployment and labour market policies in the Southern Mediterranean

Roger Albinyana

Introduction: regional cooperation on labour policies in the Euro-Mediterranean

The Employment and Labour Ministers of the Union for the Mediterranean (UfM) convened in Jordan on 26 and 27 September 2016 at a third Ministerial Conference with the aim of developing genuine cooperation at the level of labour policy.[1] The Conference was hosted by the Hashemite Kingdom of Jordan and was co-chaired by the UfM co-presidency: Jordan's Minister for Labour and the EU Commissioner for Employment, Social Affairs, Skills and Labour Mobility with the presence of the Secretary General of the UfM.

At a time of political divisiveness, challenge to multilateralism and global disbandment, the gathering of this ministerial conference six years after the previous one, which was held in Brussels in November 2010, was right considering that youth in the Southern Mediterranean, in particular, find themselves facing limited opportunities and significant challenges in advancing their lives and bettering their futures. Indeed, youth unemployment in the countries of this region is the highest in the world, and is hugely costly to the region's societies, requiring a major turnaround in policy thinking about jobs.

To this end, Ministers took account of the employment and labour developments in light of the economic, financial and migration crises, which have hit the region during the last decade and recommended that the national authorities of the 43 UfM countries develop comprehensive strategies for employment, employability and decent work for all, especially for the two vulnerable and sometimes excluded groups: youth and women. While recognizing the inherent diversity among the various national labour markets, and thus the impossibility of designing and implementing harmonized strategies, Ministers acknowledged the structural nature of youth unemployment challenges in the Arab Mediterranean countries (UfM 2016b).

With a view to tackling these common challenges, Ministers recommended policies and reforms aimed at promoting job creation, with a strong emphasis laid on both the demand and supply sides of the labour market, while the traditional mainstream approach to solving youth unemployment in most countries has mainly focussed on labour supply. On the contrary, measures identified by the Ministers encompass the need to develop sound macro-economic policies, that enable a sustainable business environment to stimulate job creation, encourage entrepreneurship (facilitating access to finance, micro-finance, business mentoring, start-up support, etc.), but also to improve employability, school-to-work transition schemes, vocational education and training (VET), development of active labour market policies, reinforcing dialogue between public and private employment services and, very important, transition from informal to formal employment (UfM 2016a).

Finally, Ministers emphasized that a well-functioning and effective social dialogue, both tripartite and bipartite, is key to democracy, good governance and to developing strategies that combine competitiveness and social progress. Indeed, prior to the Ministerial Conference, a Euro-Mediterranean Social Partners gathering was organized to bring together representatives from the business and trade union organizations from both shores of the Mediterranean. A declaration was released and considered by the Ministers (UfM 2016b).

This chapter intends to shed light on the current challenges and possible solutions that labour markets face for young people in the Southern Mediterranean countries.[2] First, we will be looking at regional trends, both from quantitative and also qualitative angles; second, we will be assessing the state of play of active labour market policies in most Southern countries from the Mediterranean region; finally, we will be identifying some policy measures that aim to tackle the most pressing socio-economic challenge that the region faces today: youth unemployment.

Labour markets in the Southern Mediterranean countries: challenges, facts and trends

Whereas youth unemployment has slowly decreased in global trends since the year 2014 when the most severe part of the financial crisis started to ease, the rates in the Southern Mediterranean countries have not improved. On the contrary, unemployment trends have been deteriorating since the onset of the global financial and economic crises, and the latest political turmoil in the region, thus underpinning one of the major factors of political and social unrest. Even before the crises, the expansion of employment opportunities lagged behind economic growth in the region.

Youth unemployment rates in the Southern Mediterranean countries in 2016 were notably higher than those observed in the EU as reflected in Figure 6.1, even though the two regions are characterized by a certain degree of country heterogeneity. In particular, southern EU countries such as Greece, Spain, Croatia or Cyprus reflect rates very much like those of the Southern Mediterranean countries, with the lowest figures in countries such as Turkey, Lebanon or Morocco. Likewise, according to data made publicly available by the International Labour Organization (ILO 2016), youth unemployment rates

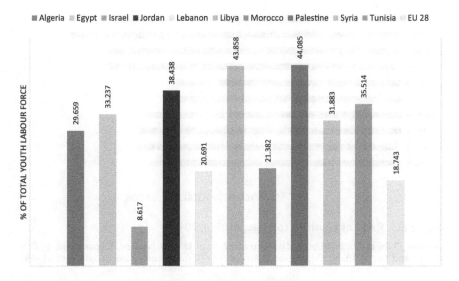

Figure 6.1 Youth unemployment rates, 2016

Source: Own elaboration with data extracted from ILOSTAT (2017). Youth comprises people ages 15–24.

in the Southern Mediterranean region, with the exception of Syria and Libya, experienced a peak in the aftermath of the revolts in 2011 although as from 2014 they stabilized with a relative declining trend.

The factors that triggered the wave of protests and uprisings in 2011 across the Southern Mediterranean countries highlighted the reality among large segments of the population who felt excluded from private and public lives, but also the significance of the demographic profile among youth in the region. Never before has the region had such a large share of youth as compared with other world regions, with the exception of sub-Saharan Africa. As shown in Figure 6.2, youth ages 15–24 account for slightly less than 20% of the population, compared with an average 12% in high-income countries, which is even lower in Northern Mediterranean countries such as Italy or Spain where the share of youth makes up around 9% of the total population.

The wave of instability and revolts in the region since 2011 has only worsened the general situation in some of these countries, not only those like Syria and Libya which have gone through armed conflict. Unemployment in the region remains a phenomenon affecting youth ages 15–24, especially young women, and has emerged as the main factor of social discontent and unrest (ILO 2015).

Demographic pressures and absence of change in economic structures are the leading causes of youth unemployment rates in the region. Indeed, a large

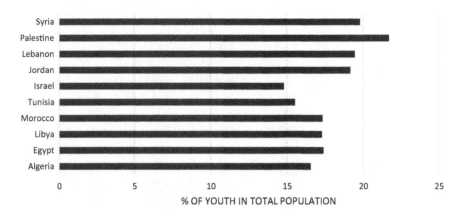

Figure 6.2 Ratio of youth to total population, 2016

Source: Own elaboration with data extracted from United Nations, Department of Economic and Social Affairs, Population Division (2017). Youth comprises people ages 15–24.

decline in infant mortality coupled with high fertility rates in recent decades has led to very high population growth rates and to an expansion of the labour force rates, a phenomenon which hit the Northern Mediterranean countries during the 1970s, but which later on softened and declined.

Furthermore, most countries in the Southern Mediterranean have witnessed little change in economic structure like industry, which has proved to be the most important vehicle of job creation in developing economies and which has been growing at very low if not negative rates. Instead of creating the environment for manufacturing, investment and trade to flourish, the public sector has forged monopolistic and uncompetitive alliances, while forgoing a sound, sustainable system of public finances (UNDP 2016). This has led to a patronized private sector unable to absorb the demographic dividend by providing a sufficient amount of job opportunities and unable to create a fertile business-friendly environment for new young, independent entrepreneurs. Moreover, in some countries, the latter have been aggravated by political shocks of a different nature, authoritarian rule, repression, coupled with the systematic distribution of unproductive rents accrued not only from the exploitation of natural resources, but also through licences, monopolies and economic controls.

In this respect, a remarkable specificity in the region is not only the duration of unemployment, which is longer for youth than for adult population when compared with other regions, but particularly youth labour force participation, which stands at the lowest levels worldwide, as shown in Table 6.1, with approximately 33% in North Africa and 31% in the Middle East in 2014, down from 37% to 35% respectively in 1991 according to the ILO.

Table 6.1 Youth labour force participation rates, by region and sex, 2014

Region	Total	Male	Female
Middle East	*31.3*	*47.2*	*13.8*
North Africa	*33.7*	*47.2*	*19.7*
World	47.3	55.2	38.9
Developed economies and EU	47.4	49.1	45.5
Eastern Europe (non-EU)	40.6	47.9	33.0
East Asia	55.0	57.0	52.9
South-East Asia and the Pacific	52.4	59.4	45.2
South Asia	39.5	55.2	22.6
Latin America and the Caribbean	52.5	62.1	42.6
Sub-Saharan Africa	54.3	56.6	52.1

Source: Own elaboration with data extracted from ILO, Trends Econometric Models, April 2015

Importantly, labour force participation among female youth in the region is somewhat half that of male youth, signalling social discrimination and exclusion from the workforce. Among young women, youth unemployment rates are also the highest in the world, with North African countries amounting to 50% on average and the EU28 standing at 18% in 2016. Figure 6.3 shows the youth unemployment rates disaggregated by sex for each country in the region and for the EU 28. Some have attributed this trend to conservative social norms (Clark et al. 1991), but the reality is that productivity and social cohesion is severely hampered, even if support for equality and women's empowerment has grown in the region, albeit slowly.

Not only does youth unemployment last longer than in any other region in the world due to insufficient labour demand, but the school-to-work transition is arduous given that education is no guarantee against unemployment. For instance, data suggest that in countries such as Tunisia, Jordan or Egypt, young people who have completed their tertiary education are two to three times more likely to be unemployed than those with primary education or less (ILO 2015). In other developing regions, as the level of education rises, the unemployment rate decreases.

The allocation of youth employment over the different sectors of activity shows how human capital characteristics and differences in the business environment influence youth employment in the different Southern Mediterranean countries. In certain countries, youth employment is mainly concentrated in agricultural, textile and clothing, and transport equipment sectors. Table 6.2 reflects which sectors attract youth workers for each Southern Mediterranean country. In particular, Table 6.2 presents how many young people (15–24 years old) will be employed in a particular sector if it increases its employment by 100 persons.

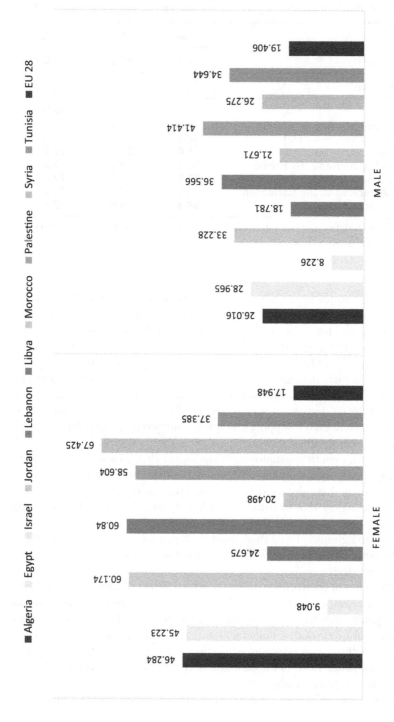

■ Algeria ■ Egypt ▨ Israel ■ Jordan ■ Lebanon ■ Libya ▨ Morocco ■ Palestine ■ Syria ▨ Tunisia ■ EU 28

FEMALE

46.284	
45.223	
9.048	
60.174	
24.675	
60.84	
20.498	
58.604	
67.425	
37.385	
17.948	

MALE

26.016	
28.965	
8.226	
33.228	
18.781	
36.566	
21.671	
41.414	
26.275	
34.644	
19.406	

Figure 6.3 Youth unemployment rates by sex, 2016

Source: Own elaboration with data extracted from ILOSTAT (2017). Youth comprises people ages 15–24.

Table 6.2 Youth employment demand by sector, 2015

Sectors	Algeria	Egypt	Israel	Jordan	Lebanon	Morocco	Tunisia
Agriculture	↑ 25	↑ 24	↓ 11	↑ 26	↑ 27	↑ 22	⇒ 17
Energy	↓ 7	↓ 9	↓ 6	↓ 10	↓ 11	↓ 9	↓ 10
Chemical Products	↑ 26	↑ 25	⇒ 15	↑ 27	↑ 28	↑ 23	↑ 21
Other Energy Intensive	↑ 25	↑ 24	⇒ 14	↑ 26	↑ 28	↑ 22	↑ 21
Electric Goods-Other Equipment Goods	↑ 25	↑ 25	⇒ 14	↑ 26	↑ 28	↑ 23	↑ 21
Transport Equipment	↑ 26	↑ 26	⇒ 15	↑ 27	↑ 29	↑ 23	↑ 22
Consumer Goods Industries	↑ 25	⇒ 18	⇒ 14	↑ 26	↑ 27	↑ 22	⇒ 20
Textiles and Clothing	↑ 24	↑ 23	⇒ 14	↑ 25	↑ 26	↑ 21	⇒ 20
Construction	⇒ 18	⇒ 17	⇒ 14	⇒ 19	⇒ 20	⇒ 16	⇒ 15
Transport	↓ 8	↓ 8	⇒ 17	↓ 8	↓ 9	↓ 7	↓ 7
Communication	↓ 8	↓ 8	⇒ 18	↓ 9	↓ 9	↓ 7	↓ 7
Business-Financial Services	↓ 5	↓ 5	⇒ 19	↓ 5	↓ 10	↓ 4	↓ 7
Public Services	↓ 11	↓ 10	⇒ 14	↓ 11	↓ 12	↓ 9	↓ 9
Recreational and Other Services	↓ 11	↓ 10	↓ 7	↓ 11	↓ 12	↓ 10	↓ 9

Source: Own elaboration from GEM-E3-MED with data extracted from UN. This figure shows that for every 100 jobs in a country's sector how many will be occupied by people ages 15–24.

Informality is another feature of job markets in the region, which employs a large proportion of young people. Jobs in the informal sector are often unstable and offer low wages and poor working conditions (Dhillon et al. 2003).[3] For example, in the period 2000–2005, 75% of new labour market entrants in Egypt were employed in the informal sector, an important surge if compared with only 20% in the early 1970s. Likewise, 69% of new job entrants in Syria were equally employed in the informal economy (European Commission 2010). Before economic reforms were implemented in the 1990s, partly in line with the Washington consensus, first-time jobseekers used to find their first jobs in the public sector. For instance, in Egypt, the public sector used to absorb 70% of the workforce in 1980, compared with 16% in the informal sector. In contrast, only 23% were employed by the public sector 20 years later, whereas 42% were employed in the informal economy (UN ESCWA 2014), a trend which has been followed in all Arab Mediterranean countries.

As mentioned earlier, youth unemployment in the region is the starkest feature in the Arab Mediterranean economies, as it has been nearly twice as high as the rates in other global regions since the early 1990s, deteriorating since 2011 (ILO 2015). Figure 6.4 shows the ratio between youth and adult unemployment rates in 2016 in the Southern Mediterranean countries and the EU 28. Mostly, youth unemployment rates are two to three times higher than adult rates, with the exception of Lebanon in which youth unemployment is more than three times higher than the adult rate. These obstacles are properly explained in the education-to-work transition, insufficient labour demand, the mismatch between job requirements and applicant qualifications or what is known in the literature as 'experience gap' (ETF 2015a).

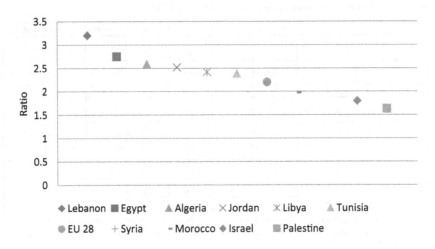

Figure 6.4 Ratio between youth and adult unemployment, 2016

Source: Own elaboration with data extracted from ILOSTAT (2017). Youth comprises people ages 15–24.

Additionally, a particularly worrying trend in the field of youth employability is the growing number of young people who are not in education, employment or training (NEETs), which is not an exclusive feature of the Southern Mediterranean countries as it hits developed economies too. Yet it aggravates social exclusion and poverty in already very unequal and fragmented societies. According to the latest estimates of the ILO, with available Eurostat statistics for 2014, the NEET rate for the 15–24 age group in Algeria is 23%, in Egypt 28%, 25% in Jordan and Tunisia while in the EU it is around 12.5%. The rate has proved to be much higher for young women and increases with low educational attainment (early drop-out) (ETF 2014).

There is a wide range of economic and social consequences of such a catastrophe. In fact, labour market conditions are one of the major pull factors explaining migration flows from certain countries to others with better labour prospects, not only to the EU but also to other parts of the world. Youth emigration from Southern Mediterranean countries has clearly increased during the last decade amidst diversification of the origin of migrants and the ways to migrate to Europe. Another consequence amongst youth is radicalization.

Instruments of active labour market policy intervention in the Southern Mediterranean countries

Active labour market policies (ALMPs) have been effectively introduced in the region, while they are designed and executed under the same rules as in most

EU countries in order to improve the employability of workers (ETF 2014). Nonetheless, overall, it is difficult to assess the effectiveness of measures, as there are very few evaluations of ALMPs in the Arab Mediterranean countries. Due to a lack of capacity (and funding), ALMPs are not properly evaluated or monitored in Arab Mediterranean countries.

The provision of ALMPs in the Southern Mediterranean countries is often the remit of a range of different institutions and organizations, such as ministries and agencies. Non-governmental organizations (NGOs) and the private sector are also involved in some countries. Indeed, private employment agencies often function as temporary work agencies or job brokers, whereas NGOs often provide services to jobseekers needing more intensive or specific professional support (e.g. vulnerable groups). Specifically, the role of private providers and NGOs differs among countries in the region. In the Maghreb countries, the public sector is the main provider of ALMPs, whilst in the Mashriq, NGOs and the private sector play a substantial role.

These various institutions and organizations often deliver independent and uncoordinated programmes that target the same groups, leading to fragmentation, duplication and inefficiencies. Due to poor coordination, many of the programmes are redundant and provide incentives for individuals to move from one programme to another, thereby promoting welfare dependency. In addition, due to weak institutional capacity, limited access to data and a lack of information, ALMPs are not well targeted. Programmes are mainly based on a one-size-fits-all logic that does not take into account the diversity of the different beneficiary profiles. The programmes are often ad hoc and target large groups, such as first-time jobseekers. Very few programmes specifically target vulnerable groups, such as young women (particularly rural women), NEETs and unskilled workers. Consequently, ALMPs often benefit individuals who would have obtained jobs without any intervention, leading to deadweight losses (ETF 2015a).

We will now assess the state of play with regard to ALMPs on a country basis among Southern Mediterranean countries, with the exception of Syria and Libya due to their current circumstances.

Algeria

Algeria has a long record of implementing ALMPs with substantial amounts of public funds accruing from the revenues of oil and gas. A National Employment Policy was adopted in 2008, whose main goal was to reduce general unemployment to below 9% in 2013. Since then, the employment policy has not changed, but it has only been strengthened. There are a number of ministries such as the Ministry of Labour, Agriculture and Industry, alongside public agencies, that have an impact on the labour market, and consequently on the level of youth unemployment. As there are no impact assessments on these various instruments and policies, the measure of their effectiveness is not evident.

Nonetheless, a lack of coordination and synergies among the various organizations involved in this strategy may be supposed.

There is a wide range of instruments implemented by all these bodies with two main functions: first, services aimed at easing social tensions by providing immediate temporary work contracts and internship schemes, as well as public work programmes for the least advantaged youth and second, services to support entrepreneurship and micro-enterprises by providing business advice and training.

In early 2011, following social unrest, the Algerian authorities decided to provide more funding to increase access to youth employment programmes. This decision included tax exemptions, hiring subsidies, government-backed credit guarantees for start-ups, as well as micro-credits for poor households. In 2013, after unemployed youth protested in the southern part of the country, the authorities decided to force employers to give preference to unemployed youth when hiring in the southern part of the country, while facing heavy sanctions in the event of non-compliance.

As regards intermediation services, they fall under the responsibility of the National Employment Agency (ANEM), which has set up some programmes (i.e. *Dispositif d'Aide à l'Insertion Professionnelle*) aimed at facilitating youth employability. Since 1990, it has been compulsory for all employers to inform ANEM about all their vacancies. In parallel, those vacancies in the civil services are publicized through the website of the Public Service Directorate. On the other hand, VET schemes such as those aimed at increasing the employability and productivity of jobseekers are still poorly developed in Algeria.

There is a wide range of employment incentive programmes to facilitate the hiring of new workers, in spite of the fact that some of the subsequent programmes cater to the same population segment, thus creating confusion. Examples include the graduate integration contract, intended for first-time jobseekers; the professional integration contract, targeting young first-time jobseekers leaving secondary education or VET programmes; the training insertion contract that targets young jobseekers without training or qualifications; social inclusion programmes that aim to reach the unemployed or those in temporary positions in the private or public sectors.

Egypt

With a Youth Employment Strategy in place, about 60% of Egypt's ALMPs identify young people exclusively as a target group. There are a number of ALMPs operational, including employment services for jobseekers, particularly through the Social Fund for Development, but most recently through the support from the EU and International Financial Institutions such as the World Bank. Most of these programmes focus on supporting job creation, which includes support to small enterprises, to micro-finance, to labour-intensive public work programmes to develop basic infrastructure, community development programmes (loans to households), and programmes targeting employment generation in rural areas which, unlike other countries in the region, concentrate a high proportion of the Egyptian population.

The main body responsible for implementing the employment strategy and policies in Egypt is the Ministry of Manpower and Migration, which is also one of the weakest ministries in the Egyptian system due to the lack of resources and quality staff (Amer 2014). The public authorities strongly rely on cooperation with non-governmental and non-profit organizations, which have become the main executors of employment-related youth programmes (Barsoum et al. 2014b). Likewise, these interventions are often possible thanks to the cooperation of international donors such as bilateral development cooperation agencies and international financial institutions.

For example, the Youth Employment National Action Plan 2010–2015 addressed the promotion of youth inclusion at its broadest level. The Plan partly aimed at expanding youth employability, reducing unemployment and providing sustainable jobs by supporting the development of micro-, small and medium-sized enterprises (MSMEs), providing ALMPs and improving the quality of systems and skills in language and new technologies.

With regard to orientation and intermediation services, the Ministry of Manpower and Migration offers, in cooperation with the ILO, career counselling, job-seekers' registration, internship offers, extensive training options, granting licences to initiate a business or collecting notices of vacancies from employers through a wide network of physical offices, but also online resources. However, the employment offices are often understaffed and under-resourced (ETF 2015c).

Egypt features different strands of VET, although there is little effective coordination between the different bodies responsible for the various schemes. This has led to an effort by public authorities to relaunch the Supreme Council for Human Resources to improve inter-ministerial cooperation and social partner engagement and avoid the fragmentation and isolation of the various initiatives existing.

The focus on entrepreneurship is not new to Egypt. The Social Fund for Development has been actively engaged in supporting the creation and nurturing of new start-ups and MSMEs. It collects and puts together funds from many different international donors to primarily target young graduates, potential small business entrepreneurs and small business owners willing to expand their activities, as well as the unemployed, disadvantaged groups such as women and those with special needs (Amer 2014). More recently, there has been growing interest in new sectors of competitive start-ups, with flourishing incubators, accelerators, high-tech and green economy sectors, which are becoming established most notably in Cairo and Alexandria.

Israel

Israel is, by and large, the country in the region with the lowest youth unemployment rate. Yet the country lacks a 'universal' ALMP, and specifically a policy aimed at youth (ETF 2015a). This is partly because most ALMPs are developed and implemented outside the government ministries, with private employers and incubators playing a major role in the design and execution of new ALMPs, which has led to particularly low levels of public spending on ALMPs compared with international standards (OECD 2013a). Moreover, Israel's compulsory education system and army service have entailed that most Israeli young people are in education, training, employment or the army, thus lowering the rate of Israeli youth counting as NEETs. These high rates of youth employment are largely because the Israeli Central Bureau of Statistics (CBS) has included the figures for youth in compulsory military service within the labour force figures since 2012. For most Israelis, military conscription (three years for men and two years for women) intervenes in the transition from school to post-secondary education or work. While military service delays entry to the labour market, it also provides skills that have market value in civilian life. Conscripts also benefit from army discharge grants allowing many to enter post-secondary education.

Orientation and intermediation services are generally provided by the Public Employment Service, whose role is to match jobseekers with employers seeking employees. Such services are structured into several physical offices, as well as online platforms, offering guidance and counselling for unemployed jobseekers, as well as advice on job placements and vocational training. In parallel, youth centres run by local authorities provide young people ages 18–30 with various local services in education, vocational training and employment facilitation services. As the Arab and ultra-Orthodox Jewish communities concentrate higher than average rates of youth unemployment, especially amongst ultra-Orthodox males and Arab females, special employment centres have been developed which are outside the remit of the Israeli Public Employment Service.

The Ministry of Education and Ministry of Economy (Israeli Manpower Training and Development Bureau) develop, maintain and finance parallel and separate systems of VET. The former has overall responsibility and the latter takes in young people who do not qualify for a place in the Ministry of Education's schools. In this regard, communication and cooperation between the ministries is good, both on a formal level and, in particular, on an informal level (ETF 2015c). Although the two key ministries exercise centralized control over aspects of VET, the education networks, the Manufacturers' Association and its affiliates and the local authorities are all in a position to lead initiatives. Furthermore, the private sector makes a significant contribution to the system through participation in skills development programmes, other initiatives and the provision of facilities.

The official Israeli body responsible for small and medium sized enterprises (SME) policy is the Ministry of Economy. The official arm of the Ministry of Economy in charge of overseeing, monitoring and implementing SME policy is the Small and Medium Business Agency (SMBA). Furthermore, a specific bill on the promotion of SMEs was passed by the Parliament in 2013. There are other governmental bodies whose functions affect SMEs, especially the Office of the Chief Scientist, which has many programmes to support research and innovation in Israeli companies, some directed specifically at SMEs. It is worth noting that the Israeli government provides strong support for high-tech start-ups and initiatives at-large in the field of research and innovation. Many multi-national companies in this field are well established in the country and employ a large number of young postgraduates. Nevertheless, young individuals wishing to establish micro-businesses outside those specific sectors might face severe difficulties due to the scarcity of financing schemes and occupational pensions.

Jordan

Jordan has no tradition of effective ALMPs, and the role of the authorities used to be strictly limited to the basic regulation of working conditions. In 2012, a National Employment Strategy 2010–2020 was launched to increase labour participation and stimulate more sustainable jobs in productive sectors. In this way, Jordan has attempted to bring under the same umbrella the country's many disparate employment initiatives and align them with the country's economic development goals. The lack of institutional planning, capacity and resources has hindered the possibilities of successfully implementing this strategy (ETF 2015a).

Orientation and intermediation services are carried out by the Ministry of Labour through physical offices and online platforms. The administration has attempted to set up one-stop shop employment offices across the country. They offer a wide range of career guidance such as information on available job opportunities, employment counselling services, information on vocational training or donor-led and funding programmes for micro-enterprises. In this regard, the Development and Employment Fund aims at reducing poverty and unemployment levels within poverty pockets and rural areas through allowing competitive Islamic loans. As a result, individuals and group entrepreneurs within the sector of MSMEs can start their own projects, create job opportunities within their communities and eventually achieve acceptable levels of life quality.

Precisely like other countries in the region, VET is highly fragmented under different ministerial units such as the Ministries of Education, Labour and Higher Education, although the E-TVET Council under the Ministry of Labour is formally intended to exert a coordination role (ETF 2015c). In addition, social partners have traditionally been engaged in implementing the National Employment Strategy and in vocational education. However, the practice is still very centralized at the national level, and there is little experience in scaling down concerted actions between government, social partners, private sector and training centres at the local level. National initiatives are supported by others such as international financial institutions and bilateral development cooperation agencies.

Lebanon

Youth employment is the most pressing issue for the Lebanese government, as it faces an intense social demand to find solutions for the unemployed, young immigrants and refugees. This problem has become more acute with the arrival of over a million refugees in Lebanon since the war in Syria began in 2011 in a country with an established population of 6 million (World Bank 2016). In this regard, the National Youth Policy Document provides the government's policy for national youth development, and the Ministry of Labour is responsible for the labour policy and different bodies responsible to supervise the labour policy such as the National Employment Office. Nevertheless, as the latter is under-staffed, with a limited budget and low technical capacity, its activities are mainly confined to administrative work (ETF 2015a). Lebanon has no labour market information system in place, which means that no accurate data are available for policy analysis and studies.

By law, the only orientation and intermediation service is provided by the National Employment Office, which has physical offices and a labour exchange portal launched in 2012, and which offers very limited services such as registra-tion for jobseekers and access to available job offers. Services often offered by analogous public agencies in other countries of the region such as counselling, mentoring or labour market analysis are not offered in Lebanon. In this regard, some international organizations such as ILO and bilateral development coop-eration agencies have been supporting the Lebanese authorities to strengthen their capacities when offering orientation and intermediation services to young jobseekers. One of the obstacles encountered in this endeavour is that Lebanese jobseekers rely more on their personal connections to find a job, which results in only a very small proportion of the young unemployed turning to the public authorities when looking for a job (ETF 2015a).

To a large extent, training is the most widely used type of publicly provided active labour market programme in Lebanon. Nonetheless, public provision is fragmented and poorly regulated: delivery schemes, training curricula and certification are not harmonized across the agencies providing training pro-grammes. With regard to service delivery schemes, some public agencies act as direct service providers but others subcontract NGOs to provide the ser-vice. Lebanon also lacks a nationwide vocational qualification framework that would set common criteria for training content and certification, thus provid-ing employers with clear signals about the skills level and aptitudes of vocational training graduates (ETF 2015c).

VET is the responsibility of the Ministry of Education and Higher Educa-tion, and is managed by the Directorate General of Vocational and Technical Education. The National Employment Office develops some short training courses on specific skills. However, these initiatives are sporadic and not framed within in a broader strategy. Its capacities (human and financial) for addressing unemployment efficiently remain very limited. Educational provision in Leba-non is highly regarded, though VET is not. The VET system lacks a coherent strategy for development.

Furthermore, the provision of support for SMEs which is a central focus of the Lebanese government seeks the creation of high-quality sustainable jobs for the youth. It is in pursuit of these objectives that a number of institutions, both public, private and international, aim to offer financial assistance, incubation, training and technical assistance. It is worth mentioning the role that Kafalat, a public financial company, plays in providing loan guarantees to MSMEs and start-ups, when accessing finance.

Morocco

A 2015–2025 National Employment Strategy under the coordination of the Ministry of Labour and Social Affairs suggested a new vision of the labour policy going beyond the traditional ALMPs. The latter in Morocco focus on private informal employment and aim to achieve better youth employability by providing access to a first professional job experience in the formal market, and also by promoting self-employment. In this regard, actions have focussed too much on unemployed graduates, when other disadvantaged groups should also be considered (e.g. women and labour force in rural areas, among others).

The National Agency for Employment and Skills Promotion is the public agency that provides orientation and intermediation services. It basically offers guidance for jobseekers by linking employment supply and demand. As in other countries of the region, the agency is understaffed, but unlike other countries in the region, private agencies of intermediation are allowed to operate as well. Overall, however, these private agencies contribute very poorly to match demand with supply (ETF 2015a).

In Morocco, VET providers in the public sector have little autonomy due to a traditionally highly centralized administration that still exerts control over public provision through the supporting work of a number of executive agencies, and exercises quite stringent controls over private sector training provision. This centralized control continues to be exercised despite the emphasis in recent years on a strong policy of regionalization. Morocco evaluates its VET system every four years.

Palestine

The Palestinian national employment strategy is based on government priorities regarding economic policy, political prisoners, women, young people and the VET sector. The strategy refers to the need to establish specialized governmental agencies dedicated to employment, including a national employment agency, a general commission for regulating cooperatives, labour offices and a VET agency. However, the Palestinian Fund for Employment and Social Protection is the only agency at present, given that strategy implementation continues to face many obstacles. Employment services offered by providers (the Ministry of Labour and other ministries such as the Ministry of Education and Higher Education, the private sector and trade unions) are mainly in the areas of job creation, vocational training and worker protection. The vision of the Ministry of Labour is to promote a workforce that is aligned with labour market needs.

The Ministry of Labour undertakes several tasks regarding employability and matching labour demand and supply. The Ministry of Labour, however, has no control over the Gaza Strip offices due to the geographic and political divide. The offices in the West Bank offer job placement services in both the domestic and Israeli labour markets.

The Ministry of Labour has been active in using these employment offices to offer a more comprehensive package of services. Hence, eight of the West Bank offices have been transformed into one-stop shops, offering a comprehensive package of career guidance, vocational training-related services, job search and job application support and information and work permits to work in Israel (except in settlements, considered illegal). Furthermore, the Ministry of Labour seeks to enhance the image of employment offices by including not only the unskilled and uneducated but also the highly educated. It has thus signed agreements with ten universities and two community colleges in order to establish career guidance offices there.

Tunisia

Tunisia has a long tradition of ALMPs implemented by the *Agence nationale pour l'emploi etle travail indépendant* (ANETI). Following the revolution in 2011, an Employment Emergency Plan (or 'Roadmap') was developed to support employment along four main axes: job creation, the promotion of entrepreneurship and micro-enterprises, the protection of existing and threatened jobs and employability and activation of unemployed through training. In addition, a National Strategy for Employment 2013–2017 was approved in December 2012 with the objective of progressively alleviating unemployment, which peaked at a maximum rate during the beginning of the transition period after 2011.

Further on, partnerships with local authorities to promote employment have become one of the cornerstones of the public labour policy. This programme aims to facilitate the integration of different categories of jobseekers to the labour market by supporting regional and local initiatives focussing on job creation and new enterprises. It is based on a participatory approach with local civil society stakeholders involved in the design, implementation and follow-up of the programmes. The partnerships with regions for the purpose of improving employment programmes are governed by a contract with annual objectives signed between local authorities, the Ministry of Vocational Training and Employment and the Ministry of Finance (ETF 2013).

The Ministry of Labour and Vocational Training has the overall responsibility for VET supported by four agencies that provide full control and coordination of the whole system. In this context, for nearly 20 years, Tunisia has been attempting to replace traditional, supply-led VET systems with a demand-led approach that is consistently applied in different areas of reform. This applies to the updating of qualifications and programmes and at least some elements of teacher training, and to the engagement of social partners, especially employers' federations. Successful reform on a large scale is difficult to achieve with limited human and financial resources, and the Tunisian case is noteworthy both for its degree of success and for the barriers and frustrations it has encountered.

There are in place some schemes undertaken by the public authorities considered as employment incentives for the youth. One of them is the integration contract for graduates from higher education, which allows the recognition of professional qualifications in a system that provides work at a private enterprise and complementary training. Another scheme is the professional integration and adaptability contract, which targets jobseekers without a higher education degree, or the cheque to support employment, or the programme to encourage employment, which enables jobseekers to obtain additional and practical skills so as to improve their employability.

Overall, Tunisia has allocated an important budget to youth employment facilitation within the framework of a number of ALMPs. In recent years and after the revolution in 2011, the budget allocated to ALMPs has been considerably increased, despite statistics provided by public agencies like ANETI not indicating a sustained improvement in terms of job quality and sustainability, or the match between the needs of the job market with those of the jobseekers (ETF 2015a).

Conclusions and policy recommendations

The Mediterranean region faces severe challenges such as high youth unemployment rates, slow job creation, skills mismatch, informal work and so forth. In recent years, a number of ALMPs have been implemented by public authorities in the region. Regardless of whether the latter have been effective in tackling the shortages of the labour markets in the region, it is obvious that they alone cannot address the systemic challenges of youth unemployment, low rates of productivity and competitiveness, or stagnant labour demand. Indeed, institutional stability, predictability and security are key factors to ensure sustained economic growth, which can then be translated into more inclusive, dynamic, open and flexible labour markets able to generate sustainable and decent jobs for young people.

To conclude the chapter, some policy recommendations may be proposed:

• **Enhance regional cooperation at the Euro-Mediterranean level**. Although this chapter has not assessed the ongoing regional dynamics in the field of labour and employment, with the exception of the last sectoral ministerial conference (read the introductory section of this chapter), there is no doubt that all initiatives undertaken at the level of the Union for the Mediterranean, especially the Med4Jobs programme, should be not only enhanced but also scaled up, multiplied and replicated. The UfM offers an undeniable platform where not only mutual learning and exchange of best practices occur, but also decisions that favour progressive integration of labour markets and progressive harmonization of labour legislation in the region could occur. Furthermore, progressive integration in numerous economic areas would be a stimulus for generating sustainable youth employment in the Southern Mediterranean countries as a recent study has estimated (Ayadi et al. 2017). Indeed, the study concludes that youth unemployment rate in the region could be reduced from 25.7% in 2015 to 17.6% in 2040 by achieving sufficient levels of integration through the elimination of trade barriers and tariffs on imports, as well as through regulatory harmonization, institutional improvement and investment de-risking.

- **Unleash the potential of stagnant labour demand in the region**. Whereas the significant existing constraints on the demand side of the labour markets are not supportive for business development and job creation, the only way ahead is to continue working to upgrade the business environment to support private sector-led development and growth, reduce state intervention that hinders the development of a robust private sector, simplify the administrative procedures for new businesses and nourish an ecosystem supportive of MSME growth by facilitating access to finance, enhancing comprehensive entrepreneurship and self-employment programmes and opening the economies to greater access to foreign markets and to foreign direct investments. In this regard, labour market regulations in the region are identified as key impediments to employment generation, and more generally, a core constraint in business expansion for almost one third of employers in the region (Gatti et al. 2014). The negative effects of a rigid regulatory framework and the resulting risk-averse behaviours of employers are particularly severe for first-time jobseekers (UNDP 2016). Moreover, poor enforcement of labour market regulations favours informality, which is widespread in the region (OECD 2009).

- **Improve the effectiveness of ALMPs and tackle the skills mismatch**. ALMPs should play a significant role in facilitating the (re-)insertion of youth into the labour market. To this end, in the design of policies and programmes dialogue and cooperation between public and private employment services, involving in this dialogue all relevant stakeholders including social partners, education and training providers and youth organizations is essential. Furthermore, core services such as orientation and intermediation, career guidance and counselling, skills development and matching, employment incentives and placement measures should be prioritized with higher budgets and more dedicated competent and better accommodated staff. Overall, ALMPs should target the most vulnerable groups by approaching rural young people and those groups at risk of becoming NEETs (ETF 2015b). Furthermore, they should encompass a gender dimension as a means of responding to the existing discrimination against women in the labour markets in the region. In this respect,

expanding the capacities of regional and local actors to identify skills supply and demand at local level with the aim of improving the matching and
use of skills is a necessity given that ALMPs continue to be excessively centralized in many countries of the region. Further, systems of monitoring
and evaluation, which do not exist or could be improved in many of the
countries analyzed, should be enforced in order to ensure accountability
over results.

Emphasis should also be laid on addressing the skills mismatch. To this end,
there is a need to improve the transition from education to work by providing
appropriate career guidance, target services to youth, and particularly to female
youth. School drop-out rates should decrease as high rates encourage NEETs.
By expanding their stay in the education system, they can obtain suitable levels
of labour market-related training. In addition, the image of VET should be
improved as an effective vehicle from education to work and this would require
in most countries revising curricula, widening collaboration with employers
and creating more solid links between general education and vocational training. In general, training programmes need to better adapted to the labour market's demand at the national but also local levels and need to be flexible enough
to respond to the needs of the most vulnerable groups, be they NEETs, rural
or female youth. Finally, there is a need to upgrade labour market information
systems in the region in order to tackle the skills mismatch more effectively,
amongst others.

There are no holistic solutions to tackling the severe challenge of youth
unemployment in the Southern Mediterranean, as the one-size-fits-all logic
does not take into account the diversity of each country. Most of the countries
concerned have had a chance to implement an agenda of reforms conducive
to structural changes in their labour markets. To date, not enough has been
achieved; although if policy makers decided to examine regional dynamics in
the Euro-Mediterranean area, the whole region, and eventually its citizens,
would certainly gain from such an approach.

Notes

1 The Union for the Mediterranean is an intergovernmental institution that brings together
the EU Member States with all the Southern and Eastern Mediterranean countries. Established in 2008, it is considered to be the continuation of the Barcelona Process launched
in 1995. It comprises all 28 EU Member States, the (non-EU) Northern Mediterranean
riparian countries (Monaco, Bosnia and Herzegovina, Montenegro, Albania and Turkey)
and all the Southern and Eastern Mediterranean countries (Mauritania, Morocco, Algeria,
Tunisia, Egypt, Jordan, Israel, Palestine, Lebanon and Syria). In fact, Syria has had its membership suspended since the year 2011 and Libya has an observer status.
2 By the term 'Southern Mediterranean countries', we encompass all Southern and Eastern
Mediterranean countries, that is, from Morocco in the West to Jordan in the East.
3 According to the ILO, the expression 'informal economy' or 'informal sector' encompasses
a huge diversity of situations and phenomena and manifests in a variety of forms across

and within economies. The formalization process and measures aiming to facilitate transitions to formality need to be tailored to specific circumstances that different countries and categories of economic units or workers face. The informal economy comprises more than half of the global labour force and more than 90% of micro and small enterprises (MSEs) worldwide. Informality is an important characteristic of labour markets in the world, with millions of economic units operating and hundreds of millions of workers pursuing their livelihoods in conditions of informality.

References

Amer, M., 2014. Patterns of Labor Market Insertion in Egypt: 1998–2012. *Economic Research Forum*, Working Paper No. 849. Egypt.

Ayadi, R., Ramos, R., Sessa, C., Paroussos, L., Albinyana, R., et al., 2017. *Youth Employment and Regional Integration in the Euro-Mediterranean Region*. Barcelona: European Institute of the Mediterranean.

Barsoum, G., et al., 2014b. *Interventions to Improve Labour Market Outcomes of Youth: An Inventory of Interventions in Egypt*. Geneva: ILO, National Report for the Youth Employment Inventory (YEI).

Clark, R., Ramsbey, T., and Adler, E., 1991. Culture, Gender and Labor Force Participation: A Cross-National Study. *Gender and Society*, 5 (1), 47–66.

Dhillon, N., Dyer, P., Yousef, T., et al., 2003. *Missed by the Boom, Hurt by the Bust. Making Markets Work for Young People in the Middle East*. Washington, DC and Dubai: Middle East Youth Initiative, Wolfensohn Center for Development at the Brookings Institution, 6–15.

European Commission, 2010. *Labor Markets Performance and Migration Flows in Arab Mediterranean Countries: Determinants and Effects, Vol. 1*. Final Report & Thematic Background Papers, Brussels.

European Training Foundation (ETF), 2013. *Youth Employment Challenges*. Turin: European Training Foundation.

European Training Foundation (ETF), 2014. *Active Labour Market Policies with a Focus on Youth*. Turin: European Training Foundation.

European Training Foundation (ETF), 2015a. *The Challenge of Youth Employability in Arab Mediterranean Countries: The Role of Active Labour Market Programmes*. Turin: European Training Foundation.

European Training Foundation (ETF), 2015b. *NEETs: An Overview in ETF Partner Countries*. Turin: European Training Foundation.

European Training Foundation (ETF), 2015c. *Governance of Vocational Education and Training in the Southern and Eastern Mediterranean*. Turin: European Training Foundation.

Gatti, R., Silva, J., and Bodor, A., 2014. *Striving for Better Jobs: The Challenge of Informality in the Middle East and North Africa*. Washington, DC: World Bank Group.

International Labour Organisation (ILO), 2015. *Global Employment Trends for Youth*. Geneva: International Labour Organisation.

International Labour Organisation (ILO), 2016. *World Employment and Social Outlook: Trends 2016*. Geneva: International Labour Organisation.

Organisation for Economic Cooperation and Development (OECD), 2009. *Is Informal Normal? Towards More and Better Jobs in Developing Countries*. Paris: Organisation for Economic Cooperation and Development.

Organisation for Economic Cooperation and Development (OECD), 2013. *Review of Recent Developments and Progress in Labour Market and Social Policy in Israel: Slow Progress towards a More Inclusive Society*. Paris: Organisation for Economic Cooperation and Development.

Union for the Mediterranean (UfM), 2016a. *Ad Hoc Working Group on Job Creation, Conclusions Document*. Barcelona: Union for the Mediterranean.

Union for the Mediterranean (UfM), 2016b. *Ministerial Conference on Employment and Labour, Declaration*. Jordan: Union for the Mediterranean.

United Nations Development Programme (UNDP), 2016. *Arab Human Development Report 2016, Youth and the Prospects for Human Development in a Changing Reality*. Lebanon: United Nations Development Programme.

United Nations Economic and Social Commission for Western Asia (UN ECSCWA), 2014. *Arab Middle Class: Measurement and Role in Driving Change*. Beirut: United Nations Economic and Social Commission for Western Asia.

World Bank, 2016. *The Welfare of Syrian Refugees. Evidence from Jordan and Lebanon*. Washington, DC: World Bank.

Chapter 7

Labour market regulations and institutions in the Mediterranean

Salvatore Capasso and Yolanda Pena-Boquete

Introduction

A substantial portion of the labour literature seems to agree that institutional rigidities are responsible, at least partially, for the poor performance of labour markets. It is strongly suggested that to achieve more efficiency those countries with 'tight' labour markets should implement deregulation policies (IMF 2003; OECD 2006). And indeed, in recent years, the International Monetary Fund (IMF) has encouraged European Union (EU) countries, especially EU-Mediterranean countries, to implement labour reforms to build a more flexible labour market (IMF 2012). The recent financial and economic crisis has amplified the tone of these policy suggestions.

In practice, although the so-called Great Recession which started in 2008–2009 has turned the deregulation of the labour market into a 'hot topic', this was already a popular subject 20 years ago, when Nickell and Layard (1999) were able to state clearly that 'we are told, Europe has the wrong sort of labour market institutions for the modern global economy'. Not all economists, however, hold this idea and, backed by the empirical literature which shows mixed results on the relationship between labour market institutions and economic performance, several authors have been critical of this view (Baccaro and Rei 2007; Howell et al. 2007). Indeed, empirical studies have delivered neither significant nor clear-cut results on the effects of employment protection legislation (EPL) on countries' economic performance. For instance, while unemployment benefits tend to increase unemployment, they boost the participation rate, with the result that the final effect on employment is uncertain (Nickell and Layard 1999).

Labour market institutions are a complex set of many interrelated variables whose effects are very difficult to disentangle.[1] Each of these variables influences a different feature of the labour market and produces different consequences on economic performance. Moreover, such institutions may interact with each other not only in a systematic way (Bassanini and Duval 2009) but also with the macro-economic shocks (Blanchard and Wolfers 2000). Certainly, some of those variables carry more weight than others, and the literature has focussed on labour taxes, employment protection legislation, unemployment benefits, unions and minimum wage.

It is, however, important to recall that the final aim of labour institutions is to protect workers. Hence a more efficient reallocation of labour resources is only one objective of optimal labour market policies. The other should be to safeguard workers' welfare during downturns. Institutions such as unemployment benefits (UB) and EPL are motivated to protect workers' consumption from income volatility (Arpaia and Mourre 2012). Thus changes in such policies should aim to achieve not only greater market efficiency but also a more adequate income redistribution.

An essential pre-condition to determine the impact on market performance, identify best practices and assess the progress of reforms on welfare, consists in correct measurement of labour market institutions (OECD 2013). This is the purpose of this chapter. In particular, we attempt to measure EPL and unemployment insurance (UI) in the Mediterranean area. The focus is on EPL and UI because there is a paucity of data for all other measures. To obtain internationally comparable data and indicators, we follow the Organisation for Economic Co-operation and Development's (OECD) methodology and build synthetic indicators for EPL and UI. Overall, our analysis shows that labour market institutions vary considerably across Mediterranean countries with EU-Mediterranean countries providing more protection for workers after dismissal. Yet EPL is not homogeneous within the different areas of the Mediterranean Basin, and some EU countries show lower values of EPL than other South-Eastern Mediterranean countries.

Of course, effective workers' protection depends on a number of variables outside the labour market: the distribution of the population in the region, the sectoral composition of the value added and the share of the informal economy are some of such variables. We focus on the informal economy and discuss how the size of the informal sector may influence the effect of labour market institutions on aggregate economic performance. The last section of the chapter offers some final remarks and policy recommendations.

Employment protection legislation

EPL is the set of rules and regulations governing the hiring and firing of workers. Such rules are generally designed to protect workers and their conditions: preserve their welfare, increase job stability and provide some economic support following dismissal (Cazes 2013; OECD 2013). While EPL does not increase labour costs directly, it raises the cost of employment adjustments in two opposite directions: it reduces the separation rate, that is, the fraction of employed workers who lose their job in the period of time, but it also reduces the exit rate out of unemployment, as firms become more cautious about hiring (Nickell and Layard 1999). Hence, while these forces will reduce short-term unemployment, they will also increase long-term unemployment. And yet the effect of more stringent EPL on aggregate unemployment remains unclear.

The empirical literature provides mixed evidence on the effects of EPL on economic growth and, in turn, on unemployment (OECD 1999). There are multiple explanations for this ambiguity. EPL may be desirable and spur growth if one considers that job contracts are incomplete and that firms may have excessive bargaining power once the workers have spent time and money on building job-specific skills (Blanchard and Tirole 2004). If this is the case, firing costs re-establish the balance and EPL stimulates firms' investments in human capital: the result is higher productivity, and consequently a higher gross domestic product growth rate (Fialová and Schneider 2009; Nickel and Layard 1999). Sound job security fosters productivity also because it ameliorates employees' attitudes and facilitates their participation in the firms' decision-making process (Levine and Tyson 1990). Yet EPL might be detrimental for growth given that it limits firms' flexibility along the business cycle (Layard et al. 2005) and restrains workers' reallocation from retrenching stagnant sectors to more dynamic expanding ones (Hopenhayn and Rogerson 1993; Bertola 1994).

Given its composite and complex nature, EPL is difficult to measure. A number of often qualitative context-specific features make it difficult to condense the degree of EPL into a single comparable and reliable indicator. To this end, by focusing on a set of common attributes, the OECD has built a synthetic indicator and provided data since 1985 for all OECD countries. More recently, this database was extended to include some developing countries, especially in Latin America and the Caribbean. Crucially, however, this dataset does not provide data on several South-Eastern Mediterranean countries. Recent studies have been attempting to fill this gap.

Following OECD methodology, Aleksynska and Schindler (2011) built a dataset which includes data on severance payments and period of notice for many developing countries over the period 1980–2005. Since this study reports only two measures of EPL, this dataset does not allow a synthetic indicator to be calculated. The International Labour Organization (ILO) provides data on a vast array of items entering the EPL which the ILO employs to construct a synthetic indicator. Unfortunately, this indicator is not comparable with that of the OECD since it hinges on a different methodology. Moreover, the ILO's dataset does not include data on the Balkan Mediterranean countries. The World Bank collects some information on severance payments but with different references on worker tenure. Hence these data cannot be used to construct an indicator based on OECD methodology.

In this chapter, we attempt to fill this gap by building for Mediterranean countries an EPL indicator of the incidence of regular contracts based on OECD methodology. This indicator does not include the legislation of temporary jobs.[2] or collective dismissal since such data are unavailable for most non-OECD Mediterranean countries. However, the index includes several variables detecting the employers' contractual firing powers such as the minimum advance notice period prior to termination, the causes for a justified dismissal, the compensation to be awarded to workers when they are fired and the duration of trial periods. Table 7.1 details the items included in our EPL indicator as well as the weights we use for aggregation. We follow OECD methodology closely and rank each item between 0 and 6 (for reference, see Chapter 2 of the OECD Employment Outlook 2013, *Protecting jobs, enhancing flexibility: A new look at employment protection legislation*).

To build the indicator, we collected data from the OECD database for most of the countries. For the other non-OECD countries (Algeria, Egypt, Morocco and Jordan), we sourced data from the ILO webpage (www.ilo.org/dyn/eplex/termmain.home). The methodology is that provided by the OECD. Detailed indicators are available upon request.

The synthetic EPL indicator in 2013 for all Mediterranean countries is displayed in Figure 7.1. The most regulated countries are Portugal, Jordan and Egypt, with an EPL equal to or higher than 3. In general, the data show that all South-Eastern Mediterranean countries, with the exception of Algeria, have higher values of the synthetic indicator than the rest of the countries in the Mediterranean. Although this may signal that these countries are more extensively regulated, in reality, other factors may influence the effective level of job regulation in the country: the capacity of law enforcement, the share of population outside the sample, higher rates of self-employed workers that are more or less unregulated (Nickell and Layard 1999) and the share of informal employment (Cazes 2013). We will analyze how these factors may affect the incidence in the economy of labour institutions in the last section of this chapter.

All synthetic indicators have a limitation: they are the result of the influence of different, sometimes opposing, forces which may become indistinguishable in the synthesis. The same applies to the EPL synthetic indicator which can

Table 7.1 Items composing EPL and their corresponding aggregation weights

Level 1	Level 2	Level 3	
Individual dismissals – regular workers	Procedural inconveniences (1/3)	1. Notification procedures (1/2) 2. Delay to start a notice (1/2)	
	Notice and severance pay for no-fault individual dismissals (1/3)	3. Notice period after	9 months (1/7) 4 years (1/7) 20 years (1/7)
		4. Severance pay after	9 months (4/21) 4 years (4/21) 20 years (4/21)
	Difficulty of dismissal (1/3)	5. Definition of unfair dismissal (1/5) 6. Trial period (1/5) 7. Compensation (1/5) 8. Reinstatement (1/5) 9. Maximum time for claim (1/5)	

Source: Elaboration based on OECD methodology

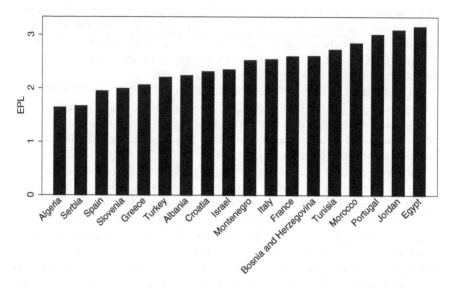

Figure 7.1 EPL indicator for Mediterranean countries following OECD methodology, 2013

hide the trade-off between sub-items pushing the index in opposite direction.
As a result, similar values in the EPL indicator might conceal really different
labour market conditions: for example, high severance payments may be associated with the possibility employers have of firing on personal motivations, or
really restricted grounds for dismissal may accompany low severance payments.
Hence, to obtain more reliable and useful aggregate information on each country's labour policy, it is useful to complement the study of the EPL indicator
with a more detailed analysis of the sub-items. We will focus on the following
sub-items: *Procedural inconvenience, Notice and severance pay for no-fault individual
dismissals* or the *Difficulty of dismissal*. The values are reported in Table 7.2.

Item I Procedural inconvenience

Although in some countries (Albania, Algeria, Jordan and Macedonia), a verbal
statement is enough, most countries require a written statement indicating the
exact reasons for a worker's dismissal. In some instances, the procedure to follow
is very strict: in Egypt, the employer needs to submit a request to the Labour
Court which decides on the worker's layoff within 15 days of the date of the
first session. This makes Egypt rank very high in the list of countries ordered
by procedural inconvenience for dismissal. A further sub-item influencing the
extent of procedural inconvenience is the warning that the employer needs to
give the employee before the notice period. Most countries do not require an
extra warning: the time from the start of the notice period is sufficient, that is,

Table 7.2 EPL indicator and sub-items for Mediterranean countries, 2013

	EPL	Procedural inconvenience	Notice and severance pay	Difficulty of dismissal
Algeria	1.6	1.5	1.4	2
Serbia	1.7	1.8	0.9	2.4
Spain	1.9	1.5	2.1	2.2
Slovenia	2	2.5	1.5	2
Greece	2.1	2.5	1.2	2.5
Turkey	2.2	2	3.4	1.2
Albania	2.2	2.5	2.4	1.8
Croatia	2.3	3	2	2
Israel	2.4	2	2.9	2.2
Montenegro	2.5	2	3.3	2.3
Italy	2.5	2.8	1.3	3.6
France	2.6	2.5	1.9	3.4
Bosnia and Herzegovina	2.6	2	1.6	4.3
Tunisia	2.7	3	2.4	2.8
Morocco	2.8	2.5	2.3	3.8
Portugal	3	3.5	2.4	3.1
Jordan	3.1	3	3.5	2.8
Egypt	3.2	4.5	1.7	3.3

about three days from when the worker is notified by a registered letter. Jordan is the only exception since it requires a one-month warning prior to serving notice of dismissal. This makes Jordan rank second in the list of Mediterranean countries with the greatest procedural inconvenience.

Item 2 Notice and severance pay for no-fault individual dismissals

All Mediterranean countries, with the exception of Italy and Egypt, have rules that ensure a form of compensation, typically a cash payment, to workers who lose their job (severance pay). Indeed, severance payment is considered to be the most "costly" component of EPL (Cazes 2013), and the literature has devoted particular attention to this issue, proposing many policy measures.

The 2009 Great Recession caused a wave of deregulation in most EU- Mediterranean countries which mainly materialized in less stringent regulations on the notice periods and severance pay: Portugal, Greece, Slovenia and Spain have significantly shortened their notice periods, making it depend on service duration, and have reduced the generosity of severance pay (Portugal reformed the system in 2009, 2011, 2012; Greece introduced new rules in 2010, 2012; Slovenia amended its regulations in 2013; Spain in 2012). Because of these reforms, the EU-Mediterranean countries display low values in notice and severance pay for the no-fault dismissals indicator.

By contrast, South-Eastern Mediterranean countries implemented extensive reforms prior to the economic crisis, usually introducing or increasing notice periods and severance pay. Algeria introduced the notice period
in 2006 and increased severance payments for cases in which the worker
committed no act of serious misconduct. Egypt first introduced the notice
period in 2003, making it dependent on the years of tenure and severance pay; it then removed severance payments in 2008. Jordan's labour code
introduced severance pay in 1996. Morocco, instead, increased severance
pay in 2003, after it had been reduced slightly for workers with more than
20 years of tenure.

South-eastern countries rank higher in the list of Mediterranean countries
for the sub-item 'Notice and severance pay for no-fault individual dismissals'
(Table 7.1) for two reasons: first, because these countries have introduced or
increased severance payments following the dismissal of workers with more
than one year of tenure, and second, because the other EU-Mediterranean
countries for their part have relaxed and reduced labour regulations on this
issue.[3] Particularly high values for notice and severance pay are recorded in
Jordan (3.5), Turkey (3.4) and Montenegro (3.3).

Item 3 Difficulty of dismissal

This item encompasses a measure of how restrictive is the definition of unfair
dismissal, the length of the trial period, and compensation, and it takes into
account whether the worker is reinstated. In a few countries (Albania, Greece,
Israel, Montenegro, Serbia, Slovenia and Turkey) a worker's limited ability or
the economic redundancy of the position are acceptable and sufficient grounds
for dismissal. Most of the countries place some extra limitations. For example,
the worker's age or job tenure are elements that may restrain dismissal. In some
countries, the employer is required to offer a possible transfer or a change in
job position prior to firing.

For most countries the trial length is six months or lower; Israel or Tunisia
in some instances, apply trial periods longer than one year. One of the main
changes introduced by the 2012 July reform in Italy consisted in restricting to
the most severe cases of unlawful dismissal the number of cases in which reinstatement can be ordered in court (e.g. discrimination). In Macedonia, Montenegro, Bosnia and Portugal, reinstatement is (almost) always possible.

Analysis of the three sub-items entering EPL reveals that countries with
the strictest regulations giving rise to procedural inconvenience are also likely
to have high values for the difficulty of dismissal, notice period and severance
pay: such examples are Jordan, Portugal, Morocco and Tunisia. The opposite
holds for countries such as Algeria, Serbia and Spain. All other countries apply
in-between models to regulate labour markets: (a) high values for the indicator capturing the difficulties of dismissal and very small values for severance
pay and notice period (Italy, France, Bosnia and Herzegovina or Egypt)[4] and

(2) high values for the indicator of notice period and severance pay and small values in the index of dismissal difficulty (Turkey).

Unemployment benefits

UI systems are designed to help workers maintain their income levels after losing a job and while they are searching for new employment over a given period of time. Thus, unemployment benefit schemes provide good income protection to the formal sector workers and can help reduce poverty (Cazes 2013). Yet UI may encourage moral hazard attitudes and increase work disincentives: to receive unemployment compensation workers may reduce their efforts in searching for a job or may even reject job offers. By reducing the 'fear' of unemployment, UI certainly increases the reservation wage and represents an efficiency cost (see Holmlund 1998; Vodopivec et al. 2005). On these grounds, the prevalent search theory framework (Mortensen and Pissarides 1999; Cazes 2013) suggests that by increasing the 'generosity' of income support (either in terms of the level of the benefits or its duration) as well as extending its coverage, UI increases the unemployment rate and makes unemployment more persistent. The time profile of benefits is generally more important than their initial level in reducing benefit dependency and the risk of long-term unemployment. For this reason, by designing declining unemployment benefits over periods of increasing unemployment spells, the policy maker may efficiently encourage workers to take up a job and deliver a more efficient job search (Nickell 2003; Arpaia and Mourre 2012; Bassanini and Duval 2006). Nickel and Layard (1999) argue that the negative effect of a higher unemployment benefit replacement rate and duration can be offset by active labour market policies.

Nevertheless, in the presence of capital market imperfections, unemployed risk-averse and risk-neutral agents are likely to accept a job although, at the market interest rate, a further search would be likely to reward them with a better job in terms of pay and productivity. In such a context, unemployment benefits act as a subsidy that funds consumption during the search, encourages further exploration and improves the allocation of resources, that is, unemployment benefits increase job match quality by allowing individuals to wait for better job offers (Nickell 2003). Moreover, a generous unemployment benefit system can play an important role in cushioning the social disruption caused by an economic recession (Cazes 2013), and it could act as a positive incentive to participate in the labour market (Nickell and Layard 1999). The higher participation due to a higher replacement rate may compensate the negative effect on the system in terms of unemployment (Nickell and Layard 1999).

In reality, it is difficult to assess whether, and to what extent, the unemployment system is generous. Some indicators such as the *UI replacement ratio* (the amount of the unemployment benefits relative to the monthly wage, i.e. proportion of net income in work that is maintained after job loss) or the *benefit duration index* (the length of time for which the benefit is available) may help in this direction but are not sufficient. The difficulties judging the unemployment system are even harder when one analyzes countries such as the South-Eastern Mediterranean for which there are no data.

The OECD has provided data on the replacement rates for all OECD countries since 1980 but it does not supply any data for the South-Eastern Mediterranean. As well as raw data, the OECD builds and publishes for those countries a gross replacement rates (GRRs) index which expresses the gross unemployment benefit levels as a percentage of previous gross earnings and a net replacement rates (NRRs) index giving the proportion of net income that is maintained after job loss. Since GRRs is built on gross values, this indicator includes taxes and social benefits. Net replacement rates are considered a more complete measure especially when compared over longer periods of unemployment. The OECD calculates GRRs and NRRs for OECD countries by aggregating two earnings levels, three family situations and three durations of unemployment.[5] Aleksynska and Schindler (2011) construct a database that contain GRRs for the period 1980–2005 for developing countries following the OECD methodology. However, they do not provide data for more recent years when some of the countries implemented unemployment insurance, such as Jordan in 2011 or Morocco in 2014.

To fill the gap, we provide an approximation of the GRRs for all Mediterranean countries. Unfortunately, we have no data on the flow of UI received by workers in the Southern Mediterranean countries for the different types of families and hence we cannot apply the OECD's methodology. For this reason, we calculate GRRs for Mediterranean countries following the *de jure* or legislative basis, that is, GRRs are calculated considering the unemployment insurance for each worker (a similar procedure can be found in the IMF paper).[6] The calculation is straightforward if the UI is expressed as a percentage of previous earnings. However, in a number of countries, UI payments are set as a percentage of a minimum wage, a subsistence minimum, or as a flat rate payment. In these cases, we calculate GRRs on a *de facto* basis, as the ratio of these payments to previous earnings, proxied by the compensation wage per employee.[7] As already stressed, we have no data to distinguish the types of families. Yet we are able to account for two durations of unemployment benefits, those who receive UI only for one or two years.

Since access to unemployment benefits depends, in general, on the length of job tenure, we calculate the GRRs for worker with nine months, four years and 20 years of work tenure (we choose the same periods as EPL in the OECD) during one or two years of unemployment. This will allow us to obtain a better picture of the insurance systems in Mediterranean countries. The synthetic indicator is calculated as the average of the six GRRs types. Data are displayed in Figure 7.2. Given that our focus is on UI, that is, the contributory scheme, we do not take other families' social benefits into account. Detailed data are available upon request.

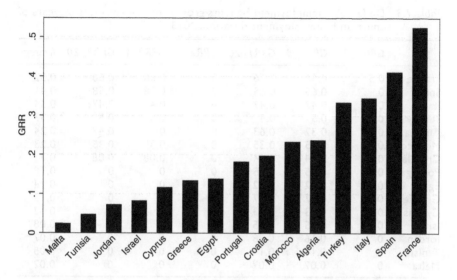

Figure 7.2 "De facto" unemployment benefits gross replacement rates for the Mediterranean countries

The data show that the "de facto" unemployment benefits replacement rates are really low for non–OECD countries (see Figure 7.2). The low coverage of unemployment insurance in southern Mediterranean countries can be mainly explained by the eligibility rules, that is, the minimum number of years that workers have to contribute. In this context, Turkey presents one of the strictest systems: workers have to contribute a minimum of 20 months over the previous three years to access benefits. If this is not the case, unemployed workers remain unprotected and have no choice but to get involved in the informal economy in order to sustain their livelihoods. This is one of the reasons why the impact of UI on work incentives is expected to be weaker in southern Mediterranean countries, although few studies have analyzed the effect of UI on labour market in developing countries (Cazes 2013).

Table 7.3 shows the "de facto" unemployment benefits replacement rates by years of tenure and the duration of unemployment benefits. Only France, Spain, Italy, Turkey, Morocco, Croatia and Algeria (for those workers with more than 20 years of experience) consider some kind of unemployment benefit in the second year.

Few countries (France, Italy, Croatia, Egypt, Greece and Cyprus) provide any kind of unemployment benefit to workers with nine months of tenure (less than one year of tenure). While South and East Mediterranean countries show the highest values in EPL for unemployment benefits, they present really small values.

Table 7.3 "De facto" unemployment benefits gross replacement rates by years of tenure and unemployment duration, 2013

	GRR1_9*	GRR1_4	GRR1_20	GRR2_9	GRR2_4	GRR2_20	Average
France	0.5	0.66	0.66	0	0.66	0.66	0.52
Spain	0	0.65	0.65	0	0.58	0.58	0.41
Italy	0.19	0.47	0.47	0	0.47	0.47	0.34
Turkey	0	0.5	0.5	0	0.5	0.5	0.33
Algeria	0	0.32	0.63	0	0	0.47	0.24
Morocco	0	0.35	0.35	0	0.35	0.35	0.23
Croatia	0.15	0.44	0.44	0	0.08	0.08	0.2
Portugal	0	0.55	0.55	0	0	0	0.18
Egypt	0.18	0.32	0.32	0	0	0	0.14
Greece	0.27	0.27	0.27	0	0	0	0.13
Cyprus	0.23	0.23	0.23	0	0	0	0.12
Israel	0	0.25	0.25	0	0	0	0.08
Jordan	0	0.16	0.28	0	0	0	0.07
Tunisia	0	0.14	0.14	0	0	0	0.05
Malta	0	0.07	0.07	0	0	0	0.02

*Note: GRR1_9: Gross replacement rate for the first year of unemployment for workers with nine months of tenure.

Labour market characteristics affecting labour institution effectiveness: the informal economy[8]

Although high values of EPL may signal the prevalence of rigid labour legislation throughout the Mediterranean Basin, particularly in the south-eastern countries, low levels of enforcement often render this legislation ineffective. Moreover, most workers in developing countries are employed in the informal economy and are therefore beyond the boundaries of regulation, meaning that employers are not directly affected by the impact of rigidities arising from labour laws. Additionally, since informal workers do not pay taxes or contribute to social security, their employment conditions are difficult to verify (Bosch and Esteban-Pretel 2015). As a result, a large proportion of workers are likely not to be covered by UB. This is particularly worrisome given that informal workers seem to be more susceptible to losing their jobs.

In this sense, the share of informal employment is an important variable playing a major role in determining the impact of labour market institutions on economic performance. This is particularly relevant to developing countries in which the share of the informal economy is larger.

Table 7.4 provides a synopsis of the prevalence of informal employment in the Mediterranean area. In all South-Eastern Mediterranean countries, the share of informal employment on total employment is over 50%. EU-Mediterranean countries have, instead, shares below 20% with the exception of Spain (27.3%) and Greece (32.8%). Note that the share of the informal economy in some EU-Mediterranean countries is also high in comparison to that in other developed economies (Schneider et al. 2010).

Table 7.4 Share of informal employment, 2013, 2015

	Share of informal employment in total employment (%)	Share of non-agricultural informal employment in non-agriculture (%)	Share of self-employed workers (%)
Morocco	79.9	75.6	
Palestine	64.3	60.1	31.9
Egypt	63.3	49.8	38.8
Albania	61	33.1	59.6
Tunisia	58.8	53.5	27.9
Algeria	53.6*		
Jordan	44.9	43	
Turkey	34.8	21.9	35.9
Greece	32.8	25.5	37
Bosnia and Herzegovina	30.1	13.2	
Spain	27.3	26.8	17.9
Italy	19	18.3	24.8
Cyprus	15.1	14.1	17.5
Croatia	13	10.8	18.1
Portugal	12.1	10.5	21.9
France	9.8	8.9	11.3
Malta	8.1	7.7	13.6
Slovenia	5	4.1	16.9

Source: Data from International Labour Organization (ILO)

Note: *Estimates for Algeria correspond to the year 2006 (Schneider 2010).

In most countries, the size of the informal sector depends on the size of the agricultural sector. Indeed, in Egypt, Albania or Bosnia and Herzegovina, the size of the informal sector is much lower if the agricultural sector is not taken into account (see Column 2 of Table 7.4). Fortuny and Husseini (2011) argue that the agricultural sector is the most difficult to analyze when studying the structure of the labour market, and it will certainly remain the last obstacle to the extension of social security. And yet, it is also true that the agriculture sector does not affect the relative size of the informal economy in those countries with the highest levels of informality, such as Morocco or Palestine. Thus the size of the agricultural sector only partly explains the level of informal employment.

Many of those operating in the informal economy are, in fact, self-employed workers, which means that for them there is no employer–employee relationship to govern, and hence they are not affected by EPL. This is particularly true in developing countries. In many instances, the self-employed are not covered by social protection, either. Fortuny and Husseini (2011) argue that even if such workers benefit from social protection, in the South-Eastern Mediterranean countries, the majority in this category are informally employed as own-account workers and 'contributing' to unpaid family workers. In fact, Nickell and Layard (1999) point out that also Southern European countries have the highest rates of self-employment among OECD countries.

Although EPL and UB cover formal sector workers only, they may also exert some effect in the informal sector due to worker mobility between formal and informal jobs (Albrecht et al. 2009). Indeed, labour market policy interventions may impact the allocation of workers across regulated (formal) and unregulated jobs (informal) as well as influencing the transition from employment to unemployment (Bosch and Esteban-Pretel 2012).

Policies that increase the cost of formal employment such as severance payment produce a reduction in the share of formal employment (Bosch and Esteban-Pretel 2012). However, such policies also increase the average employment duration in the formal sector (Albrecht et al. 2009). Bosch and Esteban-Pretel (2012) show that an increase in formal regulations tends to increase unemployment since the reallocation between formal and informal jobs has non-neutral effects for unemployment due to the shifts of workers from a low to a high job separation sector. Overall, an increase in EPL increases unemployment and reduces the share of formality. Meghir et al. (2015) show that in a market with search frictions, the informal sector reduces competition for employees and makes it harder for workers to locate to higher productivity firms by congesting the matching process. Thus, increasing the costs of informality improves the allocation of workers to better firms, it increases wages and overall welfare. In this context, policies reducing informality do not increase unemployment.

The lesson is that, more than in other contexts, labour market policies benefit from a very high degree of complementarity. For example, Bosch and Esteban-Pretel (2015) show that by combining the unemployment benefit programme with policies that reduce the cost of formality, such as lower employment taxes and firing costs, one can obtain a greater reduction in informality and a lower impact on unemployment. Albrecht et al. (2009) argue that increasing the payroll tax undoes some of the worst effects of severance taxation. In particular, payroll taxation partially reverses the incentive that severance taxation produces on unproductive matches. Bosch and Esteban-Pretel (2015) found that the UB programme associated to lower firing costs and lower employment taxes has increased the level of formality in Mexico.

Concluding remarks

This chapter discussed the implementation of labour institutions in Mediterranean countries, focussing on Employment Protection Legislation (EPL) and on Unemployment Insurance (UI). By filling a gap in the empirical literature, we supply a measure of these two institutions for the Mediterranean area. In general, South-Eastern Mediterranean countries, similarly to other developing countries,[9] show higher levels of EPL and lower levels of UI although, following the great recession of 2009, most EU-Mediterranean countries have made their labour markets less regulated and controlled.

The data show that countries with stricter regulation tend to display high values in all EPL sub-items. This is the case of Jordan, Portugal, Morocco and Tunisia. The opposite occurs, instead, for Algeria, Serbia and Spain. For intermediate levels of EPL, two different models prevail depending on the relative prevalence of the difficulty of dismissal over severance payments: Italy, France, Bosnia and Herzegovina and Egypt show high values in the indicator capturing the difficulties of dismissal and very small values in the severance pay and notice period. Indeed, Italy and Egypt do not contemplate severance pay at all. Turkey, instead, displays high values for its notice period and severance pay and small values in the difficulty of dismissal.

UI and severance payments are not to be considered alternative forms of income support: each instrument has its own features and limits (Cazes and Verick 2013). UI is worker oriented and provides periodic benefits for a prescribed duration, whereas severance payment schemes are rather job oriented and provide a lump sum payment based on employers' liability. Since severance pay lies in the power of the employer-firm, in practice, it may not be delivered to workers.

Lack of enforcement in some Mediterranean countries, even in the formal sector, ensures little worker protection in practice. Cazes (2013) argues that workers' protection may not be appropriate for most developing countries since it merely covers the small formal sector. Indeed, factors such as the share of the informal economy and self-employment certainly shape the efficiency of formal institutions and determine migration.[10]

The main lesson to be drawn is two-fold: first, there cannot be a universal institutional design that fits all countries and second, institutional implantation often fails. The results and data provided in this chapter may pave the way for future analysis of the effect of labour institutions on economic performance.

Notes

1 Labour market institutions comprise a system of laws, norms or conventions that provides constraints and incentives to individual choices in the labour market.

2 Temporary contracts can be terminated at no cost provided that the duration of the contract has expired. To prevent firms from exclusively hiring workers under temporary contracts, in most countries the use of these contracts is severely restricted. Nickel and Layard (1999) point out that the effect of EPL in unemployment can be lower since firms can reduce employment by 10% per year or more, simply by relying on workers leaving. They do not find evidence that rates of job destruction and job creation are lower in European countries with lower levels of EPL. Thus, to take into account the effects of EPL, it is important to take account of other variables such as the share of temporary jobs in the market and the size of the informal economy that may reduce its effects.

3 Most of the South-Eastern Mediterranean countries do not establish severance payments when the worker has less than one year of tenure.

4 Note that Italy and Egypt have no severance pay at all. That said, Egypt has the higher EPL index. Egypt also shows quite high procedural inconveniences.

5 For further details, see OECD (1994), The OECD Jobs Study (Chapter 8) and Martin (1996), "Measures of Replacement Rates for the Purpose of International Comparisons: A Note", OECD Economic Studies, No. 26.

6 Because of lack of data, it is not possible to calculate the NRRs. We do not include social assistance benefits in the GRRs. For the South-Eastern Mediterranean countries, there are no data either on the average wage of each type of family or on unemployment benefits. Unemployment assistance is not generally considered part of UI, and for this reason we do not include this information in GRR calculations.

7 Since comparable monthly wages are not available for all countries, we base our calculation on the national accounts data drawn from the United Nations database.

8 This section draws on J. Charmes's paper on the Informal Economy and Labour Market Policies and Institutions in selected Mediterranean Countries, 2010.

9 Cazes (2013) points out that developing countries tend to have poor UI, the mandated severance of payments being the only available protection in the case of job loss for workers.

10 Migrations may play an important role but have not been included in the models on institution labour market performance (Lehmann and Muravyev 2012).

References

Albrecht, J., Navarro, L., and Vroman, S., 2009. The Effects of Labour Market Policies in an Economy with an Informal Sector. *The Economic Journal*, 119 (539), 1105–1129.

Aleksynska, M., and Schindler, M., 2011. *Labor Market Regulations in Low - Middle-and High-Income Countries: A New Panel Database*, Working Paper No. WP/11/154. Washington, DC: International Monetary Fund (IMF).

Arpaia, A., and Mourre, G., 2012. Institutions and Performance in European Labour Markets: Taking a Fresh Look at Evidence. *Journal of Economic Surveys*, 26 (1), 1–41.

Baccaro, L., and Rei, D., 2007. Institutional Determinants of Unemployment in OECD Countries: Does the Deregulatory View Hold Water? *International Organization*, 61 (3), 527–569.

Bassanini, A., and Duval, R., 2006. *Employment Patterns in OECD Countries: Reassessing the Role of Policies and Institutions, OECD Economics Department*, Working Papers, No. 486. Paris: OECD Publishing.

Bassanini, A., and Duval, R., 2009. Unemployment, Institutions, and Reform Complementarities: Re-Assessing the Aggregate Evidence for OECD Countries. *Oxford Review of Economic Policy*, 25 (1), 40–59.

Bertola, G., 1994. Flexibility, Investment and Growth. *Journal of Monetary Economics*, 34, 215–238.

Blanchard, O., and Tirole, J., 2004. Redesigning the Employment Protection System. *De Economist*, 152 (1), 1–20.

Blanchard, O., and Wolfers, J., 2000. The Role of Shocks and Institutions in the Rise of European Unemployment: The Aggregate Evidence. *The Economic Journal*, 110 (462), 1–33.

Bosch, M., and Esteban-Pretel, J., 2012. Job Creation and Job Destruction in the Presence of Informal Markets. *Journal of Development Economics*, 98 (2), 270–286.

Bosch, M., and Esteban-Pretel, J., 2015. The Labor Market Effects of Introducing Unemployment Benefits in an Economy with High Informality. *European Economic Review*, 75, 1–17.

Cazes, S., 2013. Labour Market Institutions. *In*: S. Cazes and S. Verick, eds. *Perspectives on Labour Economics for Development*. Geneva: International Labour Organization.

Cazes, S., and Verick, S., 2013. *The Labour Markets of Emerging Economies: Has Growth Translated into More and Better Jobs?* London: Palgrave Macmillan.

Charmes, J., 2010. *Informal Economy and Labour Market Policies and Institutions in Selected Mediterranean Countries: Turkey, Syria, Jordan, Algeria and Morocco.* Geneva: International Labour Organization (ILO) Report.

Fialová, K., and Schneider, O., 2009. Labor Market Institutions and Their Effect on Labor Market Performance in the New EU Member Countries. *Eastern European Economics*, 47 (3), 57–83.

Fortuny, M., and Al Husseini, J., 2011. *Labour Market Policies and Institutions: A Synthesis Report: The Cases of Algeria, Jordan, Morocco, Syria and Turkey* (No. 994583273402676). Geneva: International Labour Organization.

Holmlund, B., 1998. Unemployment Insurance in Theory and Practice. *Scandinavian Journal of Economics*, 100 (1), 113–141.

Hopenhayn, H., and Rogerson, R., 1993. Job Turnover and Policy Evaluation: A General Equilibrium Analysis. *Journal of Political Economy*, 101 (5), 915–938.

Howell, D.R., Baker, D., Glyn, A., and Schmitt, J., 2007. Are Protective Labor Market Institutions at the Root of Unemployment? A Critical Review of the Evidence. *Capitalism and Society*, 2 (1).

International Monetary Fund (IMF), 2003. *Unemployment and Labor Market Institutions: Why Reforms Pay Off, IN: World Economic Outlook 2003.* Washington, DC: International Monetary Fund.

International Monetary Fund (IMF), 2012. *Fiscal Policy and Employment in Advanced and Emerging Economies.* Washington, DC: International Monetary Fund, Fiscal Affairs Department.

Layard, R., Nickell, S.J., and Jackman, R., 2005. *Unemployment: Macroeconomic Performance and the Labour Market.* Oxford: Oxford University Press.

Lehmann, H., and Muravyev, A., 2012. Labour Market Institutions and Labour Market Performance. *Economics of Transition*, 20 (2), 235–269.

Levine, D.I., and D'Andrea Tyson, L., 1990. Participation, Productivity, and the Firm's Environment. *In*: A.S. Blinder, ed. *Paying for Productivity.* Washington, DC: The Brookings Institution, 183–237.

Martin, J.P., 1996. Measures of Replacement Rates for the Purpose of International Comparisons: A Note. *OECD Economic Studies*, 26 (1), 99–115.

Meghir, C., Narita, R., and Robin, J.M., 2015. Wages and Informality in Developing Countries. *American Economic Review*, 105 (4), 1509–1546.

Mortensen, D.T., and Pissarides, C.A., 1999. New Developments in Models of Search in the Labor Market. *Handbook of Labor Economics*, 3, 2567–2627.

Nickell, S., 2003. Labour Market Institutions and Unemployment in OECD Countries. *CESifo DICE Report*, 1 (2), 13–26.

Nickell, S., and Layard, R., 1999. Labor Market Institutions and Economic Performance. *Handbook of Labor Economics*, 3, 3029–3084.

Organisation for Economic Co-operation and Development (OECD), 1994. *The Jobs Study: Evidence and Explanations.* Paris and France: OECD.

Organisation for Economic Co-operation and Development (OECD), 1999. *OECD Employment Outlook 1999.* Paris and France: OECD.

Organisation for Economic Co-operation and Development (OECD), 2006. *OECD Employment Outlook 2006: Boosting Jobs and Incomes.* Paris and France: OECD.

Organisation for Economic Co-operation and Development (OECD), 2013. Protecting Jobs, Enhancing Flexibility: A New Look at Employment Protection Legislation. In: *OECD Employment Outlook 2013*. Paris and France: OECD.

Schneider, F., Buehn, A., and Montenegro, C.E., 2010. New Estimates for the Shadow Economies all Over the World. *International Economic Journal*, 24 (4), 443–461.

Vodopivec, M., Worgotter, A., and Raju, D., 2005. Unemployment Benefit Systems in Central and Eastern Europe: A Review of the 1990s. *Comparative Economic Studies*, 47 (4), 615–651.

Chapter 8

Climate change and environmentally induced migration

Eugenia Ferragina and Desirée A. L. Quagliarotti

Introduction

Among the Mediterranean countries, there are profound differences in population growth rates, socio-economic conditions and natural resources availability, all factors able to undermine the process of Euro-Mediterranean cohesion and create a situation of structural weakness that makes them extremely vulnerable to destabilizing events.

In recent years, the Mediterranean region has been affected by major changes that, at first glance, do not seem to be related to each other. The revolutionary storm called the *Arab Spring* that has plagued the regimes of the Middle East and North Africa (MENA) since 2010, has ushered in a period of political instability. The popular uprisings have had strong repercussions on the economies of the Arab countries, and the responses elaborated by the new governments to stem the deterioration of the socio-economic situation have proved to be ineffective because of their substantial similarity with the misguided policies of the past.

The uncertainty that accompanied the transition phase and the persistence of the state of insecurity and instability have hindered economic revival, creating the conditions for the spread of Islamic terrorism.

At the same time, a deep economic and financial crisis has hit the Northern Mediterranean Countries (NMCs) like Greece and Portugal and, to a lesser extent, Spain and Italy. The Eurozone debt crisis has not only called into question the viability of the Euro itself, but also highlighted several weaknesses in the process of European unification. The measures imposed by the International Monetary Fund, the European Union and the European Central Bank have been able to avert the risk of default. However, the actions taken to curb public spending and increase the tax burden have contributed to fuel the economic downturn and the unemployment rate, amplifying the macro-economic imbalances between the so-called core countries, such as Germany and the North European countries and the peripheral countries such as Italy, Spain, Portugal and Greece.

The economic and social precariousness of the European countries has been exacerbated by increased migration flows coming from the MENA area.

These new migratory flows are encouraged not only by traditional push factors aimed at improving migrants' economic conditions, but also by political reasons and by factors associated to the effects of climate and environmental changes, contributing to increase the incidence of environmental migrants. In the south-eastern shore of the Mediterranean, affected by the lack of two key resources for human development, namely water and arable land, and by a strong anthropogenic pressure on natural systems, climate change assumes the role of explanatory variable in increasing social discontent, internal instability, and migratory flows, all factors that are likely to have an impact on the whole Euro-Mediterranean area.

This study aims to shed light on the complex relationships between climate change, environmental degradation and migration flows in the Mediterranean countries, and to provide insight into current research as well as political initiatives. It also intends to counter some widespread misperceptions. In particular, the chapter explores possible futures of Mediterranean migration in the coming decades, especially in respect of environmental factors. Based on an evaluation of past and current drivers of migration in the region, it will provide an assessment of how changes in drivers and their interaction may lead to different migration outcomes.

Climate change, migration and displacement

The date 29 August 2016 is fundamental for the geological history of the Earth. During the International Congress of Geology (Cape Town), the Anthropocene Working Group of the International Stratigraphy Commission, formally recognized that we are in a new geological era: the *Anthropocene*. The term 'Anthropocene' was coined and popularized by the atmospheric chemist Paul J. Crutzen and limnologist Eugene F. Stoermer in 2000, in order to identify a new geological era characterized by such strong human pressure on natural systems as to be compared to the geological forces that have shaped and transformed the Earth during its long history (Crutzen and Stoermer 2000). Geologists agree that human stress on natural systems began with the Industrial Revolution when, thanks to scientific and technological progress, humanity began to use fossil fuels and exploit natural resources unsustainably, and increased sharply from the middle of the last century, during the so-called Great Acceleration, when population growth and economic development started to change all natural systems, pushing the Earth's system into a new stage of disequilibrium with significant effects on global human and non-human mobility (Rockström et al. 2009).

Currently, the human impact on the environment is creating an emerging class of environmental migrants (Naser 2012). The Intergovernmental Panel on Climate Change has already indicated that one of the greatest effects of climate change may be on human migration (IPCC 2007). The United Nations High Commissioner for Refugees predicts that between 50 and 200 million people may be displaced by 2050 'either within their countries or across borders' (Guterres 2009). Despite these alarming predictions, the issue of environment-related migration has rarely received the necessary attention from policy makers. According to Frank Lazko and Christine Aghazarm (2010), the issue has been overlooked partly due to the lack of consensus among migration researchers and experts on the nexus between climate change, environmental degradation and migration. Many reject climate change as the primary cause of forced displacement, whereas others even refute the existence of 'environmental migration' because of the potential multi-causality associated with the choice to emigrate, which in most cases depends on a combination of complex socio-economic factors. Indeed, as there is no universal definition to identify this category of human displacement, estimates of the numbers of environmental migrants are discordant and debatable. According to the International Organizations for Migration (IOM), environmental migrants are

> persons or groups of persons who, predominantly for reasons of sudden or progressive changes in the environment that adversely affect their lives or living conditions, are obliged to leave their habitual homes, or choose to do so, either temporally or permanently, and who move either within their country or abroad.
>
> (Ionesco et al. 2017)

This working definition for environmental migrants describes a wide variety of types of environmental migration categorized according to different inter-related factors: the nature of environmental change, sudden natural disasters or progressive changes in the environment; the form of mobility, forced or voluntary; the relative permanence of the move, temporary or permanent; the nature of the boundaries crossed, internal or international. Essam El-Hinnawi of the UNEP, the first scholar who focussed on the issue, identified three broad categories of environmental displacement, namely (a) people temporarily displaced due to natural hazards, whether natural or anthropogenic, who return to their homeland when the environmental event ends and the living conditions are restored (migration primarily caused by natural disasters); (b) people permanently displaced due to drastic and marked environmental disruptions, such as the construction of dams (primarily as a result of development projects); and (c) people displaced, temporarily or permanently, due to progressive or gradual deterioration of environmental conditions, who left their home in search of a better quality of life (El-Hinnawi 1985).

Current predictions of climate change indicate that even more people are expected to be on the move since global warming will both increase the frequency and intensity of sudden-onset disasters such as storms and floods, and worsen the impact of slow-onset disasters, such as environmental degradation, droughts and desertification. Some phenomena linked to rising temperature, such as sea-level rise and melting glaciers, will combine both slow- and sudden-onset effects.

Sudden natural disasters cause the majority of human displacements worldwide. According to the Internal Displacement Monitoring Centre (IDMC), every year since 2008, climate and weather-related disasters have displaced on average 22.5 million people, representing more than 80% of the total displacement by disasters, equivalent to 62,000 people every day.[1] In 2016, new climate records were responsible for 23.5 million displacements, above the annual average since 2008, or 97% of all disaster-related displacements. Flood disasters tend to make up the majority of climate and weather-related displacements each year. In 2016, however, storms caused 12.9 million displacements worldwide – 55% of all weather-related disasters, by triggering mass displacement of populations living in exposed and vulnerable coastal areas. Gradual change in the environment also contributes to large-scale migration flows. However, while sudden natural disasters cause many people to flee at the same time, making it easier to monitor their numbers, slow-onset natural disasters rarely cause sudden mass displacement groups, making it more difficult to identify them as environmental migrants. Because the link between gradual environmental change and migration is mostly indirect, such migrants are often deemed to be economically driven. This difficulty has prompted the IDMC to call these migration flows a 'blind spot' in our current understanding of disaster displacement (IDMC 2017).

Although many experts agree that climate and environmental changes can play a decisive role in choosing to emigrate, there is disagreement about the specific ways in which environmental stress will impact migration and how significant it can be considered as determining factors in the decision to move (Black 2001). Given the multi-causal nature of migration, often triggered by a combination of push and pull socio-economic and political factors, it is difficult to extrapolate a direct causal link and isolate any one driver as necessary or sufficient. A conceptual model helpful to understand the role of the environment as a migration driver was developed for the 2011 UK Foresight Report (Figure 8.1). This model, highlighting the different interactions with other economic, social, political and demographic variables, explains how and with what effects environmental and climate changes can drive migration.

Empirical research corroborates the hypothesis that migrations related to both sudden and slow-onset events are likely to be predominantly internal, with movements being rural-rural and rural-urban. Even when international migration occurs, it develops especially over small distances, towards the nearest borders (Lazko and Aghazarm 2010). In some situations, such as sudden natural disasters, people may have little choice but to move. In other situations, where environmental change is gradual, movement is more likely to be voluntary and linked to other push factors. Moreover, it may also happen that people affected by environmental stress do not migrate either by choice or by the lack of resources needed to move. In many cases, it is precisely the severity of the environmental impact that further erodes the financial, social and even physical assets required for moving away, leading to what has been called 'trapped populations' (Geddes 2015).

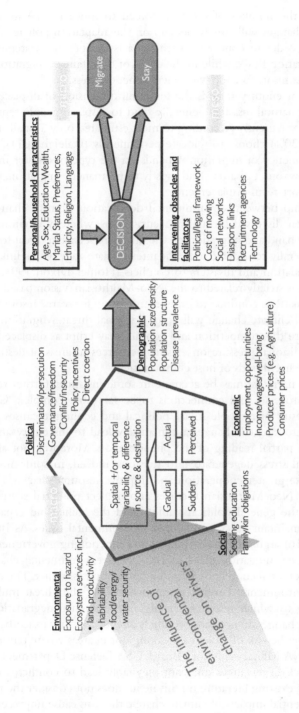

Figure 8.1 The complex drivers of migration

Source: Foresight 2011

Furthermore, the number of migrants forced to move by the impacts of environmental changes will largely depend on the adaptation policies that are implemented in order to cope with such impacts. Adaptation strategies limit the scale of migration flows, while in the event of their failure, migration takes on the role of last resort to cope with environmental stress.

Another area of enquiry regards the temporal dimension of displacements. It is argued that natural disasters generally tend to displace people temporarily rather than permanently. According to most estimates, only a small share of migrants (up to 30%) choose to relocate permanently (Raleigh 2011). In any event, the permanency of migration depends on the type of disaster in question: whereas slow-onset disasters lead mostly to permanent migration, sudden events lead to short-term displacement.

The relationship between environmental degradation, climate change and migration is often discussed through a security lens, whereby environmental stress on the one hand and migration on the other are seen as a threat to peace. Migration is generally considered to be the intermediate stage which links environmental degradation and disasters to conflicts (Homer-Dixon 1991, 1994). This assumption is strictly related to the 'Neo-Malthusian' vision based on the idea that as populations continue to grow, competition for scarce resources will also increase, and climate change will pose additional threat. Migration might further exacerbate this competition and conflict may erupt as displaced communities put additional pressure on existing resources in areas of destination, deteriorating the livelihoods of host communities.

Although this narrative may be accurate in some instances, further research has found the processes and connections to be far more complex. Conflict is actually the result of multiple social, political and economic causes and to assume that environmental changes automatically lead to insecurity and violence provides a partial reading of the phenomenon. Moreover, not all cases of environmental stress degenerate into tensions; indeed, in some instances, they can promote greater cooperation and improve resource-sharing (McLeman 2016). The Neo-Malthusian theories also neglect potential stabilization factors, such as the general political stability and the ability and capacity of government to maintain peace and address environmental issues. As Burrows and Kinney (2016) argue, a well-developed and functioning government may have adaptation or mitigation plans to cope with environmental challenges and may avoid potential conflict by providing livelihood assistance. The current paradigm in environmental conflict research is one of the 'threat multiplier' effect, according to which resource scarcity, environmental degradation and sudden climatic changes do not cause conflicts directly, but may exacerbate tensions and increase the risk of violence breaking out in areas where tensions are already high (CNA Military Advisory Board, USA Defense Department 2007). Although the lack of resources does not inevitably lead to conflict, we must consider that the existing literature on this nexus does not consider the projections for the potential impacts of climate change that can cause unprecedented levels of land degradation and resource scarcity. Assuming future migration patterns continue to follow current trends, it should be expected that migration flows triggered by climate change and other environmental events will grow as people adjust and adapt to changing conditions. In such a scenario, climate change could turn from a threat multiplier able to amplify pre-existing conflicts into a catalyst for conflicts or an active force in provoking conflicts (CNA Military Advisory Board, USA Defense Department 2014).

The following section will introduce the pre-existing and cumulative vulnerabilities that the Mediterranean region is facing with regard to climate and environmental changes before exploring the linkages between these changes and migration. The chapter will then address the most recurrent patterns of mobility as well as its impacts. Last, the chapter will introduce the key policy advances and gaps and suggest ways forward.

Due to the complexity and spatial heterogeneity of the climate–migration–conflict nexus, and to ensure greater understanding, it is necessary to examine vulnerability to the impacts of climate change that could cause displacements and/or conflicts and also analyze the response capacity of all the Mediterranean countries affected by migrations (origin, transit, destination). We begin by analyzing the current environmental status of the Mediterranean region with specific emphasis on differences both within and between countries. This analysis sets the contexts for environmental and climate changes and for the potential biophysical drivers for migration.

Environmental and climate changes in the Mediterranean region: vulnerabilities and impacts

The environmental issues in the Mediterranean countries are the result of a complex system of causes and effects within which human pressure plays a decisive role in increasing the vulnerability to the impacts of global warming. The extent of climate change effects on individual Mediterranean countries will vary over time and with the ability of different societal and environmental systems to mitigate or adapt to change. The first step to understand whether and how environmental stress will impact future migration patterns in the Mediterranean region is, therefore, to try to quantify the current to future vulnerability under climate change for different countries and then attempt to uncover the link between climate and environmental vulnerability and migration.

A noteworthy contribution in this direction is represented by the *Notre Dame-Global Adaptation Index* (ND-GAIN), a composite index that brings together over 74 variables to form 45 core indicators to measure vulnerability and readiness to climate change and other global challenges of 192 UN countries from 1995 to present. ND-GAIN assesses the vulnerability of a country by considering six life-supporting sectors, namely food, water, health, ecosystem services, human habitat and infrastructure, capturing three dimensions of vulnerability: exposure, sensitivity and adaptive capacity,[2] while it assesses readiness by considering a country's social, governance and economic ability to leverage investments towards adaptation measures. Vulnerability and readiness scores range from 0 to 1 to facilitate the comparison among countries, whereas the ND-GAIN score ranges from 0 to 100 using the formula:

$$ND - GAIN \ score = \left(Readiness \ score - Vulnerability \ score + 1\right) \star 50$$

Some Mediterranean countries, due to their geographical location or socioeconomic conditions, are more vulnerable than others to the impact of climate change. Furthermore, some are more ready to take adaptation action by leveraging public and private sector investments through government action, community awareness and the ability to facilitate private sector responses. As data show, most of the South-Eastern Mediterranean Countries (SEMCs) have a higher level of vulnerability to climate change and lower level of readiness because, in addition to their greater geographical exposure, a large share of their economies depends on climate-sensitive sectors. Moreover, their adaptive capacity is limited due to financial and environmental constraints, as well as poor institutional and technological capability (IOM 2008) (Table 8.1).

The European Project *Climate Change and Impact Research: The Mediterranean Environment*, coordinated by the National Institute of Geophysics and Volcanology and supported by the Sixth Framework Programme of the European Commission, has confirmed for the Mediterranean region the climate change trends hypothesized by the Intergovernmental Panel on Climate Change (IPCC 2014), providing a scenario with an average temperature increase of around 2°C, an increase in sea level from 6 to 11 centimetres, a 5% to 10% reduction in precipitation and an increase in frequency of extreme events such as drought, heat waves, torrential rains and cyclones.

One of the factors contributing to different levels of exposure and sensitivity to climate change is water availability. The Mediterranean countries show great inequality in terms of water resources availability, which mainly penalizes SEMCs. In these countries, natural and anthropogenic factors amplify the imbalance between water supply and demand, fuelling a structural deficit that has led to a real water crisis over the years. According to FAO, with the exception of Turkey and Iraq, all SEMCs have a per-capita water availability below 1,000 cubic metres per year, considered the minimum threshold to satisfy water requirements of both the economic system and the population (Figure 8.2).

Furthermore, excessive pumping of non-renewable water sources (fossil water) results in water exploitation indices very close to or higher than 100% (Ferragina and Quagliarotti 2015). (Figure 8.3).[3]

Water shortages will be significantly exacerbated by the impact of climate change: changing rainfall patterns and increasing temperature are projected to decrease water supply between 10% and 30%, while sea-level rise will facilitate seawater intrusion into coastal aquifers, making water unusable for agricultural and drinking purposes (IPCC 2014).

Table 8.1 Notre Dame-Global Adaptation Index (ND-GAIN Index)

Country	ND-GAIN Index		Vulnerability		Readiness	
	Rank	*Score*	*Rank*	*Score*	*Rank*	*Score*
France	17	66.7	7	0.297	23	0.631
Slovenia	19	65.9	23	0.34	20	0.658
Spain	24	62.9	10	0.308	33	0.566
Portugal	26	62	31	0.348	29	0.589
Israel	29	61.4	19	0.338	32	0.567
Italy	32	60.6	15	0.32	40	0.533
Greece	36	58.3	29	0.347	48	0.512
Cyprus	38	57.9	35	0.36	46	0.518
Malta	41	57	33	0.355	52	0.494
Croatia	42	56.9	45	0.373	49	0.511
Turkey	47	56.3	21	0.339	66	0.464
Macedonia	53	54.9	39	0.366	64	0.465
Montenegro	57	54.1	63	0.389	61	0.47
Serbia	70	51.1	82	0.41	78	0.431
Albania	73	50.6	91	0.423	76	0.434
Morocco	73	50.6	51	0.38	102	0.393
Jordan	81	50	50	0.378	108	0.378
Tunisia	84	49.6	71	0.393	106	0.385
Bosnia and Herzegovina	87	49.1	42	0.371	117	0.352
Egypt	98	46.1	93	0.426	119	0.348
Lebanon	106	45.2	78	0.408	133	0.311
Algeria	109	44.5	41	0.37	166	0.26
Libya	125	40.9	56	0.382	183	0.2
Syria	134	39.2	102	0.439	179	0.222

Source: University of Notre Dame 2018

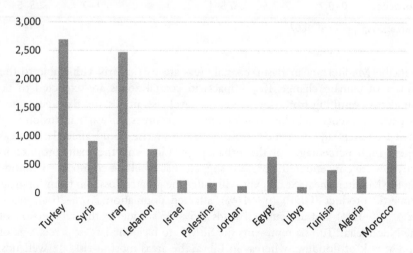

Figure 8.2 Total renewable water resources per capita, m3/year
Source: FAO, AQUASTAT (2014)

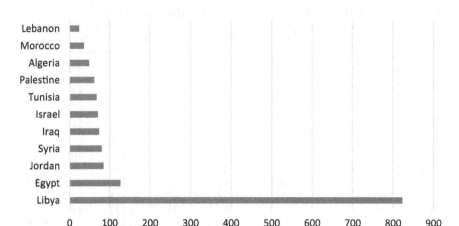

Figure 8.3 Water exploitation index %

Source: FAO, AQUASTAT (2014)

Table 8.2 The impact of sea-level rise in North African countries, percentage

Countries	Impacted area	Impacted population	Impacted GDP	Impacted agricultural land	Impacted urban area	Impacted wetlands
Egypt	1–1.5	10–20	6–16	15–35	6–12	10–11
Libya	0.25–0.50	2.5–7	1.5–3	1	6–10	10–20
Tunisia	1–2	5–10	3–7	1–1.5	4.5–10	10–11
Algeria	0–0.2	0–1.5	0.2–0.4	1	0.5–1	1–2
Morocco	0–0.2	2–2.5	0.5–1	1	1–2	2.5–5

Source: Dasgupta et al. 2007

In the Mediterranean Basin, coastal areas are particularly vulnerable to the impact of climate change. Key impacts in coastal zones are expected to be inundation resulting from slow-onset sea-level rise, floods and damage caused by extreme events including storms and storm surges, saltwater intrusion into coastal aquifers and increased erosion. Sea-level rise could affect large areas where high percentages of the urban population and the main production activities are concentrated. Forecasts suggest that of all the countries surrounding the Mediterranean Sea, Egypt will suffer the greatest losses in terms of gross domestic product (GDP) (6%–16%), affected population (10%–20%), urban areas (6%–12%) and agricultural lands (15%–35%) due to the submersion of the Nile Delta.[4] Tunisia represents the SEMC to have the largest percentage of land at risk of flooding, whereas in Libya, the areas most at risk are wetlands, followed by coastal cities (Dasgupta et al. 2007) (Table 8.2).

Anthropogenic pressure caused by economic and population growth affects physical, chemical and biological properties of soils. Land degradation may be defined as the temporary or permanent reduction in the suitability of land for agricultural purposes as a result of erosion, salinization and soil nutrient depletion. These effects are correlated with human activities such as farming and grazing but may be amplified by drought or flooding. Unsustainable agricultural practices, excessive concentration of infrastructures and economic activities in the most productive areas, and changes in land use are all factors that, albeit to different extents between the two shores of the Mediterranean Basin, have triggered serious degradation processes that limit the ecological functions of soils (FAO 2015).

High population growth rates associated with fertile land scarcity result in a decline in agricultural land area per person, favouring deforestation, expansion of agriculture into marginal lands, unsuitable cropping patterns and overgrazing. Excessive exploitation of structurally fragile soils without adequate vegetation coverage contributes to water and wind erosion, leading to a reduction in the soil's biological potential and desertification process (UNCCD 2017) (Table 8.3).

In the Arab region, desertification affects 976 million hectares, representing 68% of the total region, in addition to threatening 287 million hectares or 20% of the total area. The size of the threatened or desertified areas varies across the region: approximately 48.6% of the land area in the Mashreq, 29% in the Nile Valley and 17% in North Africa is in danger of desertification, with Libya, Egypt and Jordan among the most exposed countries (El Shaer 2015).

Climate change is likely to exacerbate aridity in the MENA region as temperature increases. In recent decades, drought frequency and severity has increased: between 2000 and 2010, drought for two or more years affected 75% of the land area in MENA countries (Erian 2011). Most climate models simulate an increase in drought frequency across most of the drylands around the Mediterranean, suggesting that severe drought is expected to be the 'new

Table 8.3 Land degradation caused by water and wind erosion in SEMCs (1000 ha)

Country	Area affected by water erosion	Area affected by wind erosion
Algeria	3,900	12,000
Egypt		1,400
Jordan	330	3,000
Lebanon	65	
Libya	1,300	24,000
Morocco	3,600	600
Syria	1,200	3,000
Tunisia	3,800	4,000

Source: Food and Agriculture Organization (FAO) and Intergovernmental Technical Panel on Soils (ITPS), 2015

norm' across the region as early as 2030, with both more consecutive dry days and soil moisture anomalies (Dai 2011). As shown in Table 8.4, the most vulnerable countries to drought are Syria (especially the north-eastern area), Tunisia (northern area), Algeria (northern area), and Morocco (northern area) (ACSAD and ISDR 2011).

From a strictly economic point of view, environmental and climate changes primarily affect those economic sectors most dependent on climate and environmental variables, such as agriculture. The risks associated with agriculture arise from the complex relationships between the sector and the climate system, in addition to the high reliance of agriculture on finite natural resources. The agricultural sector in the SEMCs shows higher vulnerability compared with the NMCs both because of its exposure to changing climatic conditions and environmental stress, and its important contribution in terms of farmers' livelihoods, national economies, food security and poverty. In these countries, environmental constraints strongly affect the potential to grow food. In addition to scarce water resources, the link between cultivated area and population is one of the major challenges facing food production in SEMCs. The per capita land share is decreasing annually because of rapid population growth rates and urbanization (World Bank 2017). By 2015, the average arable land share was about 0.15 ha per capita, which is slightly lower than the world average of 0.19 ha per capita. Furthermore, with the exception of Egypt, the dominant agricultural system in SEMCs is rain-fed agriculture, with the total average irrigated area being less than 20%. Taking into account that most of the land area receives less than 300 mm of annual rainfall and that the lower limit for rain-fed agriculture is between 200 mm and 300 mm, agricultural productivity and food security are highly correlated with the annual variability of precipitation, which has exhibited major changes in recent decades (Tolba and SAAB 2009) (Table 8.5).

Table 8.4 Areas within SEMCs vulnerable to droughts

Country	Area (km²)	High vulnerability (%)	Medium vulnerability (%)	Low vulnerability (%)	No vulnerability (%)
Algeria	2,381,741	4.53	7.11	9.62	78.74
Libya	1,759,540	0.55	1.66	6.07	91.72
Morocco	712,550	7.79	17.51	29.75	44.95
Tunisia	163,610	9.82	27.52	14.55	48.1
Egypt	1,001,450	0.43	1.61	7.71	90.24
Jordan	89,342	2.69	8.56	14.15	74.6
Syria	185,180	26.69	36.96	14.58	21.76
Palestine	6,220	8.72	36.85	14.69	39.76
Total	6,299,633	7.6525	17.2225	13.89	61.23375

Source: Arab Center for the Studies of Arid Zones and Dry Lands (ACSAD) and the United Nations Secretariat of the International Strategy for Disaster Reduction Regional Office for Arab States (ISDR), 2011

Table 8.5 Agricultural input in the Mediterranean countries

Country/Region	Agricultural land 2012–2014		Average annual precipitation 2014 (mm)	Permanent cropland 2015 (% of land area)	Arable land 2015 (% of land area)	Arable land 2015 (ha per person)
	% of total	% irrigated				
Albania	43	17.8	1.484	3	22.4	0.21
Bosnia and Herzegovina	42		1.028	2.1	20.1	0.29
Croatia	27	0.9	1.113	1.3	15.1	0.20
France	53	4.9	867	1.8	33.7	0.28
Greece	60	16.6	652	8.6	17.3	0.21
Italy	45	19.1	832	8.3	22.4	0.11
Portugal	40	12.9	854	8.2	12.4	0.11
Slovenia	31	0.3	1.162	2.7	9.1	0.09
Spain	53	14.4	636	9.4	24.7	0.27
NMCs	**44**	**11**	**958**	**5.04**	**19.65**	**0.18**
Israel	25	0.02	435	4.5	13.7	0.04
Jordan	12	9.9	111	1	2.6	0.02
Lebanon	64	20.23	661	12.3	12.9	0.02
Syria	76	9.4	252	5.8	25.4	0.25
Turkey	50	13.5	593	4.3	26.8	0.26
West Bank and Gaza	50	5.6	402	14	10.6	0.01
Middle East	**46**	**10**	**409**	**7**	**15.3**	**0.10**
Algeria	43	17.8	89	0.4	3.1	0.19
Egypt	4	95	51	0.9	2.9	0.03
Libya	9	22	56	0.2	1	0.28
Morocco	69	5	346	3.3	18.2	0.23
Tunisia	65	3.9	207	15	18.7	0.26
North Africa	**38**	**28.74**	**150**	**3.96**	**8.78**	**0.198**
SEMCs	**42**	**19**	**280**	**5.48**	**12.4**	**0.149**

Source: World Bank, World Development Indicators 2017

Note: Boldfaced values show partial total and total data.

Changes in temperature and rainfall regimes and extreme weather events will have a negative impact on agricultural production. A warmer and drier climate is projected to shift vegetation and agricultural zones northwards, for example, by 75 km for 2090–2099 relative to 2000–2009 in a 4°C world (Evans 2010), while lower rainfall and higher temperatures will shorten growing periods for cereals by about two weeks by mid-century. Crop yields are expected to decline by 30% with 1.5–2°C warming and up to 60% with 3–4°C warming (Schilling et al. 2012). The negative impact on crop yields can be only partially offset by higher CO_2 concentrations through the so-called carbon fertilization effect (Tolba and Saab 2009).[5]

The deep sensitivity of the agricultural sector to the impacts of climate change affects SEMCs in different ways. As agriculture supports about one third of the region's population and contributes 13% to the region's GDP (World Bank 2017), it represents a key challenge for sustainable development. The prevalence of poverty is extensive among farmers because of poor infrastructure, the degradation of natural resources, low rainfall and weak market linkages (Dixon et al. 2001). Moreover, lower agricultural productivity will reduce the level of food self-sufficiency, increasing SEMCs' dependency on food imports and making them extremely vulnerable to the instability of international food commodity markets and to harvest failures in other world regions.[6] As demonstrated in Table 8.6, the region is already highly dependent on food imports. The food self-sufficiency ratio at 77% in 2014 did not change significantly from its level at 71% in 2005, indicating that SEMCs did not make progress towards the goal of ensuring food security through domestic production, especially with regard to cereals, whose self-sufficiency ratio dropped from 35% in 2005 to about 30% in 2014 (Saab 2017).[7]

Table 8.6 Self-sufficiency ratio in total food commodities and cereals in SEMCs

Country/Sub-Region	Food self-sufficiency ratio (%)			Cereal self-sufficiency ratio (%)		
	2005	2011	2014	2005	2011	2014
Jordan	56.26	53.09	66.6	5.05	3.66	3.7
Lebanon	73.23	61.03	74.7	18.05	10.96	13.8
Syria	85.23	80.62	84.3	74	57.98	47.86
Palestine	81.55	72.26	79.3	19.69	10	9.48
West Asia	74.0675	66.75	76.225	29.1975	20.65	18.71
Algeria	53.48	70.04	75.2	29.88	31.96	21.65
Egypt	83.68	78.96	88	69.63	56.3	66.04
Libya	44.95	43.09	38.3	10.79	7.06	9.49
Morocco	89.6	80.4	100	46.09	58.96	68
Tunisia	71.78	68.49	89.5	47.82	46.79	42.42
North Africa	68.698	68.196	78.2	40.842	40.214	41.52
Total	71.38275	67.473	77.2125	35.01975	30.432	30.115

Source: Saab 2017

The extreme vulnerability of the Mediterranean countries to the impacts of climate change reveals the urgency in undertaking a combined action of mitigation and adaptation strategies. Mitigation measures aim to limit atmospheric concentrations of greenhouse gases through their reduction (e.g. renewable energy and energy efficiency) and their sequestration and storage (e.g. afforestation). The implementation of these strategies will reduce global warming but will not stop it completely by the end of the century as the climate system is characterized by a strong inertia. This requires the adoption of adaptation measures to minimize the expected negative impacts on both natural and social systems. In such a scenario, migration may act both as an adaptation strategy to address climate change in vulnerable ecosystems, such as drylands, mountains and low-elevation coastal zones, and as a last resort when all other adaptation strategies fail. The predominance of one over the other will largely depend on the adaptation policies implemented not only to mitigate the impact of climate change, but also to facilitate and manage these migration flows. Supporting adaptive capacity is the only human response to the challenges of climate change in the Mediterranean region.

The environmental factor in migration dynamics in the Mediterranean countries

The interweaving of environmental constraints, socio-economic divides and institutional weakness creates a rupture between the two shores of the Mediterranean that triggers political instability and migratory pressure. All the Mediterranean countries are particularly likely to experience some adverse effects of climate change, which can take the form of both slow-onset environmental degradation and sudden-onset disasters. As a result, migration flows related to environmental and climate changes are expected to increase. However, the way in which these new migratory flows may reshape human settlements in the Mediterranean region will depend on the specific vulnerability of countries to the impact of climate and environmental changes which, in turn, is a function of their unique exposure, sensitivity and adaptive capacity.

A recent study published in the journal *Sustainability* combined data on international migration flows with the climate vulnerability indices to explore global and country-level patterns of the climate-migration relationship over the past 20 years. As Maps 8.1 and 8.2 show, people generally tend to migrate from more to less vulnerable countries, confirming that migration can be an effective adaptation strategy to environmental risks. Nevertheless, there are also cases of countries, such as those of sub-Saharan Africa where, although having a high climate vulnerability score, international migration is not as significant as could be expected. Moreover, migrants from this area tend to move to countries with greater or similar climate risks and with a lack of sufficient capacity to deal with them.

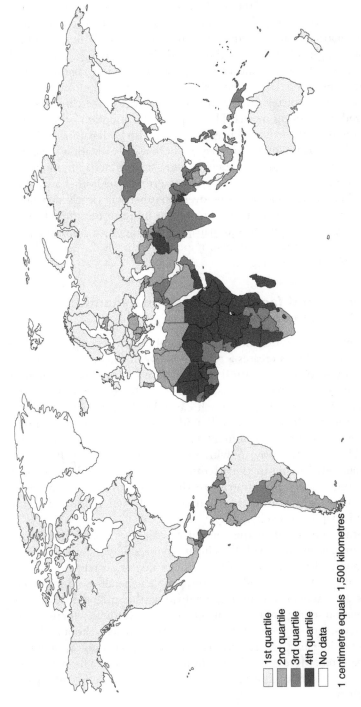

Map 8.1 Climate vulnerability score, 2010

Source: Grecequet et al. 2017

* Shading reflects climate vulnerability quartiles, with cut-off points of 0.35 (25th percentile), 0.43 (50th percentile) and 0.54 (75th percentile). Mean climate vulnerability score was 0.44, with a range of 0.47 (min = 0.22; max = 0.69).

1 centimetre equals 1,500 kilometres

1st quartile
2nd quartile
3rd quartile
4th quartile
No data

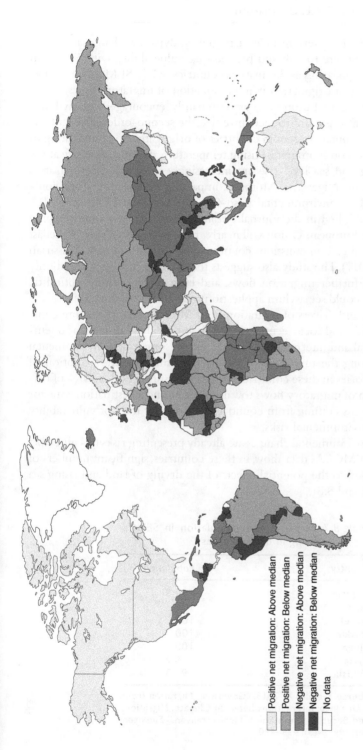

Map 8.2 Net migration rate per thousand populations, 2010–2015

Source: Grecequet et al. 2017

*Net migration rate is an occurrence-exposure rate, calculated as the difference between in- and out-migration flows, divided by total person-years lived in the five-year window. Negative (darker shading) and positive (lighter shading) net migration rates indicate population loss and gain due to migration, respectively. Negative and positive net migration rates are further cut at 50th percentiles, with values of −1.46 and 2.45 per thousand, respectively. Mean net-migration rate was 0.44 per thousand, with a range of 121.18 (min = −38.90 per thousand; max = 82.28 per thousand.

Positive net migration: Above median
Positive net migration: Below median
Negative net migration: Above median
Negative net migration: Below median
No data

Focussing on the Mediterranean level, migration dynamics change according to the level of exposure to risk and pre-existing vulnerability, with European countries mainly appearing as destination countries, while SEMCs simultaneously become areas of origin, transit and destination of migratory flows.

Refugees arriving in Europe are predominantly encouraged by civil war and unrest, but it is important to recognize that the second-order effects of climate and environmental changes in countries of origin are also contributing to instability and decision to migrate. Rising temperature, drought, desertification, erosion, flooding and sea-level rise are increasingly threatening several areas along the axis from Nigeria to Morocco, impacting on the migratory component triggered by environmental push-factors (Werz and Hoffman 2016). New research published in the journal *Science* predicts that migrants applying for asylum in the European Union will nearly triple over the average of the last 15 years by 2100 if carbon emissions continue on their current path (Missirian and Schlenker 2017). The study also suggests that cutting emissions could only partially prevent further migration flows, and even under a more optimistic scenario, Europe could see asylum applications rise by at least a quarter.[8]

The dynamics and drivers of migration in SEMCs appear to be more complex. Demographic and socio-economic trends, especially high rates of unemployment, internal and international conflict and, in some cases, environmental pressure, are among the multitude of factors that influence the evolution of migration trajectories in these countries. SEMCs constitute both an area of origin and transition of migratory flows towards Europe and a destination zone for millions of migrants coming from countries with higher level of vulnerability to climate and environmental risks.

Climate and environmental changes are already presenting risks to vulnerable populations in SEMCs. As data show, in these countries, significant numbers of people are exposed to the potential effects of the drying of land and rising sea levels (Tables 8.7 and 8.8).

Table 8.7 Percentage of population in SEMCs living in dryland areas

Country	Population (%)
Algeria	65.8
Egypt	100
Israel	100
Jordan	100
Libya	100
Syria	96.2
Tunisia	98.3

Source: Geddes A. 2015. "Governing Migration from a Distance: Interactions between Climate, Migration, and Security in the South Mediterranean." *European Security*, 24(3): 473–490.

Table 8.8 Urban and rural population in SEMCs within the low-elevation coastal zones (LECZ), 2000

Country	Population in the LECZ				
	Total	Total urban	Urban (%)	Total rural	Rural (%)
Algeria	739,375	196,507	26.58	542,868	73.42
Egypt	25,461,200	3,735,020	14.67	21,726,180	85.33
Iraq	2,664,710	370,008	13.89	2,294,702	86.11
Israel	245,770	80,894	32.91	164,876	67.09
Jordan	679	3	0.44	676	99.56
Libya	645,381	125,268	19.41	520,113	80.59
Morocco	1,739,490	202,621	11.65	1,536,869	88.35
Palestine	72,214	0	0	72,214	100
Syria	98,900	18,541	18.75	80,359	81.25
Tunisia	1,388,660	355,506	25.6	1,033,154	74.4

Source: Geddes A. 2015. "Governing Migration from a Distance: Interactions between Climate, Migration, and Security in the South Mediterranean." *European Security*, 24(3): 473–490.

However, population exposure does not necessarily mean that these people will migrate either internally or internationally because, as already outlined, migration is multi-causal and the effects of environmental change interact with other factors such as economic and political changes.

In the SEMCs, internal migration is far more significant in scale than international migration and often takes the forms of rural–urban migration. Rural–urban migration is the major social transformation that is affecting SEMCs and environmental stress may amplify this trend (Table 8.9). The decline in rural population and the continuing migration from rural to urban areas are due to weak economic structure, inadequate infrastructure, high unemployment rates and low level of per capita income in rural areas. In addition, worsening rural livelihoods associated with soil degradation and water scarcity further operate as a driving force for internal migration flows.

Urban migrants may become more exposed to other environmental risks and hazards. New city migrants tend to be extremely vulnerable as they are often located in hazardous districts of cities affected by low levels of water, health and other services. In addition, most of the SEMCs' major cities, economic activities and transportation hubs are placed in low-lying coastal areas. As a result, a rise in sea level could be disastrous for many densely populated coastal cities, especially for migrants concentrated in informal urban settlements particularly exposed to such risks (UN-Habitat 2012). It is, therefore, likely that people in urban areas will seek better living conditions by migrating towards third countries, and will not return to the countryside where they originally came from. It could also happen that the lack of an effective government strategy able to mitigate the migratory pressure and to stem the deterioration of socio-economic conditions in urban centres (growth of urban populations, creation of informal

Table 8.9 Urbanization in SEMCs

Country	Urban population					Population in urban agglomeration of more than 1 million		Population in the largest city	
	Thousands 1990	Thousands 2015	% of total population 1990	% of total population 2015	% growth 2015	% of total population 1990	% of total population 2015	% of urban population 1990	% of urban population 2015
Algeria	13,496	28,200	52	71	2.8	7	7	13	9
Egypt	24,962	40,451	43	43	2.3	23	25	40	46
Iraq	12,177	25,090	70	69	3.3	36	32	34	26
Israel	4,211	7,721	90	92	2.1	58	56	49	47
Jordan	2,610	7,664	73	84	4.2	24	13	33	15
Lebanon	2,247	5,137	83	88	4.5	48	38	58	43
Libya	3,360	4,898	76	79	0.7	19	18	26	23
Morocco	12,039	20,950	48	60	2.2	21	22	22	22
Palestine	1,339	3,328	68	75	3.2	–	–	20	19
Syria	6,090	10,802	49	58	-1.8	33	48	28	33
Tunisia	4,771	7,536	58	67	1.5	18	18	31	26
Turkey	31,923	57,449	59	73	2.3	26	38	21	25

Source: World Bank, World Development Indicators 2017

settlements, development of illegal activities, increase in food insecurity, pressure on resources) triggers political discontent and tensions within urban areas.

In SEMCs, migration and displacements in themselves will not lead to conflict unless other structural problems are already in place. The supplementary stress linked to climate change could amplify an already difficult reality upon which the distribution and access to resources and mobility could play decisive roles. Most of the available literature on environmental change, displacement and conflict in SEMCs focuses on Syria and the climate change–related drought that occurred in the country prior to the outbreak of civil war. Between 2007 and 2010, severe drought plagued Syria, causing as many as 1.5 million people to migrate from the countryside into cities like Damascus, Aleppo and Dara'a. Some experts argue that this displacement contributed to the uprising connected to the start of the Syrian conflict. Three separate studies provide support for the Syria–climate conflict thesis: (a) a short briefing document by Francesco Femia and Caitlin Werrell of the Center for Climate and Security in Washington DC, which was the primary reference point for proponents of this view (Femia and Werrell 2012); (b) a peer-reviewed article by Peter Gleick, one of the foremost scholars of water issues worldwide (Gleick 2014); and (c) a further peer-reviewed article by Colin Kelley and colleagues, mostly earth scientists at the Universities of California and Columbia (Kelley et al. 2015). All three studies explain the role played by anthropogenic climate change in the Syrian civil war through a three-step argument: first, that anthropogenic CO_2 emissions were a significant contributor to the severe drought occurring in Syria, second, that drought led to large-scale internal migration and third, that internal migrants were an important determining factor in sparking the 2011 uprising. This unilinear direct connection between climate-related drought, migration and conflict in Syria is difficult to support and overlooks the role of political and socio-economic factors in determining people's vulnerability to environmental stress and the root causes of the rebellion against the Assad regime (Eklund and Thompson 2017).

Conclusions

In recent decades, an emerging literature based mostly on individual data and household surveys has investigated how climate and environmental changes may affect migration (Wodon et al. 2014; Swearingen and Bencherifa 2000; Gray and Mueller 2012; Gray and Bilsborrow 2013; Bohra-Mishra et al. 2014). The main findings show that, though climatic shocks and environmental stress may trigger both internal and international migration, the relationship appears complex and the effects are often country specific (Gray and Wise 2016). In addition, several conflicting results have emerged, such as the low or negligible effect of environmental variables on migration flows (Mueller et al. 2014), or reverse effects, namely situations where adverse climate factors reduce rather than increase emigration flows (Gray and Mueller 2012). Another critical issue is the lack of macro studies focussing on climate and environmental changes and migration, which renders the generalization of existing micro-evidence extremely difficult. More recently, important data collections, such as the *Global Bilateral Migration Database* developed by Özden et al. (2011), have inaugurated a new series of macro studies on the impact of climate change and environmental degradation on human movements (Beine and Parsons 2015; Cattaneo and Peri 2016; Maurel and Tuccio 2016). If, on the one hand, such studies have confirmed some of the outcomes of previous micro-based evidence, on the other, they have raised new important issues, suggesting that the effects on migration appear to be mainly indirect and mediated by other socio-economic characteristics (Falco et al. 2018)). At the same time, knowing whether climate change and natural disasters lead to more migration is crucial to better understand the different channels of transmission between climatic and environmental shocks and migration and to formulate evidence-based policy recommendations (Mbaye 2017).

The emergence of climate change as a global issue has helped to recast the literature on the impacts of weather variability and climate shocks on migration flows, but empirical data and analysis of threats of, and possible solutions to, climate-induced migration continue to be limited (Salehyan 2005; Gleditsch et al. 2008; IPCC 2014). Predominantly, this literature is based on causal chain analysis, which considers climate change as a push factor, including the role of climate variability in contributing to environmental degradation which, in turn, fuels migration flows, and the role of climate extremes in triggering sudden population movements. Furthermore, distinctions are made between climate-induced voluntary migration, predominantly linked to slow-onset processes, and forced migrations in response to sudden-onset climate hazards.

The Mediterranean constitutes a geographically complex region with deep international and intra-national gradients in environmental, socio-economic and political conditions. The great diversity of the region means that generalizations about the linkages between climate and environmental changes and migration cannot be made. According to the IPCC, the Mediterranean region is a hot spot of climate change whose impacts will affect especially SEMCs because of their greater sensitivity and lower adaptability to climate shocks. By the end of the century, SEMCs are projected to become considerably hotter and drier. The combined effect of higher temperature and reduced precipitation will increase the occurrence and severity of frequent and intense extreme weather events such as droughts, an effect that is already materializing in many areas of the south-eastern shore. It is further estimated that an additional 80–100 million people will be exposed by 2025 to water stress, which is likely to result in increased pressure on groundwater resources, which are currently being extracted beyond the aquifers' recharge potential. The physical impacts of climate change will directly translate into economic impacts. In several SEMCs, economic growth and poverty levels are deeply dependent on agriculture. With an average share of 15% in GDP, 40% in employment and 85% in total water use, agriculture is a sector of strategic significance in SEMCs, from the economic, social and environmental standpoint. Furthermore, agricultural yields, especially in rain-fed areas, are expected to fluctuate more widely, ultimately falling to a significantly lower long-term average.

While our understanding of climate dynamics and economic impacts is increasing, we still have a lack of knowledge on the social implications of climate and environmental changes, and specifically on how environmental degradation, climate variability and climate change may induce human mobility. Focussing on the Mediterranean countries, what can be said is that migration dynamics change according to the level of exposure to risk and pre-existing vulnerability, with European countries mainly appearing as destination countries, while SEMCs simultaneously become areas of origin, transit and destination of migratory flows. Even if refugees arriving in Europe are predominantly encouraged by civil war and conflicts, it is important to recognize that climate and environmental changes in countries of origin are also contributing to instability and the decision to migrate. In SEMCs, internal migration is far more significant in scale than international migration, taking the form of rural-urban migration, exposing urban migrants to other environmental risks and hazards, such as coastal flooding, water scarcity and decreasing water quality, all factors that are likely to affect public health and worsen living conditions. The lack of an effective government strategy to mitigate migratory pressure and to prevent the deterioration of socio-economic conditions in urban centres may amplify political discontent and tensions in the host areas, triggering migration towards third countries.

In the Mediterranean region, the effects of climate change and environmental deterioration on migration flows cannot be attributed to a single driver. Whilst the environmental variable has become increasingly important, artificially isolating it from other intervening factors in explaining causal links risks excluding important factors influencing how such threats may affect human mobility. Even within a community affected by the same environmental stress, the vulnerability level and the decision to migrate is influenced by demographic characteristic, socio-economic conditions, the degree of dependency on natural resources and the level of adaptive capacity to climate and environmental changes.

Such a scenario reveals the urgency not only in undertaking a combined action of climate change mitigation and adaptation strategies, but also in implementing measures and actions able to decrease the level of vulnerability to environmental stress.

Furthermore, rather than being considered as a problem to be avoided, migration must be seen as an adaptation strategy itself. Coordination of environmental and migration policies with broader development aims is crucial for avoiding the negative impacts of these movements. Supporting adaptive capacity in its broadest meaning is the most effective response to the challenges of climate change in the Mediterranean region.

Notes

1 IDMC's global estimates cover disasters triggered by sudden-onset hydro-meteorological and climatological hazards such as floods, storms, wildfires and extreme winter conditions, and geophysical hazards such as earthquakes, volcanic eruptions and landslides. They do not include displacements associated with slow-onset disasters such as drought and environmental degradation. Nor do they cover those associated with technological and biological hazards, such as industrial accidents and epidemics, except when they are triggered by a natural hazard.

2 Exposure refers to changes in biophysical factors that affect human society and its supporting sectors (changes in crop yields, marine biodiversity, etc.). Sensitivity refers to the degree to which human society and its supporting sectors are affected by climate disturbances, with sensitivity indicators including, for example, countries' dependency on climate-sensitive sectors (e.g. agriculture) and the proportion of the population that is sensitive to climate hazards due topography (e.g. living in low-lying coastal areas). Adaptive capacity refers to the ability to respond to the negative consequences of climate change, with indicators of adaptive capacity serving as proxies of possible actions that may ameliorate the impacts of climate change (fertilizer and pesticide use, access to electricity, area of protected biomes, engagement in international environmental conventions, etc.) (Grecequet et al. 2017).

3 The water exploitation index is the mean annual total abstraction of freshwater as a percentage of the mean annual total renewable freshwater resource at the country level. It gives an indication of how the total water demand puts pressure on available water resources. It also identifies those countries that have high demand in relation to their resources, and therefore are prone to suffer problems of water stress. For this assessment, the following threshold values/ranges for the water exploitation index have been used to indicate levels of water stress: (a) non-stressed countries < 10%; (b) low stress 10% to < 20%; (c) stressed 20% to < 40%; and (d) severe water stress ≥ 40%. The threshold values/ranges above are averages and it would be expected that areas for which the water exploitation index is above 20% would also be expected to experience severe water stress during drought or low river-flow periods.

4 Much of the Nile Delta is already at or below sea level and is one of the world most densely populated deltas. Therefore, even a marginal sea-level rise combined with storm surges could create disastrous flooding, for example, in Alexandria, Egypt's second city. Increased erosion of the Nile Delta has already been attributed to upstream engineering projects such as the Aswan High Dam and as a result the land levels of the delta are falling at the same time as sea levels are rising (Stanley and Clemente 2017).

5 Though rising CO_2 can stimulate plant growth, it also reduces the nutritional value of most food crops. Rising levels of atmospheric carbon dioxide reduce the concentrations of protein and essential minerals in most plant species, including wheat, soybeans, and rice. This direct effect of rising CO_2 on the nutritional value of crops represents a potential threat to human health.

6 Despite the many possible contributing factors, the outbreak of protests in several MENA countries in 2011 as well as earlier riots in 2008 coincides with large peaks in global food prices.

7 Heavy cereal import dependency not only is a matter of economic choices, but also is linked to water and land constraints that avoid self-sufficiency already today, and may even intensify with population growth and the impact of climate change (FAO 2016).

8 Comparing asylum applications to the EU filed from 103 countries between 2000 and 2014 with temperature variations in the applicants' home countries, researchers found that the more temperatures in a country's key agricultural region rose above 20°C in the growing season, the more people left their homes for another country. Combining the asylum-application data with projections of future warming, they found that an increase of

average global temperatures of 1.8°C – an optimistic scenario in which carbon emissions flatten globally in the next few decades and then decline – would increase applications by 28% by 2100, translating into 98,000 extra applications to the EU each year. If carbon emissions continue on their current path, with global temperatures rising between 2.6°C and 4.8°C, applications could increase by 188% by 2100, leading to extra 660,000 applications filed each year.

References

Arab Center for the Studies of Arid Zones and Dry Lands (ACSAD) and the United Nations Secretariat of the International Strategy for Disaster Reduction Regional Office for Arab States (ISDR), 2011. *Drought Vulnerability in the Arab Region: Case study – Drought in Syria, Ten Years of Scarce Water (2000–2010)*. Damascus/Cairo: ACSAD, ISDR.

Beine, M., and Parsons, C., 2015. Climatic Factors as Determinants of International Migration. *The Scandinavian Journal of Economics*, 117 (2), 723–767.

Black, R., 2001. *Environmental Refugees: Myth or Reality?* Working Paper 34. Geneva: United Nations High Commissioner for Refugees (UNHCR).

Bohra-Mishra, P., Oppenheimer, M., and Hsiang, S.M., 2014. Nonlinear Permanent Migration Response to Climatic Variations but Minimal Response to Disasters. *Proceedings of the National Academy of Sciences*, 111 (27), 9780–9785.

Burrows, K., and Kinney, P.L., 2016. Exploring the Climate Change, Migration and Conflict Nexus. *International Journal Environmental Research Public Health*, 13 (443), 5–17.

Cattaneo, C., and Peri, G., 2016. The Migration Response to Increasing Temperatures. *Journal of Development Economics*, 122, 127–146.

Crutzen, P.J., and Stoermer, E.F., 2000. The "Anthropocene." *Global Change Newsletter*, 41, 17–18.

Dai, A., 2011. Drought Under Global Warming: A Review. *Wiley Interdisciplinary Reviews: Climate Change*, 2 (1), 45–65.

Dasgupta, S., et al., 2007. *The Impact of Sea Level Rise on Developing Countries: A Comparative Analysis*. World Bank Policy Research Working Paper No. 4136. Washington DC: World Bank.

Eklund, L., and Thompson, D., 2017. Differences in Resource Management Affects Drought Vulnerability Across the Borders between Iraq, Syria, and Turkey. *Ecology and Society*, 22 (4), 9.

El-Hinnawi, E., 1985. *Environmental Refugees*. Nairobi: UNEP.

El Shaer, H.M., 2015. Land Desertification and Restoration in the Middle East and North Africa (MANA) Region. *Sciences in Cold and Arid Regions*, 7 (1), 7–15.

Erian, W., 2011. *Drought Vulnerability in the Arab Region: Case Study-Drought in Syria, Ten Years of Scarce Resources (2000–2010)*. Damascus: Arab Centre for the Studies of Dry Areas and Arid Zones (ACSAD).

Evans, A., 2010. *Resource Scarcity, Climate Change and the Risk of Violent Conflict*. World Development Report 2011 Background Paper. Washington DC: World Bank.

Falco, C., Galeotti, M., and Olper, A., 2018. *Climate Change and Migration: Is Agriculture the Main Channel?* Working Paper No. 100. Milan: Bocconi.

Femia, F., and Werrell, C., 2012. *Syria: Climate Change, Drought and Social Unrest*. Available from: https://climateandsecurity.org/2012/02/29/syria-climate-change-drought-and-social-unrest/

Ferragina, E., and Quagliarotti, D.A.L., 2015. Gli effetti delle dinamiche globali sui paesi mediterranei: rischio e vulnerabilità ambientale. *In*: E. Ferragina, ed. *Rapporto sulle economie del Mediterraneo. Edizione 2015*. Bologna: il Mulino.

Food and Agriculture Organization (FAO), 2016. *Climate Change and Food Security: Risks and Responses*. Rome: FAO.

Food and Agriculture Organization (FAO), Intergovernmental Technical Panel on Soils ITPS, 2015. *Status of the World's Soil Resources (SWSR) – Main Report*. Rome: FAO and ITPS.

Foresight., 2011. *Migration and Global Environmental Change*. Final Project Report. London: The Government Office for Science.

Geddes, A., 2015. Governing Migration from a Distance: Interactions between Climate, Migration, and Security in the South Mediterranean. *European Security*, 24 (3), 473–490.

Gleditsch, N.P., Raleigh, C., Jordan, L., and Salehyan, L., 2008. *Social Dimensions of Climate Change: Assessing the Impact of Climate Change on Migration and Conflict*. Washington DC: World Bank.

Gleick, P., 2014. *Water, Drought, Climate Change, and Conflict in Syria*. Boston, MA: American Meteorological Society (AMS).

Gray, C., and Bilsborrow, R., 2013. Environmental Influences on Human Migration in Rural Ecuador. *Demography*, 50 (4), 1217–1241.

Gray, C., and Wise, E., 2016. Country-Specific Effects of Climate Variability on Human Migration. *Climatic Change*, 135 (3–4), 555–568.

Gray, C.L., and Mueller, V., 2012. Natural Disasters and Population Mobility in Bangladesh. *Proceedings of the National Academy of Sciences*, 109 (16), 6000–6005.

Grecequet, M., DeWaard, J., Hellmann, J.J., and Abel, G.J., 2017. Climate Vulnerability and Human Migration in Global Perspective. *Sustainability*, 9 (720), 1–10.

Guterres, A., 2009. *Climate Change, Natural Disasters and Human Displacement: A UNHCR Perspective*. Geneva: United Nations High Commissioner for Refugees (UNHCR).

Homer-Dixon, T.F., 1991. Environmental Scarcities and Violent Conflict: Evidence from Cases. *International Security*, 19 (1), 5–40.

Homer-Dixon, T.F., 1994. On the Threshold: Environmental Changes as Causes of Acute Conflict. *International Security*, 16 (2), 76–116.

Internal displacement Monitoring Centre (IDMC), 2017. *Global Report on Internal Displacement*. Geneva: IDMC.

International Organization for Migration (IOM), 2008. *Migration, Development and Environment*. Geneva: IOM.

Intergovernmental Panel on Climate (IPCC), 2007. *Climate Change 2007. Synthesis Report*. Geneva: IPCC.

Intergovernmental Panel on Climate (IPCC), 2014. *Climate Change 2014. Synthesis Report*. Geneva: IPCC.

Ionesco, D., Mokhnacheva, D., and Gemenne, F., 2017. *The Atlas of Environmental Migration*. London: Routledge.

Kelley, C.P., et al., 2015. Climate Change in the Fertile Crescent and Implications of the Recent Syrian Drought. *Proceedings of the National Academy of Sciences of the United States of America*, 112 (11), 3241–3246.

Lazko, F., and Aghazarm, C., 2010. *Migration, Environment and Climate Change: Assessing the Evidence*. Geneva: International Organization for Migration (IOM).

Maurel, M., and Tuccio, M., 2016. Climate Instability, Urbanisation and International Migration. *The Journal of Development Studies*, 52 (5), 735–752.

Mbaye, L., 2017. *Climate Change, Natural Disasters, and Migration*. Bonn: IZA World of Labor.

McLeman, R., 2016. Migration as Adaptation: Conceptual Origins, Recent Developments, and Future Directions. *In*: A. Milan, B. Schraven, K. Warner, and N. Cascone, eds. *Migration, Risk Management and Climate Change: Evidence and Policy Responses*. Dordrecht: Springer, 213—229.

Missirian, A., and Schlenker, W., 2017. Asylum Applications Respond to Temperature Fluctuations. *Science*, 358 (6370), 1610–1614.

Mueller, V., et al., 2014. Heat Stress Increases Long-Term Human Migration in Rural Pakistan. *Nature Climate Change*, 4, 182–185.

Naser, M.M., 2012. Climate Change, Environmental Degradation, and Migration: A Complex Nexus. *William & Mary Environmental Law & Pol'y Review*, 36 (3–4), 713–768.

Özden, Ç., Parsons, C.R., Schiff, M., and Walmsley, T.L., 2011. Where on Earth Is Everybody? The Evolution of Global Bilateral Migration 1960–2000. *The World Bank Economic Review*, 25 (1), 12–56.

Raleigh, C., 2011. The Search for Safety: The Effects of Conflict, Poverty and Ecological Influences on Migration in the Developing World. *Global Environmental Change*, 21S, S82–S93.

Rockström, J., et al., 2009. A Safe Operating Space for Humanity. *Nature*, 461, 472–475.

Saab, N., 2017. *Arab Environment in 10 Years*. Beirut: Arab Forum for Environment and Development (AFED).

Salehyan, I., 2005. *Refugees, Climate Change, and Instability. Human Security and Climate Change*. An International Workshop at Holmen Fjord Hotel, Asker. San Diego: University of California, 21–23 June.

Schilling, J., et al., 2012. Climate Change, Vulnerability and Adaptation in North Africa with Focus on Morocco. *Agriculture, Ecosystems and Environment*, 156, 12–26.

Stanley, J.D., and Clemente, P.L., 2017. Increased Land Subsidence and Sea-Level Rise are Submerging Egypt's Nile Delta Coastal Margin. *GSA Today*, 27 (5), 4–11.

Swearingen, W.D., and Bencherifa, A., 2000. An Assessment of the Drought Hazard in Morocco. *In*: D.A. Wilhite, ed. *Drought: A Global Assessment*, Vol. 1. New York: Routledge.

Tolba, M.K., and Saab, N.W., 2009. *Arab Environment: Climate Change. Impact of Climate Change on Arab Countries*. Beirut: AFED.

United Nations Convention to Combat Desertification (UNCCD), 2017. *Global Land Outlook. First Edition*. Bonn: UNCCD.

United Nations Human Settlements Programme (UN-Habitat), 2012. *The State of Arab Cities 2012 Challenges of Urban Transition*. Nairobi: UN-Habitat.

University of Notre Dame, 2018. *Notre Dame Global Adaptation Initiative (ND-GAIN)*. South Bend: University of Notre Dame.

Werz, M., and Hoffman, M., 2016. Europe's Twenty-First Century Challenge: Climate Change, Migration and Security. *European Review*, 15, 145–154.

Wodon, Q., Liverani, A., Joseph, G., and Bougnoux, N., eds., 2014. *Climate Change and Migration: Evidence from the Middle East and North Africa*. World Bank Study. Washington, DC: World Bank.

World Bank, 2017. *World Development Indicators*. Washington DC: World Bank.

Chapter 9

International migrations in the northern countries of the Mediterranean

Continuity and changes, before and after the crisis

Corrado Bonifazi and Salvatore Strozza

Introduction

The world economic crisis since 2008 has constituted an important turning point in international migration trends. This process is particularly evident in the southern countries of the European Union (EU). Subject to the greatest consequences of the slump (Alessandrini et al. 2013), these nations are still displaying great difficulties overcoming it in full, and, in terms of migration, have undoubtedly experienced the most significant changes in Europe (Strozza and De Santis 2017a). In the two decades straddling the turn of the century, the four countries considered (Italy, Spain, Portugal and Greece) were the main poles in the world attracting international migratory flows (Strozza 2010; Arango and Finotelli 2010), overturning a tradition that for at least a century had them marked as the most important points of departure from the continent (Bonifazi and Strozza 2002). According to some scholars (King and Rybaczuk 1993; King et al. 1997, King 2000; Ribas-Mateos 2004; Peixoto et al. 2012), the result has been the development of the so-called Southern Europe model of immigration, rather different from the one of the 'old(er)' European immigration countries. 'The timing of inflows, the position in the migration cycle, the level and type of labour demand, the socio-economic structures, the public perception and the immigration policies are all significantly different in those contexts' (Peixoto et al. 2012: 141). The main characteristics of the North–Western Mediterranean model of immigration have been singled out in the similarity in the process of transition from emigration to immigration countries, the considerable variation in the national origin of immigrants with different demographic characteristics, the labour-oriented nature of most inflows with immigrants mainly absorbed into the least protected segments of the labour market, often overqualified for the jobs they perform and overexposed to temporary contracts and unemployment risks, more or less similar migration policies with the common treat of the use of repeated regularization procedures in order to regulate *ex post* what they were unable to regulate *ex ante* (Peixoto et al. 2012). Supported by research during the 1990s and early 2000s, this model could be considered dynamic.

According to Baldwin-Edwards (2012), Northern Mediterranean countries have accumulated more experience and techniques for the management of migration. Furthermore, an issue that merits further investigation is the effect of the 2008 economic recession on migration trends (Martin 2009).

With the recession, the situation has changed completely: the number of foreigners arriving have fallen, labour immigration has slowed greatly and family and forced migration have acquired growing significance. The structural composition of resident foreign populations has changed, integration processes have found themselves dealing with a negative economic trend and naturalizations have increased owing to the effect of large segments of immigrants settling down. And, surprisingly, emigration abroad by young people in the aforementioned countries, a phenomenon believed to have been relegated to the family annals, has started up again.

These changes have completely altered the template for migratory policies, highlighting all the limits of the EU's approach to managing the phenomenon. The situation has also cast light on the need for flexible tools in this ambit, especially in the countries under examination, that can rapidly and effectively tackle changes in the trends and characteristics of the migratory processes. Against this background, this chapter sets out to analyze how the phenomenon has evolved in the four Mediterranean countries of the EU since the 1990s, identifying the main aspects and characteristics before and during the recession, also with reference to the situation in the labour market. This analysis will also enable definition of the contextual problems that most directly influence the development of the Northern Mediterranean model of immigration and the construction of migratory policies in the countries under consideration.

Dynamics and characteristics of migratory flows

However succinct and limited, net migration values and rates estimated for the period between 1960 and 2014 for the three geographical areas making up the historic core of the EU-15, with the addition of Norway and Switzerland, are sufficient to describe the salient moments characterizing the phenomenon (Table 9.1). In the first 30 years (1960–1989), only the countries of the central zone, corresponding roughly to the 'Western Europe' of the Cold War, recorded significant net immigration. By contrast, in the last 25 years, all three regions have recorded a considerable positive net migration, which in the case of the southern and northern countries has grown notably from one decade to the next (Strozza and De Santis 2017b). Traditionally an area of emigration, after 20 years (1970–1989) of net migration approaching zero, the southern region first became an area of immigration, and in the last decade went so far as to assume the role of main pole of attraction in the whole European Union, with a net figure of over 8.8 million immigrants. The net migration rate in this area (+7.2 per 1,000 inhabitants, on average every year) reached more than double the figure recorded by the countries traditionally receiving immigration in

Table 9.1 Net migration for EU-15 countries plus Norway and Switzerland aggregated by geographical area,[a] for the decades from 1960 to 2009 and the five years from 2010 to 2014 (absolute values in thousands and average annual values per 1,000 inhabitants)

Geographical area	Period					
	1960–1969	1970–1979	1980–1989	1990–1999	2000–2009	2010–2014[b]
	Net migration (absolute values in thousands)					
North	-103.5	54.2	20.1	1,092.4	3,586.8	1,755.7
Centre[c]	4,572.1	2,047.2	2,704.7	4,451.9	3,124.3	3,159.6
South[d] of which:	-3319.0	134.5	-280.6	2,082.2	8,837.8	689.7
– Greece[d]	-385.8	156.0	189.0	696.2	31.4	-260.8
– Italy[d]	-994.1	-221.7	-245.7	329.9	2,908.9	1,421.6
– Portugal	-1,240.1	219.3	-129.6	164.3	283.3	-124.1
– Spain	-699.0	-19.1	-94.4	891.9	5,614.3	-347.0
Total	1,149.6	2,235.9	2,444.2	7,626.5	15,548.9	5,604.9
	Net migration rates (average annual values per 1,000 inhabitants)					
North	-0.1	0.1	0.0	1.3	4.0	3.7
Centre[c]	2.9	1.2	1.6	2.5	1.7	3.3
South[d] of which:	-3.3	0.1	-0.2	1.8	7.2	1.1
– Greece[d]	-4.5	1.7	1.9	6.7	0.3	-4.9
– Italy[d]	-1.9	-0.4	-0.4	0.6	5.0	4.7
– Portugal	-14.2	2.4	-1.3	1.6	2.7	-2.4
– Spain	-2.2	-0.1	-0.2	2.3	13.0	-1.5
Total	0.3	0.6	0.7	2.0	3.9	2.7

Source: Our elaborations of Eurostat data integrated with national statistics

Notes: [a] North: Denmark, Finland, Ireland, Norway, Sweden and the United Kingdom; Centre: Austria, Belgium, France, Germany, Luxembourg, the Netherlands and Switzerland; South: Greece, Italy, Portugal and Spain. [b] For this period, the estimated net migration rates also contain statistical adjustments. [c] The resident population in Germany at the beginning of 2000 and 2010 has been revised to take account of the results of the 2011 census. [d] The resident population in Greece at the beginning of 1990, 2000, 2010 and 2015 has been revised to account for the results of the last three censuses. The resident population in Italy at the beginning of 2010, contrary to what was done in the past, is a statistical reconstruction (ISTAT 2015) and not an intercensal reconstruction. This results in differences compared with estimates published in the past of net migration for the periods 2000–2009 and 2010–2014 not just for Italy, but also for the southern geographical area and the regional total.

Central Europe in the 1960s (2.8 per 1,000), that is, the period of active policies for recruiting foreign labour. Owing to the economic crisis, in the last five years, the appeal of southern countries has declined greatly, while the central countries of Western Europe have regained their attraction.

Thanks to the details on the single countries in southern Europe, it is possible to highlight the time differences in the past and recent migration trends in the four states. The positive net migration recorded by Greece in the 1970s and 1980s and by Portugal in the first of the two decades are essentially linked to net returns of their own citizens following the economic crises (1973 and 1980) which had led the traditional European receiving countries to launch policies closing the doors to new arrivals of workers and encourage the unemployed to return to their country of origin. In the case of Portugal, arrivals from the former colonies following the so-called decolonization process and the democratization process that took place after the Carnation Revolution *(Revolução dos Cravos)* in 1974 also need to be considered. In the 1980s and 1990s, even Greece received flows of 'national' origin: the Pontiac Greeks and Albanians of Greek descent. Estimates of net migration in the 1970s and 1980s for Spain and Italy provide negative values, even if close to a balance between arrivals and departures. Despite these results, it should be remembered that in these countries, especially in the early 1970s, there was an intensification of the returns of the nationals previously emigrated and, from the 1980s and particularly in the second part of the decade, a growing foreign immigration. The proposed estimates indicate instead a negative balance while the values are positive considering the direct registration of migratory flows. This contradiction is probably due partly to errors in the indirect estimates of net migration, for the different degree of coverage of the resident population at the censuses, partly to the sub-registration of emigration, that may have been particularly important in a period in which minors were the possibilities to settle permanently abroad.

It is in the 1990s that, owing to the effect of growing foreign immigration, the net migration rate becomes positive in all four countries, with a particularly significant intensity in Greece (almost 700,000 people in the decade, equivalent to around seven arrivals on average every year per 1,000 inhabitants), owing to the exodus of citizens from nearby Albania heading towards the Hellenic peninsula (as well as towards Italy) after the end of the socialist regime and following the 1996–1997 economic crisis, known as the collapse of the financial pyramids. In the other three countries, the period of the most intense net immigration is instead the first decade of the new millennium: Spain is the country which, in terms of mere numbers (5.6 million) and impact on the resident population (13 arrivals on average every year per 1,000 inhabitants), recorded the most intense immigration, followed by Italy (2.9 million people, equivalent to five immigrants per year per 1,000 residents) and Portugal (almost 300,000, fewer than three arrivals every year per 1,000 residents). With the economic crisis, the situation changed radically. In the five-year period from 2010 to 2014, Spain, Greece and Portugal recorded negative net migration figures which seem to have brought the period of mass immigration that began with the fall of the Berlin Wall to a definitive close (Triandafyllidou 2014). This observation also holds for Italy, even though it diverges from the other three countries, given that the residual estimate of net migration, revised to account for the underestimation of the population in the 2011 census, nevertheless gives a positive value of 1.4 million. This constitutes a sizeable surplus that can be put down to at least two reasons: first, underestimation of the departures, especially of foreigners, and second, the constant large number of arrivals from abroad owing to the registration of several hundred thousand workers from non-EU countries in the last two regularization opportunities, the substantial flow of arrivals for family reunification, which underwent no major reductions compared to the past, and the significantly growing inflow of refugees and asylum seekers, who in part settled down and therefore registered in the Municipal Population Registers.

The direct collection of migration flow data without doubt enables further analysis, allowing to distinguish between nationals and foreigners.[1] The data available need to be treated with a certain amount of caution: the figures are affected by the well-known limits of statistics on migratory movements (see Salt et al. 1994; Bilsborrow et al. 1997; United Nations 1998; Bonifazi and Strozza 2006; Kraler et al. 2015). Notwithstanding, availability and comparability of data improved with the introduction of the European Regulation (EC) No. 862/2007 on *Community statistics on migration and international protection*. In the case of Greece and Portugal, these advances are the direct result of action by Eurostat (and/or National Statistical Institutes) which in some cases estimates values starting from the available information. Thanks to this information, it can be observed that, in the four countries under consideration, a progressive increase in the annual emigration figures has been recorded since 2010, in addition to a reduction in the number of immigrations (Figure 9.1). Since 2008, this reduction has been truly drastic in Spain (from almost 960,000 to less than 600,000), while it has been gradual in Italy (from around 530,000 to less than 280,000 in 2014) as well as in Portugal. In truth, in Portugal as in Greece, the decrease in intensity had already arrived before the crisis: in the latter, the number of immigrants fell from 116,000 in 1998 to 63,000 in 2003, subsequently levelling out at around 60,000 until 2015 (in 2016, there was a significant recovery in immigration); in Portugal, the drop was greater, from 78,000 in 2000 to 15,000 in 2012, then rising again (to almost 30,000) in the last two years under examination. Between 2011 and 2015, net migration, calculated as the difference between recorded inflows and outflows, proved negative in Spain, Greece and Portugal. Only in Italy has it continued to be positive, even though the rate fell progressively following 2007–2008 until 2015.

The year 2008, that is, the point at which the financial crisis fully manifested itself, starting from the USA and affecting the whole world and striking the real economy with an extraordinarily intense and long-lasting impact, seems to represent the perfect watershed between two different phases in the international

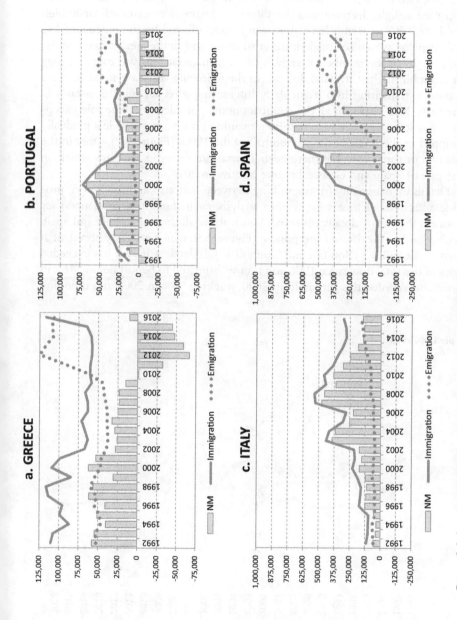

Figure 9.1 Immigration, emigration and net migration (NM) in Greece, Portugal, Italy and Spain, 1992–2016 (absolute values)

migration concerning the southern EU countries. Indeed, during the 1990s and early 2000s, the net migration rate in Italy was tendentially on the rise; after the first two to three years of the last decade, the rates in Greece and Portugal recorded a slight decrease, and the values for Spain were extraordinarily high until 2007. These trends have also been largely affected by the process of EU enlargement, which has made it easier to move within the area of free circulation (in 2007, the number of arrivals of Romanian citizens was extraordinary in Spain but highest in Italy). Instead, in the following years, a general decrease was seen, translating into particularly intense negative net migration rates in the years 2012–2013 for all the countries under consideration. The sole exception was Italy, whose values, despite remaining positive, nevertheless gradually dropped to the levels of the second half of the 1990s (Figure 9.2). Only in the last two or three years has there been a certain recovery in the rates which, in the case of Spain and Greece, became positive in 2016.

Details by nationality (distinguishing between nationals and foreigners) provide additional elements for further analysis, even though in substance they confirm the trends already observed. This is above all the case in Italy and Spain with regard to the foreign component (Figure 9.3), which is clearly prevalent at least in the inflows (Bonifazi and Conti 2017). Indeed, in Italy it has exceeded 80% of the total flow since 1996 and is now estimated to be just below 90%; in Spain, it exceeded this threshold in 2000, reaching 96% in 2007 and dropping

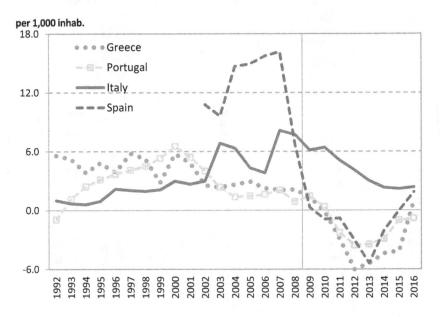

Figure 9.2 Net migration rates in Greece, Portugal, Italy and Spain, 1992–2016 (annual average values per 1,000 inhabitants)

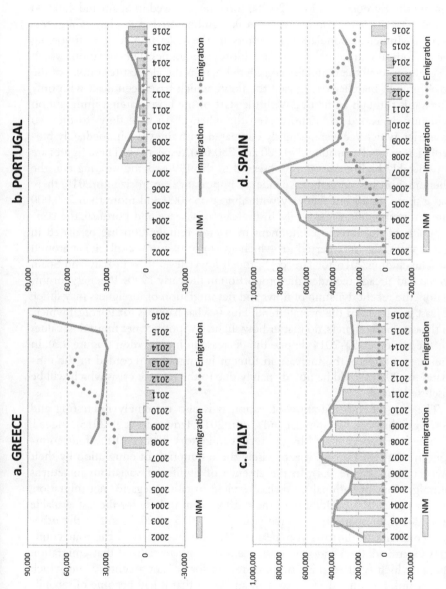

Figure 9.3 Immigration, emigration and net migration (NM) of foreign citizens in Greece, Portugal, Italy and Spain, 2002–2016 (absolute values)

to 85% in the last two years. However, it appears evident that the overall immigration trends recorded in the past 25 years reflect the evolution in time of the inflow of foreign nationals. In 2007, the year that Romania and Bulgaria entered the European Union, 920,000 foreigners arrived in Spain and 490,000 in Italy. For the latter country, some peaks can be noted in foreigners' registration in Municipal Population Registers in the years immediately following the periodical extraordinary regularization programmes. This situation, which is common to all the countries considered here, is the clearest testimony of the governments' inability to regulate the flows, which have been dealt with only afterwards through amnesties. With the start of the crisis, foreign immigration evidently decreased in intensity, even though in 2015 total flows to the two countries, which recovered slightly compared with the years immediately preceding, remained at around 290,000 and 250,000, respectively. These figures are considerably higher than those observed in the 1990s, demonstrating that the phenomenon has nevertheless made an important leap in size. In 2016, there was a more significant recovery with almost 355,000 and more than 260,000 foreign immigrants, respectively. In the case of Greece and Portugal, the contribution of the foreign component to overall immigration has oscillated in recent years (the only period for which any information is available) at around 50% (excluding 2016 for Greece), a much lower level than in Italy and Spain which had already recorded this proportion in the early 1990s. Precisely for this reason, the recent dynamic of flows and net migration of foreigners may differ, at least in part, from the overall trend. This is what happens for Portugal which, in the case of foreigners, no matter how slight, saw positive net migration values for the period 2010–2014 despite the decrease in immigration (Figure 9.3). In the case of Greece, the increase in foreign immigration recorded in the estimates for 2016 should be noted, mainly due to the refugee crisis which will be discussed ahead.

The case of the migration of nationals is also extremely interesting and deserves a brief aside (Bonifazi and Conti 2017; Izquierdo et al. 2015). Indeed, if there is an aspect shared by the recent migratory history of the four countries in southern Europe, it is precisely the resumption of emigration by their own citizens (Figure 9.4). In the absence of significant variations in returns (immigrations of nationals), this has resulted in rising negative net migration, at least since 2010, peaking with the outflow seen in Italy for the last available year (2016), in Spain in the three years from 2013 to 2015, and in the other two countries in the two-year period 2012–2013. Hence, in the four countries examined, the economic crisis seems to have revitalized that emigration abroad which typified this European region for at least a century and which had shrunk for some decades to such an extent that it had become of secondary importance compared with foreign immigration, prevalently becoming the stuff of memories or a past legacy. Though in the receiving countries, the net inflow of foreigners is known to often combine with a net outflow of citizens (Bonifazi and Strozza 2002; Pugliese 2002; Strozza 2010), this new emigration

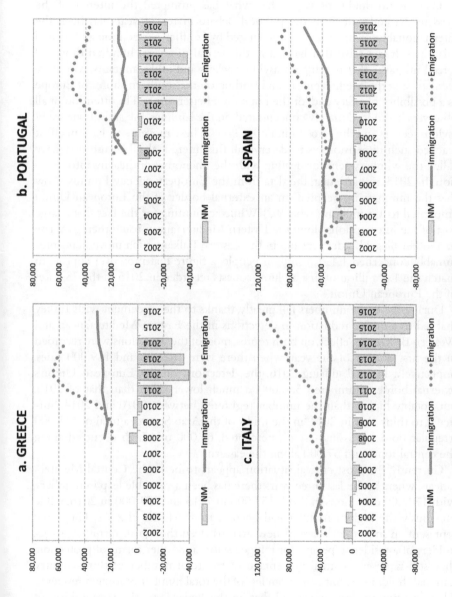

Figure 9.4 Immigration, emigration and net migration (NM) of nationals in Greece, Portugal, Italy and Spain, 2002–2016 (absolute values)

abroad of southern Europeans certainly represents a novelty and, in some ways, a break from the previous situation of economic crisis from 2008. What is more, it is a transformation capable of attracting the attention of the public opinion.

There is no doubt, however, that what has prompted the interest of the mass media and enlivened the political debate in recent years has been the international humanitarian crisis, generated by conflict, persecution and natural calamities. It is a crisis that has led to the arrival of several hundred thousand forced migrants, that is, refugees, asylum seekers and other migrants, who have seen crossing the Mediterranean and landing on the southern shores of Europe as a possibility of safety and/or the hope for a better future. The attention of all observers has indeed mainly concentrated on the landings, the arrivals via sea of asylum seekers and the forced migratory flows. These movements have in effect reached such dimensions as to deserve all this interest, also because they have called the whole system for dealing with the phenomenon heavily into question. In 2015, in particular, the data from the European agency Frontex show that the numbers intercepted on an external border of the European Union amounted to 1.8 million (Table 9.2). While accounting for the fact that a large part of the interceptions along the Eastern Mediterranean route then gave rise to another illegal border crossing in the Eastern Balkans, such movements presumably concerned 1.1–1.3 million people, a figure that moreover appears to match the 1.3 million of first asylum requests recorded in 2015 in the 28 states of the European Union.

During 2016, the numbers fell greatly, thanks to the agreement with Turkey that led to a drastic reduction in detections in the Eastern Mediterranean and Western Balkans. In effect, on both routes, most of the detections were recorded in the first quarter of the year, when there were 162,000 and 119,000 cases, respectively. In total, during 2016, the detections on the European Union's external borders numbered 556,000, a much lower value than that of 2015, but notably higher than the number registered between 2010 and 2014. Suffice it to think that in 2011, in the midst of the Arab Spring, a total of 141,000 irregular border crossings were intercepted, 64,000 of which occurred along the central route and 57,000 along the eastern.

Currently, the most critical situation appears to be in the Central Mediterranean, where in the last three years there has been a veritable leap in numbers, with 170,000 detections in 2014, 157,000 in 2015 and 181,000 in 2016, while previously the highest number had been at most 64,000 in 2011. They now represent an important share of new arrivals, even though in terms of stocks, holders of a residence permit for refugee status and other forms of protection, they still represent a small percentage of the total number of third-country nationals holding permits, and even less of the total number of foreign residents. Then, it must also be considered that, in the Italian case, the composition of the flow changes too, with an important share attributable to African countries. Suffice it to think that among the top three nationalities of arrivals in Italy in 2016 we find Nigerians (37,500), Eritreans (20,700) and Guineans (13,500),

Table 9.2 Number of detections of illegal border crossings in the European Union, 2010–2016 (absolute values)

Routes of illegal entries	2010	2011	2012	2013	2014	2015	2016
Central Mediterranean (Italy, Malta)	4,450	64,261	15,151	45,298	170,664	153,946	181,419
Eastern Mediterranean (Greece, Cyprus, Bulgaria)	55,688	57,025	37,224	24,799	50,834	885,386	182,277
Western Balkans	2,371	4,658	6,391	19,951	43,357	764,038	130,261
From Albania to Greece	35,297	5,269	5,502	8,728	8,841	8,932	50,121
Western Mediterranean (Spain)	5,003	8,448	6,397	6,838	7,272	7,164	10,231
Eastern Border (Russia, Ukraine, Belarus)	1,052	1,049	1,597	1,316	1,275	1,920	1,349
Black Sea	0	0	1	148	433	68	0
Western Africa (Canary Islands)	196	340	174	283	276	874	671
Others	3	1	0	4	10	9	0
Total	**104,060**	**141,051**	**72,437**	**107,365**	**282,962**	**1,822,337**	**556,329**

Source: Frontex (2016) and data from the Frontex site

while along the eastern route by far the most numerous are Syrians (84,600), Afghans (43,100) and Iraqis (28,000). In the first months of application, the agreement between the European Union and Turkey appears to have achieved its aim. However, it seems unlikely to be a definitive solution to a problem in which the whole system for dealing with forced migrations will require an overhaul by the European Union once the Dublin Regulation falls out of use.

Hence, not only have the dimensions of foreign immigration changed, but in the years of the economic crisis, regular flows for work reasons have also dropped. Indeed, the use of the legal channels for the work recruitment was largely reduced, as happened in Italy with the '*decreti flussi*' (decrees on migratory flows). In turn, these have been greatly surpassed in numbers by arrivals for family reunification and, in some cases (in Italy and Greece), also by the so-called forced migrations of refugees and asylum seekers.

Evolution of the size and characteristics of the foreign presence

In the last 25 years, there has been a truly remarkable increase in the numbers of resident foreigners in the four countries of southern Europe, in three out of four cases representing almost 10% of the total population (Table 9.3). On the basis of the data from the censuses carried out around 1991, foreigners living on a long-term basis in the four nations in question totalled fewer than

Table 9.3 Foreign population resident in Greece, Italy, Portugal and Spain, 1991–2016 (absolute values in thousands, percentage of the total number of residents and percentage annual average rate of variation)

Year/Period	Greece	Italy	Portugal	Spain
	Absolute values (in thousands)			
1991	353	356	107	353
2001	762	1.335	233	1.572
2009	928	3.570	440	5.387
2016	798	5.026	389	4.418
	% of the total number of residents			
1991	1.6	0.6	1.1	0.9
2001	7.0	2.3	2.2	3.8
2009	8.4	6.1	4.2	11.6
2016	7.4	8.3	3.8	9.5
	Annual average rate of variation (%)			
1992–2001	7.7	13.2	7.8	14.9
2002–2008	2.8	14.1	9.1	17.6
2009–2015	−2.1	4.9	−1.8	−2.8

Source: Elaboration of Eurostat data and national statistics

1,200,000 which, accounting for census underestimates the number of the foreigners residing in these countries, can be rounded up to around 1,500,000 at most.[2] The numbers censused in Greece, Italy and Spain were similar (around 350,000 people in each country), with a much lower figure in Portugal (just over 100,000). At the time, foreigners still accounted for a negligible share of the resident population, with the highest impact recorded in Greece remaining below 2%.

The intensification of arrivals during the 1990s led to a significant increase in the foreign population counted in the round of censuses in 2001. In all, they amounted to almost 4 million, over three times the number found ten years earlier. Spain accounted for almost 1.6 million (less than 4% of residents), Italy over 1.3 million (2.3%), Greece 760,000 (7%) and Portugal 230,000 (2.2%). The first two countries show the highest percentage variation: almost 15% and just over 13% on average a year, respectively. The Hellenic peninsula nevertheless remained the area with the highest incidence of foreigners, mainly due to the mass emigration observed from nearby Albania.

It is, however, in the early years of the new millennium that the greatest incoming flows were recorded on the Iberian and Italian peninsulas. As a consequence, at the beginning of 2009, that is, more or less at the start of the economic crisis, the figures for foreign citizens resident in the four countries leapt to over 10 million, two and a half times the number counted in the 2001 census and almost nine times more than revealed by the previous census. The highest figure was recorded in Spain, with almost 5.4 million foreigners registered with the *Padrón Municipal*, equal to just under 12% of the resident population. Italy followed with under 3.6 million non-Italian citizens resident in the country according to the estimates drawn up by ISTAT (2015) in the statistical reconstruction of the population. It is a share that exceeded 6% of the total number of people living on a long-term basis in Italy, an incidence that is lower than what was seen in Greece where the foreigners numbered just under 900,000 but accounted for 8.4% of the population. After Spain and Italy, the country that experienced the most intense relative growth in people of foreign nationality is Portugal which, owing to the favourable economic situation at the beginning of the millennium, saw the population without a Portuguese passport double, reaching 440,000, with a demographic impact that nevertheless remained relatively low (just 4.2%).

The intense and lengthy economic slump, generated by the US financial crisis, also appeared as a watershed for international migrations, marking the passage between two successive historical phases. For the countries in southern Europe, it meant the end of the intense and predominant immigration for work reasons, a growth in the importance of other types of migration and the emergence of a growing return flow (see previous section). In three of the four countries considered, the stock of resident foreigners has shrunk in the last seven years owing to net emigration, but also owing to many foreigners gaining citizenship of the host country. Numbers of foreigners resident in Spain have gone down by almost 1 million, weighing in at the beginning of 2016 at just above 4.4 million (less than 10% of the population), a lower figure than that recorded by the Italian Municipal Population Registers, where over 5 million foreigners, 8.3% of the residents in Italy, are registered. Therefore, in the more recent period, Italy has overtaken Spain, at least as far as foreigners in the population registers of the two countries are concerned. Italy is the only case in which the resident foreign population has continued to grow, even during the recession, but at a much lower rate compared with the previous two periods (4.9% against 13.2% in 1992–2001 and 14.1% in 2002–2008). In Greece and Portugal, the reduction in the number of foreigners has been less intense (respectively −2.1% and −1.8% on average per year) than in Spain (−2.8%), but nonetheless significant. At the most recent date, foreign residents on the Hellenic peninsula had fallen below 800,000 and in Portugal to below 400,000, with a consequent decrease in their impact on the total population (from 8.4% to 7.4% and from 4.2% to 3.8%, respectively), which in the case of Greece dropped to lower than the figure for Italy (8.3%). During the economic crisis, the countries of southern Europe, which in the first decade of the new millennium had become the main European pole of attraction for international migration (Strozza 2010; Strozza and De Santis 2017b), lost a large part of their appeal.

At the same time, the number of naturalizations have been assuming growing importance: the number of foreigners who with time achieve the minimum conditions required to apply increases, even though the national legislation substantially remains restrictive. In the period 2009–2015, there were almost 960,000 naturalizations in Spain, mainly by Latin Americans (almost two thirds of the total), with particularly high figures in the two-year period 2013–2014 (430,000). In Italy, there have been over 650,000 new Italians, with an extraordinary growth in the last three years (in the period from 2013 to 2015 almost 410,000, of which just under 180,000 in 2015). In Greece and Portugal, the numbers are obviously smaller: on the basis of the Eurostat data, almost 130,000 and over 155,000 naturalizations, respectively, were recorded in the period from 2009 to 2015. Among the countries in southern Europe, it is Portugal that has the highest naturalization rate, probably owing to the presence of a large share of foreigners originally from Brazil and the *Países Africanos de Língua Oficial Portuguesa* who, given the colonial connections, have an advantage in acquiring citizenship, as by law they have to meet fewer requirements. Without doubt, in the four countries considered, one of the significant novelties in the recent period is precisely the fact that the number of new citizens has become statistically relevant, leading to growth in the national population of those from a foreign background, which is generally difficult to survey because a combination of several identification criteria are needed (at least current citizenship with previous or birth citizenship).

If we are to limit our attention to the foreign population at the time of the survey, it is possible to examine its composition according to the main countries of citizenship, and its evolution in time, resulting from the migratory flows, births and deaths of foreigners and changes in citizenship taking place in the period between two successive counts. The data considered refer to three distinct surveys which cover approximately the last 15 years: the situation at the 2001 census is followed by the situations deducible from administrative data collections datable (more or less) to the beginning of the economic crisis and the most recent date (Table 9.4). In the case of Greece, the source containing the most information is the censuses. Hence, the data refer to the last two censuses and to an intermediate date with statistics available on stay permits.

A first sweeping glance shows that the most significant changes in composition by citizenship took place at the beginning of the new millennium, prior to the economic crisis. By way of example, it is to be noted that Romanians became the largest foreign group in Italy and Spain, Brazilians in Portugal, while Ukrainians also increased significantly in three of the four countries considered, as well as Chinese. On the one hand, this underlines the Europeanization of the migration flows that have affected the countries of southern Europe and, on the other, the globalization of the international migratory currents, to which this region has not proved immune. If we exclude Greece, where Albanians, who arrived above all in the 1990s, count for over half of the foreigners (together with Bulgarians and Romanians, they make up two thirds), in the other countries there is an evident mix of origins: in Spain, the first seven nationalities need to be considered to reach half of the residents, and in Italy and Portugal, the first five. While in the case of Spain, heterogeneity has increased over time, in the case of Italy, it has in part fallen, owing to the growing importance assumed by the Romanian community. In Spain, next in the rankings after Romanians and Moroccans (in both cases, counting just under 700,000 residents) are British and Italians (almost 300,000 and just under 200,000, respectively) and then Chinese and Ecuadorians (both groups counting over 150,000). Hence, we see the presence of immigrants from all of the continents, from the less developed regions but also from the richest nations in the world, even though a significant part of the Italians probably arrived from Argentina rather than Italy itself.

In Italy, Romanians are clearly the most numerous group (over 1,150,000, 23% of the foreign population), followed a long way behind by two historical communities, Albanians and Moroccans (just over and just under 450,000, above and below 9%, respectively), then Chinese and Ukrainians, groups which have grown so considerably throughout the period in question that they now exceed some nationalities whose immigration stretches back further (e.g. from the Philippines and Tunisia). In Portugal, Brazilians and Cape Verdeans, groups linked to the country's colonial past (as well as citizens of Angola, Guinea-Bissau and São Tomé and Príncipe) are followed in the classification by Ukrainians and Romanians, two nationalities that focus attention on the importance of East–West migration on the European continent, as is even more evident in the case of the foreign presence in Greece and Italy. In the same way, colonial links emerge in Spain when looking through the classification, with significant

Table 9.4 First ten foreign citizenships in Greece, Italy, Portugal and Spain, 2001–2016 (absolute values in thousands, percentages by citizenship and gender)

First ten countries of citizenship	Greece A.v. (thousand)	% by citi.	% women	First ten countries of citizenship	Italy A.v. (thousand)	% by citi.	% women	First ten countries of citizenship	Portugal A.v. (thousand)	% by citi.	% women	First ten countries of citizenship	Spain A.v. (thousand)	% by citi.	% women
2001 Census				**2001 Census**				**2001 Census**				**2001 Population Registers (Padrón)**			
Albania	438.0	57.5	41.3	Morocco	180.1	13.5	39.8	Angola	37.0	15.9	49.1	Morocco	307.5	15.5	32.9
Bulgaria	35.1	4.6	60.4	Albania	173.1	13.0	43.7	Cape Verde	33.1	14.2	48.7	Ecuador	259.5	13.1	50.7
Georgia	22.9	3.0	57.0	Romania	74.9	5.6	53.5	Brazil	31.9	13.7	46.8	Colombia	191.0	9.7	57.6
Romania	22.0	2.9	43.4	Philippines	54.0	4.0	61.1	Guinea-Bissau	15.8	6.8	37.3	UK	128.1	6.5	50.6
USA	18.1	2.4	51.5	Former Yug.	49.3	3.7	46.8	France	15.4	6.6	54.1	Germany	113.8	5.8	50.3
Russia	17.5	2.3	62.7	Tunisia	47.7	3.6	35.1	Ukraine	10.8	4.6	18.6	Romania	67.3	3.4	39.0
Cyprus	17.4	2.3	52.5	China	46.9	3.5	48.5	Spain	9.0	3.9	55.8	France	59.8	3.0	52.6
Ukraine	13.6	1.8	75.5	Germany	35.1	2.6	64.7	São Tomé	8.5	3.7	54.0	Argentina	56.7	2.9	49.5
UK	13.2	1.7	60.1	Senegal	31.2	2.3	15.5	Germany	8.4	3.6	49.0	Portugal	52.1	2.6	46.3
Poland	12.8	1.7	54.2	Peru	29.5	2.2	62.7	UK	8.2	3.5	49.0	Italy	46.2	2.3	39.2
2005 Permits to Stay				**2009 Population Registers (Anagrafe)**				**2009 Estimated Residents**				**2009 Population Registers (Padrón)**			
Albania	481.7	69.6	31.4	Romania	658.8	19.4	54.3	Brazil	107.0	24.3	53.8	Romania	764.4	14.2	46.5
Bulgaria	44.0	6.4	65.2	Albania	422.1	12.4	45.9	Ukraine	52.5	11.9	42.7	Morocco	727.2	13.5	37.8
Romania	25.4	3.7	47.2	Morocco	368.6	10.8	43.6	Cape Verde	51.4	11.7	52.1	Ecuador	420.3	7.8	50.6
Ukraine	19.8	2.9	81.7	China	154.1	4.5	48.1	Romania	27.8	6.3	42.3	UK	312.6	5.8	49.2
Pakistan	15.8	2.3	1.2	Ukraine	134.4	3.9	79.6	Angola	27.6	6.3	50.4	Colombia	296.8	5.5	54.8

2011 Census				2016 Population Registers (Anagrafe)				2016 Estimated Residents				2016 Population Registers (Padrón)			
Russia	13.6	2.0	82.6	Philippines	105.4	3.1	57.2	Guinea-Bissau	24.4	5.5	38.8	Bolivia	226.6	4.2	56.9
Georgia	13.3	1.9	67.4	India	85.7	2.5	42.0	Moldova	21.1	4.8	42.5	Italy	163.5	3.0	41.1
India	10.0	1.5	9.0	Moldova	85.3	2.5	65.7	UK	15.4	3.5	48.6	Germany	157.3	2.9	49.7
Moldova	9.9	1.4	71.3	Tunisia	79.2	2.3	38.6	China	13.3	3.0	46.8	Bulgaria	152.5	2.8	45.9
Egypt	9.5	1.4	12.3	Poland	77.9	2.3	72.7	São Tomé	11.7	2.7	54.6	China	150	2.8	46.1

2011 Census				2016 Population Registers (Anagrafe)				2016 Estimated Residents				2016 Population Registers (Padrón)			
Albania	480.9	53.1	46.9	Romania	1,151.4	22.9	57.2	Brazil	82.6	21.2	61.6	Romania	695.1	15.7	50.0
Bulgaria	75.9	8.4	62.2	Albania	467.7	9.3	48.4	Cape Verde	38.7	9.9	53.4	Morocco	680.5	15.4	45.2
Romania	46.5	5.1	54.9	Morocco	437.5	8.7	46.0	Ukraine	35.8	9.2	51.3	UK	296.6	6.7	49.6
Pakistan	34.2	3.8	4.3	China	271.3	5.4	49.4	Romania	30.5	7.9	45.2	Italy	191.6	4.3	42.8
Georgia	27.4	3.0	66.3	Ukraine	230.7	4.6	78.8	China	21.4	5.5	49.2	China	172.2	3.9	49.7
Ukraine	17.0	1.9	78.8	Philippines	165.9	3.3	56.9	Angola	18.2	4.7	53.5	Ecuador	159	3.6	47.6
UK	15.4	1.7	57.6	India	150.5	3.0	40.3	UK	17.2	4.4	47.5	Germany	142.1	3.2	50.5
Cyprus	14.4	1.6	49.5	Moldova	142.3	2.8	66.5	Guinea-Bissau	17.1	4.4	45.9	Colombia	135.9	3.1	55.9
Poland	14.1	1.6	61.7	Bangladesh	118.8	2.4	29.2	Spain	10.0	2.6	49.8	Bulgaria	130.5	3.0	49.0
Russia	13.8	1.5	79.9	Egypt	109.9	2.2	31.5	São Tomé	9.6	2.5	55.1	Portugal	101.8	2.3	40.1

Source: Elaboration of Eurostat data and national statistics

numbers of foreigners originating from the Latin American countries. Nevertheless, at the most recent date, their numbers are much lower than in the past, above all due to the numerous acquisitions of Spanish citizenship seen in recent years (between 2008 and 2015 almost 215,000 Ecuadorians, over 150,000 Colombians, 75,000 Peruvians, just under 70,000 Bolivians and around 40,000 Argentinians became Spanish).

The complexity of the presence of immigrants and persons of immigrant origin hence lies in both the wide range of countries of origin and the different degrees of (progressive) belonging to the adopted countries. In the countries of southern Europe too, a numerically large group of new citizens, immigrants and their descendants who have (acquired) the passport of the country where they live is coming into being. This group probably has a different structure by country of origin from that of the foreign population since those who arrived longer ago, with long-term plans and, in the case of the countries on the Iberian Peninsula, belonging to the former colonies, are probably over-represented.

Gender composition is just one of the elements that at times differentiates the various immigrant communities. In general, the North Africans and citizens of the Indian subcontinent are mainly male, and the East Europeans and Latin Americans mainly female. In terms of the degree of the imbalance and, in some cases, its direction, there are specific characteristics for the single nationalities of these geographical areas. However, it must be noted that in time, (a) the imbalances within the single nationalities have progressively reduced, a likely signal of the stabilization process of the immigrant communities; and (b) the differences between the various nationalities within the same host country are still notable only in Italy and Greece.

These two countries are also those which, being more involved in the forced migrations of recent years, have recently been affected by a growing presence of refugees, asylum seekers and other (irregular) immigrants requesting aid from emergency reception centres. This is an additional aspect in the complexity and intricacy of a multifaceted migration phenomenon which shows various elements of similarity, but today, perhaps more than in the past, also differences between the four countries in southern Europe.

Evolution of foreign employment

The situation of foreigners in the labour market has also changed. At the start of the economic crisis, owing to the periodical extraordinary amnesties adopted above all by Italy and Spain, the foreigners resident in the four countries of southern Europe counted a total of over 10 million. The population of working age (ages 15–64) approached 7.7 million and the employed counted over 5 million, according to Eurostat estimates based on the European Union Labour Force Survey. In the four countries considered, the employment rate among foreigners (between 65% and 73% of the population ages 15–64) was higher than in the European states with a longer tradition of immigration and was always higher than that of their native citizens (from one to nine percentage points more), with levels of unemployment (in three cases out of four around 10%) that were more or less in line with those estimated for the latter, with the only exception of Spain where the rate proved to be seven percentage points higher. In some ways, this situation reflected the stage of immigration, with a young foreign population who, despite the growing presence of families, continued to feature a preponderant working component, given that employment continued to be the formal and/or substantial condition for permanence in the country and the success of their migratory projects. With the economic crisis, the picture changed radically, with the worst labour market indicators recorded for the two-year period 2012–2013.

In 2013, the average number of foreigners employed in the four countries decreased by over 600,000 compared with 2008, with a particularly large decrease in absolute terms in Spain (about 900,000 units less) and in relative terms in Portugal (the number of foreigners employed has halved) (Table 9.5). Italy is the only one of the four countries to record a growth in foreign employment (almost 500,000 more units) which partly offset the decrease in employment of Italian citizens (−1.4 million), such that in the considered period of five years the loss of jobs is under 1 million. In the following three years, there was a slight recovery in employment rates in all four countries considered. This recovery concerns both nationals and foreigners, indiscriminately for men and women (Figure 9.5). Foreign women residing in Italy are the only exception: they have not experienced a marked decrease in the employment rate in the years of the crisis, and therefore do not show a recovery in the last three years. The general improvement in the labour market situation is confirmed by the reduction in the unemployment rate which is generalized for nationals and foreigners, as well as for men and women (Figure 9.6). The situation of the last year (2016) appears to be better than that of 2013 but remains significantly worse than that recorded at the beginning of the economic crisis (2008).

In 2016, nearing the end of the long and intense crisis, the employment rates of foreigners dropped sharply (from eight to 17 percentage points less compared with the rates recorded in 2008, with figures between 51% and 61%) and now they are lower than those estimated for foreigners resident in other European states of the 'old' EU-15 and in line with or lower than the figures for nationals. At the same time, unemployment has reached noteworthy levels (over 16% in Italy, but more than 30% in Greece and Spain) with clearly higher values (from five to 10 percentage points) compared to those, which are also growing, of the people with citizenship of the country where they reside.

Compared with 2013, the number of foreigners employed in the four countries increased by just over 200,000, a growth mainly attributable to residents in Italy. It should be remembered, however, that especially in the case of Spain it is not possible to overlook the fact that several hundred thousand foreigners have acquired Spanish citizenship. According to statistics released by the Spanish National Institute of Statistics coming from the labour force survey, between

Table 9.5 People in employment distinguished by citizenship and gender. Greece, Italy, Portugal and Spain, 2008, 2013 and 2016. Annual average values in thousands and changes in thousands.

COUNTRY/	Nationals			Foreigners		
Year or Period	Men	Women	Total	Men	Women	Total
GREECE	Absolute values (in thousands)					
2008	2,473	1,672	4,145	248	128	376
2013	1,878	1,329	3,207	149	102	251
2016	1,954	1,430	3,384	137	88	226
	Absolute changes (in thousands)					
2008–2013	−595	−343	−938	−100	−25	−125
2013–2016	76	101	178	−11	−14	−25
2008–2016	−519	−242	−761	−111	−39	−150
ITALY	Absolute values (in thousands)					
2008	12,525	8,491	21,016	988	695	1,683
2013	11,411	8,177	19,587	1,173	995	2,168
2016	11,535	8,328	19,863	1,318	1,060	2,378
	Absolute changes (in thousands)					
2008–2013	−1,115	−314	−1,429	185	300	485
2013–2016	124	152	276	145	65	210
2008–2016	−991	−163	−1,153	330	366	696
PORTUGAL	Absolute values (in thousands)					
2008	2,427	2,138	4,565	116	105	221
2013	2,061	1,984	4,045	55	58	113
2016	2,162	2,104	4,266	48	57	105
	Absolute changes (in thousands)					
2008–2013	−366	−155	−520	−60	−47	−108
2013–2016	101	121	222	−7	−1	−8
2008–2016	−265	−34	−299	−68	−48	−116
SPAIN	Absolute values (in thousands)					
2008	10,128	7,360	17,488	1,580	1,249	2,828
2013	8,270	6,813	15,083	967	952	1,919
2016	8,855	7,359	16,214	1,055	914	1,969
	Absolute changes (in thousands)					
2008–2013	−1,858	−547	−2,405	−613	−297	−910
2013–2016	585	546	1,131	88	−38	50
2008–2016	−1,273	−1	−1,274	−525	−335	−860

Source: Elaborations of Eurostat data

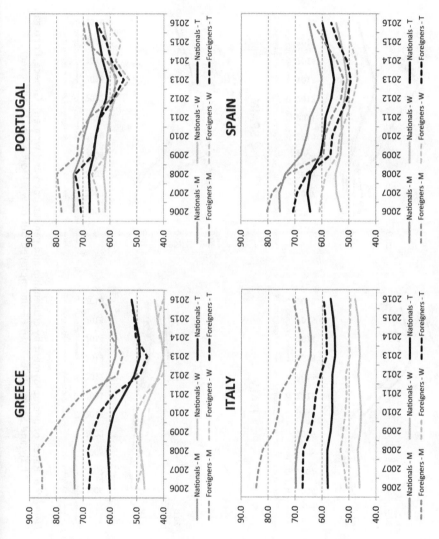

Figure 9.5 Rates of employment by citizenship and gender (men and women). Greece, Portugal, Italy and Spain, 2006–2016 (% employed out of the population ages 15–64)

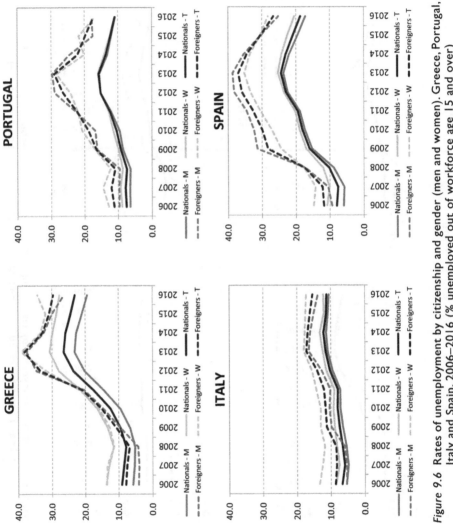

Figure 9.6 Rates of unemployment by citizenship and gender (men and women). Greece, Portugal, Italy and Spain, 2006–2016 (% unemployed out of workforce age 15 and over)

2013 and 2016 foreign employment increased by only 50,000 units but the number of employed with dual citizenship has grown by almost 220,000 cases (increasing from less than 300,000 to over 500,000 employed). Foreign workers are now a structural component of the national labour markets of southern European countries, even if they have suffered the economic crisis more significantly than the national labour force. The employment rate of foreigners has undoubtedly decreased considerably, so that high work participation can no longer be considered a typical characteristic of the four countries of Southern Europe in comparison with the other Western European reception countries. At the same time, not only unemployment but also underemployment increased (for Italy, see Strozza and De Santis 2017a) and probably precarious employment and/or irregular economy could instead represent a further characterization (or at least a confirmation) of the immigration model of the countries of Southern Europe. Moreover, modes and sectors of employment often vary from one foreign nationality to another and also the economic crisis has produced extremely different effects among the various foreign nationalities that make up the universe of the foreign population (Strozza and De Santis 2017a).

Towards a new conceptual and operative picture?

In the second half of the 1990s and the early years of the new millennium, the countries of southern Europe, which in the past had traditionally been areas of emigration, became the main European pole of attraction for international migratory flows. Spain and Italy climbed up the European rankings to arrive, behind Germany, together with the United Kingdom in the top places for the number of foreigners resident in their territory. However, with the economic crisis important new elements emerged: (a) the migration flows of foreigners decreased and in some cases the net migration became negative, owing to the prevalence of departures over arrivals; (b) owing both to armed conflicts and politico-institutional crises in countries of Africa and the Middle East and their geographical position in the Mediterranean, some of these countries (Greece and Italy), for the first time in their history, became the prime destination of immense flows of refugees and asylum seekers; (c) the emigration of nationals grew in the years of the most intense economic crisis, with negative net migration which took a long time to regain the levels observed in the previous years; (d) at the same time, and perhaps also as a consequence of the economic crisis, there was an increase in the acquisitions of citizenship by those immigrants present in the country for longer as well as by those from the former colonies who had fewer difficulties in obtaining a passport from their country of adoption. Employment rates decreased due to not only a greater presence of family members, but also the greater difficulties in finding work, as shown by the growth in unemployment rates. The impact of economic crisis on labour market performances of immigrants in the four countries deserves more attention than it was possible to reserve to the issue in a work devoted to the analysis of the evolution of migratory flows. The different impacts of the crisis among nationals and foreigners, the difference between countries and regions, the growth of precariousness and a probably larger involvement in informal or irregular economy are contributing to redefine the characteristics of immigration in this part of the EU.

All these changes, probably ascribable not only to the economic crisis but also to the evolution of the migration flows (e.g. the importance assumed by family reunification and asylum seekers) and the foreign population itself (e.g. acquisitions of citizenship), call for renewed reflection on what has been defined the southern Europe migratory model (King and Rybaczuk 1993; King et al. 1997; King 2000; de Filippo and Carchedi 1999; Ribas-Mateos 2004; Peixoto et al. 2012), as well as careful reconsideration of immigration policies and, above all, policies for immigrants in light of the international context and changes underway in the populations and societies of the four Mediterranean countries.

Notes

1 In this chapter, we use the criterion of citizenship to distinguish between nationals and foreigners.
2 This evaluation does not take into account the non-resident component, both regular and irregular. For an assessment of the irregular foreign presence, which was particularly large for those years, refer to the existing literature (Schoorl et al. 1996; Huntoon 1998; Strozza 2004). For more recent evaluations, see the results of the CLANDESTINO project.

References

Alessandrini, P., Bettin, G., and Pepe, M., 2013. *Viaggio nell'economia*. Bologna: Il Mulino.

Arango, J., and Finotelli, C., 2010. *Past and Future Challenges of a Southern European Migration Regime: The Spanish Case*, IDEA Working Papers, 8.

Baldwin-Edwards, M., 2012. The Southern European 'model of immigration'. A sceptical view. *In*: M. Okólski, ed. *European Immigrations: Trends, Structures and Policy Implications*. Amsterdam: Amsterdam University Press, 149–157.

Bilsborrow, R.E., Hugo, G., Oberai, A.S., and Zlotnik, H., 1997. *International Migration Statistics: Guidelines for Improving Data Collection Systems*. Geneva: International Labor Office.

Bonifazi, C., and Conti, C., 2017. La transizione dell'Italia da paese di emigrazione a paese d'immigrazione. *In*: S. Strozza and G. De Santis, eds. *Rapporto sulla popolazione. Le molte facce della presenza straniera in Italia*. Bologna: Il Mulino, 29–60.

Bonifazi, C., and Strozza, S., 2002. International Migration in Europe in the Last Fifty Years. *In*: C. Bonifazi and G. Gesano, eds. *Contributions to International Migration Studies*. Rome: Irp-Cnr, 33–105.

Bonifazi, C., and Strozza, S., 2006. Conceptual Framework and Data Collection in International Migration. *In*: G. Caselli, J. Vallin and G. Wunsch, eds. *Demography: Analysis and Synthesis. A Treatise in Population, Volume IV*, USA: Elsevier Inc., 537–554.

de Filippo, E., and Carchedi, F., 1999. I mercati del lavoro e la collocazione degli immigrati. Il modello mediterraneo. *In*: F. Carchedi, ed. *La risorsa inaspettata. Lavoro e formazione degli immigrati nell'Europa mediterranea*. Rome: Ediesse, 19–35.

FRONTEX, 2016. *Risk Analysis for 2016.* Available at https://frontex.europa.eu/assets/Publications/Risk_Analysis/Annula_Risk_Analysis_2016.pdf

Huntoon, L., 1998. Immigration to Spain: Implication for a Unified European Union Immigration Policy. *International Migration Review,* 32 (2), 423–450.

ISTAT, 2015. *Ricostruzione statistica delle serie regionali di popolazione del periodo1/1/2002–1/1/2014.* Explanatory note, Rome, 14 January.

Izquierdo, M., Jimeno, J.F., and Lacuesta, A., 2015: *Spain: From Immigration to Emigration?* Documentos de Trabajo, 1503. Madrid: Banco de España.

King, R., 2000. Southern Europe in the Changing Global Map of Migration. *In*: R. King, G. Lazaridis, and C. Tsardanidis, eds. *Eldorado or Fortress? Migration in Southern Europe.* London: Macmillan, 1–26.

King, R., and Rybaczuk, K., 1993. Southern Europe and the International Division of Labour: From Mass Migration to Mass Immigration. *In*: R. King, ed. *The New Geography of European Migrations.* London: Belhaven Press, 175–206.

King, R., Fielding, A., and Black, R., 1997. The International Migration Turnaround in Southern Europe. *In*: R. King and R. Black, eds. *Southern Europe and the New Immigrations.* Brighton: Sussex Academic Press, 1–25.

Kraler, A., Reichel, D., and Entzinger, H., 2015. Migration Statistics in Europe: A Core Component of Governance and Population Research. *In*: P. Scholten, H. Entzinger, R. Penninx, and S. Verbeek, eds. *Integrating Immigrants in Europe: Research-Policy Dialogues.* London: Springer, 39–58.

Martin, P., 2009. *The Recession and Migration: Alternative Scenarios.* International Migration Institute Working Papers 13, Oxford.

Peixoto, J., Arango, J., Bonifazi, C., Finotelli, C., Sabino, C., Strozza, S., and Triandafyllidou, A., 2012. Immigrants, Markets and Policies in Southern Europe: The Making of an Immigration Model? *In*: M. Okólski, ed. *European Immigrations: Trends, Structures and Policy Implications.* Amsterdam: Amsterdam University Press, 107–146.

Pugliese, E., 2002. *L'Italia tra migrazioni internazionali e migrazioni interne.* Bologna: Il Mulino.

Ribas-Mateos, N., 2004. How Can We Understand Immigration in Southern Europe? *Journal of Ethnic and Migration Studies,* 30 (6), 1045–1063.

Salt, J., Singleton, A., and Hogarth, J., 1994. *Europe's International Migrants: Data Sources, Patterns and Trends.* London: HMSO.

Schoorl, J., Brujin, B., Kuper, E. J., and Heering, L., 1996. Migration from African and Eastern Mediterranean Countries to Western Europe. Presented at the Mediterranean Conference on Population, Migration and Development, Council of Europe, Palma di Maiorca, October 15–17.

Strozza, S., 2004. Estimates of the Illegal Foreigners in Italy: A Review of the Literature. *International Migration Review,* 38 (1), 309–331.

Strozza, S., 2010. International Migration in Europe in the First Decade of the 21st Century. *Rivista Italiana di Economia Demografia e Statistica,* LXIV (3), 7–43.

Strozza, S., and De Santis, G., eds., 2017a. *Rapporto sulla popolazione. Le molte facce della presenza straniera in Italia.* Bologna: Il Mulino.

Strozza, S., and De Santis, G., 2017b. Migrazioni internazionali e popolazioni immigrate in Europa e in Italia. *In*: S. Strozza and G. De Santis, eds. *Rapporto sulla popolazione. Le molte facce della presenza straniera in Italia.* Bologna: Il Mulino, 7–28.

Triandafyllidou, A., 2014. Migrant Livelihoods During the Greek Crisis: Coping Strategies and the Decision to Return. *Mondi Migranti,* 3, 7–30.

United Nations, 1998. *Recommendations on Statistics of International Migration, Revision 1.* New York: United Nations/Nations Unies (Statistical Papers, Series M, 58, Rev. 1).

Chapter 10

Migration and trade in the Mediterranean

*Giorgia Giovannetti, Mauro Lanati
and Alessandra Venturini*

Introduction

In the last ten years, contrary to the general perception, international migration flows in Europe have been quite stable (around 5 million each year according to the European Commission 2017). What has dramatically changed is, however, the migrants' composition, with a sharp increase in migrants pushed by conflict and political instability. Even if the majority of refugees are hosted in neighbouring countries (Turkey, Pakistan, Lebanon, cf. www.unhcr.org/figures-at-a-glance.html), given its geographical proximity, Europe, between 2013 and 2016, received about 3 million asylum seekers (40% of the world total). This increase is shaping most of the current discussion on migration movements in the Mediterranean (UN, 2017).

While the asylum seekers phenomenon attracts considerable media attention and policy concerns as to whether and how national and European institutions should manage and share the cost of arrivals, its management is complicated by the mixed nature of the flows which combine real asylum seekers and a larger number of economic refugees escaping both poverty and insecurity. Short-run solutions seem unlikely to curb the outflows, and long-run solutions need to be found as well as a better understanding of the effect of migration in sending countries.

In what follows, we confine our analysis on the links between economic migration and trade, and in particular on trade triggered by highly educated emigrants.

Our societies are increasingly knowledge based, and are therefore ever more reliant on high-skilled workers. Hence, in many countries, investment in education seems to be the point of departure for a better future, with the possible drawback of a potential increase in highly educated migrants, termed the 'brain drain'.

In the last ten years, migration of the highly educated has increased. To be more precise, the share of the highly educated among migrants, measured as the share of tertiary educated on the total outflows, has increased against the share of the poorly educated. This is the result of two different forces: on the one hand, an increase in tertiary educated in the countries of origin where investment in education has produced a steady increase in access to university, including females; on the other, the increase in the demand for highly educated workers in the destination countries coupled with special policies such as the European Blue Card to make the move more appealing and rewarding for highly skilled migrants.

This increase in highly skilled migration, however, has rekindled the worries of a 'brain drain'. The idea is that the country of origin, by investing in state university education, is losing the return on its investment since the highly educated graduate may well search for a job abroad, thereby not providing any return to their country and reducing the potential human capital available at home (Docquier and Rapoport 2012). If this outflow of skilled migrants is very large, it can slow the growth of the origin country, also reducing its attractiveness to foreign direct investment.

Although the loss of human capital due to highly skilled outflows in the origin country can be measured, it is much more difficult to measure the net effect of the highly skilled outflows where short-run and long-run effects are deeply intertwined and difficult to separate. Highly skilled migrants send more remittances back home; frequently they return, transfer their knowledge to the origin country or may invest there. The relative facility of emigration for the highly skilled can also be an incentive for the native population to invest in higher education and in the case of limited emigration it can augment the average level of human capital of the country and produce a 'brain gain' (Stark et al. 1997).

Against this background, Fargues and Venturini (2015) show that, in the case of the Mediterranean, the size of highly skilled outflows is not an appropriate predictor to measure the effect of the highly skilled outflows on the economy and society of the origin country. Nor is the share of highly educated migrants on the total highly educated population, which instead could be the key driver of the economic and social development of the origin country. The most striking case is Lebanon where the share of tertiary educated migrants on the total educated Lebanese (at home and abroad) represents 40% of the total tertiary educated Lebanese (at home and abroad) – that is, the brain drain index – is. This number, as pointed out by Choghig Kasparian (2015), is very important even if compared with the already very high share of the highly educated in the country. It suggests a model of diffused and integrated highly educated diaspora, sending back large remittances and contributing with investment and technological transfer to increase the quality of life and well-being at home.

The opposite case is Morocco which, as pointed out by Mohamed Khachani (2015), has a smaller value of the brain drain index, but also a smaller share of those educated to tertiary level. Hence, the outflows of the highly educated are perceived as a major loss for investment in human capital of the resident population.

In evaluating the impact of highly skilled emigrants on the development of the country of origin, very little attention has been so far devoted to analyzing the impact of highly skilled migration on trade and productive integration with destination countries. This channel, however, can be very important since trade is a crucial driver of economic growth in developing countries. An exception is the article by Giovannetti and Lanati (2016) which analyses the link not only between emigration and exports from the origin country but also between skills level of the migrants and the quality level of the good exported.[1]

The Mediterranean represents an interesting case to analyze, not only because there has been a recent increase in highly educated migrants, but also because both migrants and exported goods tend to move mainly from Southern shore countries to European countries, especially Southern European. The existing analyses suggest an important role played by migrants in favouring the penetration of national goods abroad. According to Giovannetti and Lanati (2016), migrants promote international trade by reducing transaction costs and thus supporting exports. This effect is higher for those goods for which the country of origin has a comparative advantage. Hence, low-skilled emigrants trigger exports of low-tech goods, whereas highly skilled migrants are more likely to favour high-quality technological exports. Given the increase in average literacy and the improvement in education systems in Mediterranean countries, it is important to ascertain whether the growth in highly skilled migrants has resulted in an increase in exports of higher quality.

The objective of this chapter is to explore this channel of transmission. We consider both the preference channel – highly skilled migrants earning a higher wage prefer and consume higher-quality goods – and the distribution channel, highlighting that highly educated migrants can promote more easily than low-skilled migrants goods coming from their country of origin with more technological content. The former become high-tech ambassadors of goods from their home country.

The chapter puts together two strands of the literature: the one on the relationships between trade flows and migrant networks and the one measuring quality in trade. After a description of the data, we estimate the impact of different types of migrant networks (skilled versus unskilled) on trade flows, separating exports and imports according to their quality.

Trade and Migration

The existing literature

Since the seminal work of Gould (1994), numerous contributions have investigated the relationship between stocks of migration and bilateral trade flows. As Parsons and Winters (2014) pointed out, despite the heterogeneity of the countries considered and issues associated with identification (i.e. proving causation), the very fact that many studies characterized by different approaches, samples and techniques seem to point to a strong and positive role of migration facilitating international trade is, in the end, quite convincing and persuasive. For instance, to cite a few, Girma and Yu (2002) have found that a 10% rise in immigration from non-Commonwealth countries was associated with a 1.6% rise in UK exports.[2] Felbermayr and Jung (2009) have utilized newly available panel data on developing countries' diaspora to rich OECD nations in a theory-grounded gravity model, for the years 1990 and 2000, and found a robust, causal pro-trade effect. Most recently, Parsons and Vézina (2018) have conducted a natural experiment to identify causality from migration to trade – which is arguably one of the most convincing methods for addressing endogeneity issues – namely the exodus of the Vietnamese boat people to the United States between 1975 and 1994, and they have found a robust positive causal impact of migration on trade.

For the purposes of this chapter, three main stylized facts emerge from the strand of literature which explores the impact of migrants' networks on international trade:

- The impact of migrants is stronger for so-called differentiated goods with respect to the homogeneous goods according to the classification proposed by Rauch (1999).
- The impact of networks is greater for imports than for exports (see e.g. Bratti et al. 2014).
- Highly skilled migrants tend to have a stronger effect compared with the total stock of migrants (see Herander and Saavedra 2005; Felbermayr and Jung 2009; Felbermayr and Toubal 2012).

The main channel through which the pro-trade effect of migrants' networks operates is the role of networks in reducing the asymmetries of information in international transactions. In other words, migrants provide important information in the destination market about the distribution channels, types of products consumed, preferences of residents and so forth which reduce the transaction costs, and therefore facilitate international trade. In line with this hypothesis, Rauch and Trindade (2002) found that the impact of networks is larger for products which have no reference price in organized exchanges and that, therefore, are considered sufficiently differentiated such that prices do not provide all the relevant information for international trade. In this respect, Giovannetti and Lanati (2016) found that the pro-trade effect of migrants is a function of the quality of products – other than the degree of product differentiation – and largely depends on the countries' specialization along the quality spectrum, as highlighted by Fontagné et al. (2008).

The gap between pro-import and pro-export effects is commonly attributed to the preference channel of migrants in the countries of destination. Indeed, it is likely that, rather than having information reducing transaction costs, migrants derive larger utility from goods produced in their own country with respect to the native population. Genc et al. (2012) summarize the main empirical findings in this strand of literature and show a discrepancy between elasticities of imports and exports of about 0.03.

Several studies such as Felbermayr and Jung (2009), Herander and Saavedra (2005) and Felbermayr and Toubal (2012), show that the ability of networks in receiving, providing and processing information on trade opportunities, proxied by the skill of migrants, is associated to larger trade flows. In other words, the role of migrants in promoting international trade increases when migrant networks are better at receiving and processing information on trade and investment opportunities. In this regard, Docquier and Lodigiani (2010) show that the size and quality of the diaspora stimulate the inflows of capital in the form of foreign direct investment (FDI) especially in the long run.

Vertical specialization in terms of quality

The evidence that emerges from influential contributions such as Fontagné et al. (2008) and Hallak (2006) points to vertical specialization between North and South which takes place within product categories for different levels of quality. Their results are possible thanks to the availability of trade data at high levels of disaggregation (from six to ten-digit codes).

On the *supply side*, the quality of exported products is strongly related to the stage of development of the source country. The model proposed by Falvey and Kierzkowski (1987) provides a first theoretical explanation of this stylized fact. The authors assume that products of different quality require different intensity in terms of factors of production for their production. Therefore, countries relatively more endowed in skilled labour will have a comparative advantage in the production of high-quality products. Giovannetti and Lanati (2016) arrived at similar conclusions by using a Ricardian model of trade where the underlying (and successfully tested) hypothesis is that high-quality goods show a degree of variability in terms of costs of production (technology) compared to those of lower quality.

Concerning the *demand side*, Fontagné et al. (2008) show that importers from developing countries consume different types of goods: richer countries consume and import goods of higher quality, whereas developing countries import predominantly goods of lower quality. This stylized fact is in line with the gaps in terms of both income and preferences found in the countries in the North and South, respectively.

The relations between trade and migration in the Mediterranean

Trade relations between the southern and northern shores of the Mediterranean are very uneven and depend largely on the geographical distance between countries, their history and the language spoken (Zachman et al. 2012). These relationships are mainly managed through Euro-Mediterranean Association

Agreements, which are in force with most of the partners (with the exception of Syria and Libya) but confined to trade in goods.

Comparative advantages of different countries are changing as firms are integrated in global value chains (Del Prete et al. 2017) which have created advantages in traditional sectors (such as textiles and clothing) but also in high technology sectors (aeronautics, automotive, ICT). The extension of tax-free zones, especially in Morocco, has also helped the trade integration. Despite these recent changes, Europe remains the main destination for exports from the southern shore of the Mediterranean.

Europe is the preferred destination for migrants from Southern Mediterranean countries. History and common language seem to play a more important role than pure geographical distance (Algerians migrate mainly to France, Moroccans to Italy and Spain, etc.). In this context of integration, we study the relationships between trade flows and migrations, separating migrants into highly skilled and low skilled and dividing exports according to their quality level.

The data we use and some descriptive statistics

Our dataset analysis is based on a large sample (177,360 observations) which encompasses four cross sections for the years 1995, 2000, 2005 and 2010. The data on the stocks of migrants born in Southern Mediterranean countries and resident in selected European countries are from Brucker et al. (2013). This dataset provides longitudinal data on migrants differentiated by skill from 1995 to 2015 (five-year intervals). The proxies for dyadic costs associated to international transactions, such as geographic distance, linguistic distance, colonial past as well as source and destination GDP, are from CEPII. Data on international trade are from the BACI dataset from CEPII,[3] which provides HS 6-digit annual trade flows data from 1995 onwards. We exploit the disaggregated nature of trade data to distinguish bilateral trade flows in quality terms, building on the strategy based on export unit values first proposed by Fontagné et al. (2008) and subsequently adopted by Giovannetti and Lanati (2016). Following the alternative strategy used in Fontagné et al. (2008), we define market segments by percentiles in each year and the relative unit value ratio for each trade flow as: s: $r = (UV_{s/} UV_{World})$ where the reference group is the weighted average of unit values with respect to all trade flows for each HS 6-digit category.[4] This methodology has the advantage of ensuring stability of the shares of the market segments for the world total. Following this classification and given the possibility of some selection bias due to the relatively small size of the subgroups (i.e. some country pairs may appear solely in some specific quality classes and not in others), the spectrum of traded goods based on r is divided into terciles ($k = 1, 2, 3$), the first segment $k = 1$ represents the subsample with trade flows of relatively low quality, while $k = 3$ stands for the subsample with trade flows of relatively high quality.

Other than a time span covering more than 20 years, the BACI dataset guarantees a representative sample at cross-section level, given that it includes trade flows for more than 200 countries. Such wide coverage provides a fairly large number of observations for each quality segment, which helps address the concerns associated to small sample bias.[5] Considering that the data on migrant stocks from Brucker et al. (2013) are available solely for a selected number of European countries of destination and only for a limited number of years, the merged dataset includes both the following countries of origin (exporters): Algeria, Cyprus, Egypt, Israel, Jordan, Lebanon, Libya, Malta, Morocco, Syria, Tunisia and Turkey, and the following European destinations (exporters): Austria, Belgium, Denmark, France, Germany, Greece, Ireland, Netherlands, Portugal, UK, Spain and Sweden.

Table 10.1 shows the total stocks of migrants resident in the selected European destination countries and the corresponding growth rate for the period 1995–2010. Turkey is the main country of origin, followed by other Maghreb countries such as Morocco, Algeria and Tunisia, respectively. Among these countries of origin, Morocco reports the highest growth rate in the period considered.

Furthermore, migration from Southern Mediterranean countries towards the EU is predominantly *low-skilled*, although the share of the highly skilled has been growing considerably over time, a trend which is common across all the selected countries of origin as clearly emerges from Table 10.2

Table 10.1 Stock of migrants resident in selected EU countries (for country of origin)

Country	Stock 1995	Growth Rate 1995–2010
TURKEY – TUR	1,574,693	+19%
TUNISIA – TUN	214,338	+17%
SYRIA – SYR	51,887	+81%
MOROCCO – MAR	65,0190	+111%
MALTA – MLT	31,200	+20%
LIBYA – LBY	7,622	+145%
LEBANON – LBN	75,694	+45%
JORDAN – JOR	12,270	+39%
ISRAEL – ISR	23,683	+53%
EGYPT – EGY	69,951	+106%
CYPRUS – CYP	83,261	+31%
ALGERIA – DZA	528,867	+37%

Note: The Table shows the total stock of migrants resident in the EU countries of destination in 1995 (according to their country of origin). The second column shows the correspondent growth rate of the stock from 1995 to 2010. The total stock and the growth rate are calculated by the authors. Source Brucker et al. (2013)

Table 10.2 Share of high- and low-skilled migrants over the total stock (by country of origin)

Country	1995 Low skilled	1995 High skilled	2010 Low skilled	2010 High skilled
TUR	0.729	0.058	0.680	0.088
TUN	0.798	0.106	0.655	0.192
SYR	0.437	0.273	0.355	0.320
MAR	0.703	0.133	0.456	0.222
MLT	0.568	0.258	0.553	0.360
LBY	0.539	0.242	0.284	0.535
LBN	0.479	0.306	0.380	0.373
JOR	0.469	0.284	0.329	0.426
ISR	0.508	0.270	0.352	0.424
EGY	0.453	0.283	0.252	0.428
CYP	0.556	0.258	0.516	0.356
DZA	0.873	0.070	0.678	0.179

Source: Brucker et al. (2013)

Note: The table shows the shares of low and high skilled migrants over the total stock (by country of origin) for the years 1995–2010. The shares are calculated by the authors.

Bringing the data to an econometric model

Our goal in this chapter is to explore whether and to what extent migrants' networks influence international trade. To do so, we rely on the most popular and effective empirical strategy used to study this relationship is the gravity model for international trade. Head and Mayer (2015) clearly point out the advantages of using such a model. By exploiting the information included in the dataset provided by Brucker et al. (2013), we are also able to distinguish the impact of migrants' networks on trade for different skill levels and its variation for different levels of quality of traded products. Our empirical strategy is similar to that proposed by Giovannetti and Lanati (2016), where international trade flows are divided according to different levels of quality and the same gravity equation is estimated for each quality class k, a technique in line with the work of Rauch and Trindade (2002). We estimate

$$lnX_{ni,g,t}^{k} = S_{i,g,t} + S_{n,g,t} + \ln\left(GDP_{i,t} {}^\star GDP_{n,t}\right) + \theta_k \text{lndist}_{ni}$$
$$+ \theta_k \text{lang}_{ni} + \theta_k \text{colony}_{ni} + \theta_k \text{lnmig}_{ni,t} + \theta_k \delta_{ni,g,t}^{*}$$

(10.1)

where i is the exporting country while n is the importing country. stands for trade flows from i to n at time t of product g of quality k. The longitudinal dimension of the dataset allows for the inclusion of a comprehensive set of fixed effects which, along with the availability of a sufficiently large amount of information, enables us to isolate and estimate more accurately the parameters of interest. $S_{i,g,t}$ and $S_{i,g,t}$ represent year*exporter*category HS06 and year*importer*category HS06 fixed effects, respectively, which capture all the factors that affect bilateral trade and do not vary by year, country and product category. In other words, the specific characteristics of a country in a given year and for given product categories are entirely accounted for through the inclusion of the fixed effects in our regression. The model allows us to isolate the impact of the coefficient and to reduce potential distortions in the estimates associated with omitted variable bias. Furthermore, by including this comprehensive set of fixed effects the impact of so-called multilateral resistance can be captured, as shown by the influential contribution of Anderson and Van Wincoop (2003). Indeed, the intensity of bilateral trade exchanges not only depends on the attraction of the country of destination but also is related to the potential attractiveness of alternative destinations. By the same token, the competitiveness of a source country should be considered relative to the competitiveness of alternative sources. As illustrated by Anderson and Van Wincoop (2003), a model which doesn't successfully account for this multilateral resistance effect can lead to major distortions in the estimates. The inclusion of our set of fixed effects allows this issue to be addressed.

Despite the high number of controls included in the gravity specification, some potential issues of endogeneity remain. For instance, there might exist variables that are not controlled for which affect trade and the stocks of migrants simultaneously, causing the estimates to be biased and inconsistent. Giovannetti and Lanati (2016) addressed these endogeneity concerns with an IV strategy in which networks are instrumented with past stocks.[6] Here, to partially address and alleviate the simultaneity bias issue we simply estimate Equation 10.1 with the 2- and 4-years lagged impact of networks on trade because current trade flows are unlikely to have an effect on past migration. The results available upon request are very similar to the ones reported in Table 10.3, which we find reassuring.

The term $\ln (GDP_{i,t} *GDP_{n,t})$ in Equation 10.1 captures the 'size' of trading partners in the gravity model; $Indist_{ni}$ represents weighted geographical distance between trading pairs (CEPII); $lang_{ni}$ is a binary variable which takes the value of 1 when trading pairs share the same official language, 0 otherwise (CEPII); $colony_{ni}$ is a dummy variable which takes the value of 1 if the trading countries have had a colonial relationship, zero otherwise (CEPII). As mentioned earlier, $Inmig_{ni,t}$, which represents the number of migrants resident in country n and born in country i at time t and proxies for the role of migrants in affecting bilateral trade exchanges, is our variable of interest. is the error term.

Because our proxy for quality of trade is the unit value, which is the ratio between the value and the quantity of exports, observations with zero trade flows and zero or no quantities are automatically dropped. Hence, for each country pair we are unable to track trade exchanges for all products g of quality k over time, which prevents us from performing panel data analysis. Despite this loss of information, however, we are able to consistently estimate the pro-trade effect of immigrants using a very large number of observations. Furthermore, the lack of zero trade flows in our dependent variable allows us to avoid the issue of treatment of zeroes in gravity log-log specifications, as warned by Santos Silva and Tenreyro (2006) and Head and Mayer (2015), and we can, therefore, rely on pooled Ordinary Least Squares (OLS) as the workhorse estimator for this econometric exercise.

Results

The first column of Table 10.3 reports the estimates of the gravity model applied to international trade flows, where we introduce the total bilateral stock of migrants among other standard dyadic trade determinants (i.e. the estimate of Equation 10.1). Gravity variables have the expected sign, in line with the underlying theory. The product of GDP, which as mentioned earlier proxies the size of the trading partners, has a positive sign: the larger the income of the country pair, the greater the trade between them. Geographical distance, which proxies for the dyadic costs associated with international trade, has a negative sign. Countries with a common language trade relatively more with each other, while the colonial past does not seem to play any significant role. This result is not surprising since, given the composition of our sample, the past colonial relationship is likely to be highly collinear with the common language. As for the impact of migrant networks, the impact is positive and statistically significant at 1% and the magnitude of the elasticity of total stock is 0.17, a value that is very much in line with the mean value of the network elasticities estimated in this strand of literature (see Genc et al. 2012).

The lower part of Table 10.3 illustrates the trend of the coefficients for different levels of quality of the traded products. The estimates are essentially in line with the findings in Giovannetti and Lanati (2016). The pro-trade effect of migrants reflects the comparative advantage of their country of origin: as illustrated by Fontagné et al. (2008), developing countries have a comparative advantage in the production of goods of relatively lower quality. Migrants certainly have more information on the types of products, distribution channels and so forth, which reduces the transaction costs of trade in goods of lower quality. Indeed, the network effect is larger in the first tercile (low quality) while the lowest impact is for high quality products.

In the second and third columns, we report the estimates including the stock of high-skilled (Column 2) and low-skilled (Column 3) migrants, according to the classification proposed by Brucker et al. (2013). The impact of the network of highly skilled migrants residing in Europe and coming from the Mediterranean is slightly larger than the impact of the total stock. Considering the total bilateral trade flows, the migrants' skills seem to have a significant effect in reducing transaction costs and the elasticity of the network grows as the migrant skill level increases. These results are in line with the literature (see e.g.

Table 10.3 The impact of migrant networks on traded products of different quality

	(1)	*(2)*	*(3)*
Dependent Variable *Skill Level*	*In* $x_{ni,g,t}$ *Total*	*In* $x_{ni,g,t}$ *High skilled*	*In* $x_{ni,g,t}$ *Low skilled*
$\ln(\text{GDP}_{i,t}{}^*\text{GDP}_{n,t})$	0.177***	0.184***	0.175***
	(5.02)	(5.05)	(4.85)
$\ln(\text{mig}_{ni,t})$	0.110***	0.118***	0.103***
	(3.43)	(3.33)	(3.19)
$\ln(\text{dist}_{ni})$	−0.961***	−1.015***	−0.950***
	(−4.90)	(−5.59)	(−4.43)
Colony_{ni}	0.026	0.016	0.023
	(0.20)	(0.13)	(0.17)
Lang_{ni}	0.882***	0.903**	0.889***
	(3.44)	(3.53)	(3.52)
N	97055	97055	97055
S_{ngt}	X	X	X
$F_{(5, 131)}$	X	X	X
R_{sq}	27.8	27.2	25.6
	0.80	0.80	0.80
Skill Level	Total	High skilled	Low skilled
Coefficient	$\ln(\text{mig}_{ni,t})$	$\ln(\text{mig}_{ni,t})$	$\ln(\text{mig}_{ni,t})$
Quality Segment k			
0–33th LOW	0.142***	0.155***	0.133***
34th–66th MEDIUM	(3.16)	(2.92)	(3.16)
67th–100th HIGH	0.134***	0.118**	0.128***
	(3.55)	(2.60)	(3.39)
	0.126***	0.140***	0.116***
	(2.84)	(2.84)	(2.50)

Source: The estimates are obtained using the STATA command *reghdfe* written by James Correia. The samples are divided in classes (based on terciles) according to the level of quality of traded products. The number of observations in each segment is approximately one third of the total number of observations. The estimated equation is:

$$lnX^k_{ni,g,t} = S_{i,g,t} + S_{n,g,t} + \ln\left(\text{GDP}_{i,t}{}^*\text{GDP}_{n,t}\right) + \theta_k l n dist_{ni}$$
$$+ \theta_k lang_{ni} + \theta_k colony_{ni} + \theta_k ln mig_{ni,t} + \theta_k \delta^k_{ni,g,t}$$

The upper part of Table 10.3 shows the coefficients obtained estimating the gravity equation over the whole sample. The lower part shows the estimates of our parameter of interest ln $(\text{mig}_{ni,t})$ estimated for each level of quality k.

Note: t-statistics are included in parentheses. * $p < 0.10$, ** $p < 0.05$, *** $p < 0.01$. Standard Errors are clustered by trading pair. The model includes the intercept.

Felbermayr and Jung 2009). An interesting figure, however, emerges from the statistics reported in the lower part of Table 10.3. As in Giovannetti and Lanati (2016), the trend of elasticity of the network that reflects the comparative advantage of their countries of origin emerges independently of the skill level of migrants. In other words, the greatest elasticity is for low-skilled products.

However, the impact of highly skilled migrants is relatively higher for high-quality goods. In contrast to the case of the low-skilled and total stock, the coefficient of the network $Inmi_{gni,t}$ does not decrease progressively with the increase in product quality. We interpret this variation in the trend as mainly due to the so-called preference channel. Highly skilled migrants are likely not to have a binding budget constraint and can thus afford (have preferences for) relatively higher quality goods.

Conclusions

This chapter contributes to a broader vision of the impact of migration on the economic and social growth of the country of origin and to a more complex assessment of the benefits and potential damage of (highly) qualified migration to the economic development of the country of origin.

We show that, in the case of the Mediterranean countries, migration in general favours the growth of exports in the country of origin and that the growth ofsskilled migration favours the growth of products with a higher technological content. This means that, on the one hand, skilled emigration reduces the level of human capital in the country of emigration, but on the other, it favours the production of goods with higher technological content in the country of origin as well as the employment of more skilled workers, making a virtuous circle of development possible.

These considerations allow us to reassess the impact of skilled migration, the so-called brain drain.[7] Migration seems to be less harmful to the country of origin, since it is likely to trigger production and trade of goods with higher technological content, thereby boosting growth and skilled employment in the country of origin, potentially leading to a brain gain.

The final evaluation of the impact of migration on the growth of the country of origin depends on many factors, some of which lie beyond its control. Our results suggest that, in the case of Mediterranean countries, skilled migrants can positively affect the high-quality goods trade. This, in turn, contributes positively to the ongoing debate on 'skilled migrations' whose benefits are known in terms of larger remittances, higher propensity to invest in their homeland, increased human capital and important contacts for development of their country. Hence, arguments against selective policies in destination countries, such as the Blue Card, can be countered, based on the effects on high-quality trade growth from the origin country.

Notes

1 They use the price of the good as a technological indicator.
2 The result is reached by interacting a Commonwealth Dummy variable with the stocks of immigrants in the UK.
3 The BACI dataset, made available by CEPII for subscribers of COMTRADE, is a harmonized international trade dataset. It includes values and quantities traded for more than 5,000 products and more than 200 countries, starting in 1994 and ending in 2016. The

full description of the dataset is available at: www.cepii.fr/cepii/en/bdd_modele/presen tation.asp?id=1
4 More detailed information about the empirical strategy used is outlined in Fontagné et al. (2008) and Giovannetti and Lanati (2016).
5 We depart from Giovannetti and Lanati (2016) by dividing the sample into terciles rather than quartiles: this guarantees a larger number of observations in each sample which addresses potential issues deriving from small sample bias.
6 The same stocks are not available for this analysis given that prior to 1995, there are only three lags available, which can only partially match our four cross sections for 1995, 2000, 2005 and 2010.
7 See, for instance, Beltrame (2008) for an example for Italy.

References

Anderson, J.E., and Van Wincoop, E., 2003. Gravity with Gravitas: A Solution to the Border Puzzle. *The American Economic Review*, 93 (1), 170–192.

Beltrame, L., 2008. Globalizzazione e fuga dei cervelli. *Rassegna Italiana di Sociologia*, XLIX (2), 277–295.

Bratti, M.L., Benedictis, D., and Santoni, G., 2014. On the Pro-trade Effects of Immigrants. *Review of World Economics*, Weltwirtschaftliches Archiv, 150 (3), 557–594.

Brucker, H., Capuano, S., and Marfouk, A., 2013. *Education, Gender and International Migration: Insights from a Panel-Dataset 1980–2010*. Mimeo [url: www.iab.de/en/daten/iab-brain-drain-data.aspx].

Del Prete, D., Giovannetti, G., and Marvasi, E., 2017. Global Value Chains: New Evidence for North Africa. *International Economics*, 153 (4), 675–701.

Docquier, F., and Lodigiani, E., 2010. Skilled Migration and Business Networks. *Open Economies Review*, 21 (4), 565–588.

Docquier, F., and Rapoport, H., 2012. Globalization, Brain Drain, and Development. *Journal of Economic Literature*, 50 (3), 681–730.

European Commission, 2017, *10 Trends Shaping Migration*. European Political Strategy Center.

Falvey, R., and Kierzkowski, H., 1987. Product Quality, Intra-Industry Trade and (im)Perfect Competition. *In*: H. Kierzkowski, ed. *Protection and Competition in International Trade: Essays in Honor of M. Corden*. Oxford and New York: Basil Blackwell, 143–161.

Fargues, P., and Venturini, A., ed., 2015. Migration from North Africa and the Middle East. Skilled migrants. *Development and Globalization*. London: I.B. TAURIS.

Felbermayr, G.J., and Jung, B., 2009. The Pro-trade Effect of the Brain Drain: Sorting Out Confounding Factors. *Economics Letters*, 104 (2), 72–75.

Felbermayr, G.J., and Toubal, F., 2012. Revisiting the Trade-Migration Nexus: Evidence from New OECD Data. *World Development*, 40 (5), 928–937.

Fontagné, L., Gaulier, G., and Zignago, S., 2008. Specialization Across Varieties and North-South Competition. *Economic Policy*, 23 (53), 51–91.

Genc, M., Gheasi, M., Nijkamp, P., and Poot, J., 2012. The Impact of Immigration on International Trade: A Meta-Analysis. Oxford Handbook of Innovation. *In*: P. Nijkamp, J. Poot, and M. Sahin, eds. *Migration Impact Assessmemt. New Horizons in Regional Science*, ch. 9, 301–337. Northhampton, MA: Edward Elgar Publishing Limited.

Giovannetti, G., and Lanati, M., 2016. Do High-Skill Immigrants Trigger High Quality Trade? *The World Economy*, 40 (7), 1345–1380, July.

Girma, S., and Yu, Z., 2002. The Link Between Immigration and Trade: Evidence from the United Kingdom. *Weltwirtschaftliches Archiv*, 138 (1), 115–130.

Gould, D.M., 1994. Immigrant, Links to the Home Country: Empirical Implications for US Bilateral Trade Flows. *The Review of Economics and Statistics*, 302–316.

Hallak, H.C., 2006. Product Quality and the Direction of Trade. *Journal of International Economics*, 68 (1), 238–265.

Head, K., and Mayer, T., 2015. Gravity Equations: Workhorse, Toolkit, and Cookbook. *In*: G. Gopinath, E. Helpman, and K. Rogoff, eds. *Handbook of International Economics*, Vol. 4. Amsterdam: Elsevier, 131–195.

Herander, M.G., and Saavedra, L.A., 2005. Exports and the Structure of Immigrant Based Networks: The Role of Geographic Proximity. *The Review of Economics and Statistics*, 87 (2), 323–335.

Kasparian, C., 2015. Young and Highly Skilled: Emigration from Lebanon. *In*: P. Fargues, and A. Venturini, eds. *Migration from North Africa and the Middle East. Skilled migrants, Development and Globalization*. London: I.B. TAURIS.

Khachani, M., 2015. Highly Skilled Migration: Morocco. *In*: P. Fargues, and A. Venturini, eds. *Migration from North Africa and the Middle East. Skilled migrants, Development and Globalization*. London: I.B. TAURIS.

Genc, M., Gheasi, M., Nijkamp, P., and Poot, J., 2012. The Impact of Immigration on International Trade: A Meta-Analysis. *Migration Impact Assessment: New Horizons*, 301.

Parsons, C., and Vézina, P.L., 2018. Migrant Networks and Trade: The Vietnamese Boat People as a Natural Experiment. *The Economic Journal*, 128 (612), F210–F234.

Parsons, R.C., and Winters, L.A., 2014. *International Migration, Trade and Aid*, Working Paper 90. Oxford: International Migration Institute (IMI), Oxford Department of International Development (QEH), University of Oxford.

Rauch, J.E., 1999. Networks Versus Markets in International Trade. *Journal of International Economics*, 48 (1), 7–35.

Rauch, J.E., and Trindade, V., 2002. Ethnic Chinese Networks in International Trade. *The Review of Economics and Statistics*, 84 (1), 116–130.

Santos Silva, J., and Tenreyro, S., 2006. The Log of Gravity. *The Review of Economics and Statistics*, 88 (4), 641–658.

Stark, O., Helmenstein, C., and Prskawetz, A., 1997. A Brain Gain with a Brain Drain. *Economic Letters*, 55, 227–234.

UN, 2017. *International Migration Report 2017*, ST/ESA/SER.A/403.

Zachman, G., Tam, M., and Granelli, L., 2012. How Wide Is the Mediterranean. *Brussels, Bruegel Policy Contribution*, 8.

Chapter 11

Bound to share aims and instruments

The future of Euro-Mediterranean migration policies

Alessandro Romagnoli

Introduction

The migrant flows of the Mediterranean Sea currently represent a serious threat for both the European Union and its Mediterranean partners: they weaken both the social cohesiveness and the decision-making ability of the EU's 27 Member States and the socio-economic conditions of the countries of the south-eastern shores of the sea. This is not the first time that the area has faced such a threat, but the current situation is different from that emerging between the 1950s and the 1980s because the structure of the Mediterranean migration system has turned out to be more complex and articulated with respect to the traditional one-directional flow of people from sending to receiving countries.

After three to four decades of originating migration flows towards the centre of Europe until the 1990s, most of the countries fronting onto the shores of the Mediterranean are becoming destination or transit points for the new movements of people feeding the Euro-Mediterranean migration system. Countries once sending people abroad (such as Spain, Italy, Greece and Turkey) are now landing places, whereas other 'sending' countries like Tunisia, Egypt and Morocco have also become 'transit stations' for non-resident refugees and workers seeking safety and employment. Thus, two new attracting poles have grown in recent decades within the migration network characterizing the basin, in addition to central Europe: on the one hand, the EU southern countries, where one third of the migrants come from West Africa and Southern Mediterranean regions, – and, on the other, the Mediterranean Asian coast where there is a mounting concentration of workers and people displaced from the neighbouring territories. However, the chance for EU citizens to move around the territory of all the member countries gave rise to additional worker flows from EU economies towards Mediterranean, Centre and North European ones as will be shown later in the chapter. In this perspective, the 'migration problem' (or rather, the set of phenomena usually labelled by this term) represents the challenge that the evolution of the Euro-Mediterranean migration system, emerging after the Second World War, presents to all the countries of the area.

The Euro-Mediterranean Partnership which started in 1995 did not consider the Mediterranean migration system a matter to be concerned with. This was for several reasons: first, the Barcelona Declaration rejects the economic core of the phenomenon, as it mentions migration *en passant* when debating 'human development' and the 'political and security' partnerships. Furthermore, EU policies and official documents fail to acknowledge previous migration experience or the migration-development/growth nexus. On that subject, the pledge that 'the EU and its Member States will step up efforts to seize the opportunities for development offered by migration, while addressing its challenges' (COM 2017: 740) cannot be considered as recognizing that migration is a constituent element of a capitalist economy and hence a priority both for the EU economic system and for those of its neighbouring partners. Therefore, in accordance with the framework of Euro-Mediterranean Partnership (EMP) cooperation programmes, the policies implemented by the EU and/ or by the countries of the Mediterranean north shore to tackle the problem have sought to combine the protection of their own borders with the recruitment of globalized flexible foreign workers. For their part, the countries on the south-eastern shores of the Mediterranean seconded the EU, hoping that the unemployment of their young people and the problem of immigrants, returnees and people displaced in transit could be partially solved by the goodwill of their neighbours opposite. In so doing, the blast waves of the economic crisis and the flare-ups of the Arab Spring, both shifting flows of people outside their countries, ruled out both such management of the migration flows and the cooperation policies following the Barcelona Declaration.

Yet the reasons behind the crash of migration policies go beyond the failed conceptualization of the problem. What also counts is the current impotence of the European Union and the aloofness of its South-Eastern Mediterranean partners. The inability of the EU authorities and its members to cope with the inflows of people arises from two basic faults: the widespread misunderstanding of the different natures, forms and economic functions that international migrations take, and the EU's tendency to entrust its Member States with their management. By contrast, the lack of concern of the signatories to the Barcelona process derives from internal political instability and/or from the free-riding attitude and compliance of their foreign policies with the European Union: a case in point is the participation of the South-East Mediterranean countries in EU policies aiming to control European frontiers by implementing suitable measures and structures on their territories. Moreover, the failure of the model of economic cooperation resulting from the Mediterranean partnership is due to both the lack of awareness of a shared responsibility for all the economic phenomena unfolding on the sea and the lack of a common and participated Euro-Mediterranean policy. For the aforementioned reasons, the discussion on future guidelines aimed at tackling the subject should consider these basic requirements and provide a conceptual and operative framework for Mediterranean cooperation which is more suitable for an economic space of a globalized world, as is the Mediterranean Sea.

As a preliminary step, this analysis will depict the 'Mediterranean economy' by grouping the countries fronting onto the sea in three blocks of somewhat homogeneous economies. Searching for the economic divergences in the structure and performance of the basin, the importance of contrasting demographic dynamics for the sustainability of a better economic path will emerge, for both low-income and high-income countries. Thus the discussion will demonstrate that international economic migration is a typical feature of capitalist economies which, in a context of a diversified level of development, constitutes a common problem and a challenge whose solution requires participated and shared management. The next step to succeed in achieving this aim is to gain insights into the economic nature of migration and the characteristics of the Mediterranean migration system. Some general methodological suggestions and policy recommendations conclude the chapter.

Diverging structural conditions in the Mediterranean economic space

The term 'Mediterranean space' is generally applied to define the area occupied by the 25 states giving onto (or situated near) the sea in question. These countries are part of three continents (namely Europe, Asia and Africa) and differ in language, religion, history and customs. All these elements have interacted in the process of upgrading the economies, determining, for example, their long-standing or recent industrialization and accession to, or disengagement from, their free trade areas. Taking into consideration these and other economic features (that also mirror non-economic aspects) the Mediterranean countries can be split into three economically homogeneous groups: the European Union Mediterranean countries, the Balkan-Anatolian countries and the South-Eastern Mediterranean countries.

At first glance, the different economic conditions of the three aggregations can be highlighted by the per capita gross domestic product (GDP), a parameter measuring annual average personal income. The 2016 per capita GDP values of each country calculated as a percentage of the French value enable the comparative economic levels to be assessed, as they measure the distance of each economy from the best performing one of the area. As highlighted by Table 11.1, the economies belonging to the European Union occupy the highest positions and a greater range than those of the other groups, being between one and half of the French per capita GDP (Croatia excepted). The economic level of the Balkan-Anatolian countries fluctuates between 33.49% of the French value registered by Turkey and 11.15% of Albania (about 22 points), while the South-Eastern Mediterranean countries stand between the Lebanese value (16.62%) and that of the West Bank and Gaza (6.11%), that is a span of about ten points. Moreover, the Mediterranean space presents the concentration of the economies in different segments of each cluster: the most densely populated EU Mediterranean countries (France, Italy and Spain) represent the highest-income economies; Turkey excels in its group, even though its per capita GDP is about one third that of France; by contrast, the most densely populated Southern Mediterranean

Table 11.1 Per capita GDP of Mediterranean countries in percentage of the French value, 2016 (constant 2010 US$)

Countries	%	Countries	%
EU Medit. countries		Montenegro	17.74
Portugal	53.19	Albania	11.15
Spain	74.85	Macedonia	12.42
France	100		
Italy	81.6	*S-E Medit. countries*	
Slovenia	57.97	Syria	...
Croatia	34.2	Lebanon	16.62
Greece	54.11	Jordan	7.75
Malta	63.25	Israel	80.41
Cyprus	67.41	West Bank and Gaza	6.11
		Egypt	6.48
Balkan-Anatolian countries		Libya	...
Turkey	33.49	Tunisia	10.15
Bosnia and Herzegovina	12.62	Algeria	11.53
Serbia	13.92	Morocco	7.6

Source: Author's elaboration from World Bank, (2017) World Development Indicators

countries (Morocco and Egypt) are the lowest-income countries of the cluster at the bottom of the ranking. Finally, on average, most of the economies belonging to the second and third groups (excluding Turkey and Israel) present a per capita GDP value of between nearly one third and one quarter that obtained by the worst economy of the first cluster (i.e. Croatia).

This introductory analysis of the economic conditions of the Mediterranean peoples highlights the differences in the average income of the citizens living in the area, thereby depicting the structure of the 'Mediterranean economy'. The divide that characterizes such a set of economic systems, whose GDP in 2016 was USD 8,088,585,000 (10.66% of world GDP) is based on the income produced by a limited group of economies. According to the World Bank national accounts, almost four fifths of Mediterranean GDP is accounted for by France (30.48%), Italy (22.98%), Spain (15.30%) and Turkey (10.68%). The contribution of all the other 21 economies to Mediterranean GDP is less than 20% of the total income produced in the area (see Table 11.2). On further inspection of the disparities in the economic conditions among the Mediterranean countries a real divide emerges between the European Union Mediterranean economies and all the others giving onto the sea. Indeed, the EU Mediterranean countries produce just over three quarters (75.24%) of the whole value for the area, the Balkan-Anatolian economies little more than one tenth (11.70%), while the South-Eastern Mediterranean countries account for 13.06%. This is a crushingly different weight for the three economic groups of countries as well as between the four 'Mediterranean economic powers' and all the other economies.

Table 11.2 Country shares of the total GDP produced in the Mediterranean area, 2016 (current US$)

Countries	%	Countries	%
EU Medit. countries	75.24	Montenegro	0.05
Portugal	2.53	Albania	0.15
Spain	15.3	Macedonia	0.13
France	30.48		
Italy	22.98	*S-E Medit. countries*	13.06
Slovenia	0.55	Syria	. . .
Croatia	0.63	Lebanon	0.61
Greece	2.38	Jordan	0.47
Malta	0.14	Israel	3.93
Cyprus	0.25	West Bank and Gaza	0.17
		Egypt	4.11
Balkan-Anatolian countries	11.7	Libya	. . .
Turkey	10.68	Tunisia	0.52
Bosnia and Herzegovina	0.21	Algeria	1.97
Serbia	0.48	Morocco	1.28
		Total Mediterranean	100

Source: Author's elaboration from: GDP (current US$), World Development Indicators, World Bank

The previous structural imbalance highlights the 'Mediterranean economy' polarized around EU countries and shapes international trade in the area, facilitated by the different levels of economic integration along the shores.[1] All the European countries giving onto the sea have joined a common currency area, whereas those of the other shores are economies without trade relations with like neighbours, even if they have sometimes signed trade agreements with them (as in the case of the Maghreb countries). As a result, the main origin and destination international trade partners of EU Mediterranean countries are the members of the Union, which also attract the economies of both the Balkan-Anatolian and Maghreb countries. Few states in the Eastern Mediterranean have diversified their trade partners and present less intensive trade flows with Europe (Table 11.3). Despite the unbalanced trade, financial and labour flows carried out between the countries giving onto the sea, the 'Mediterranean economy' emerges as a space with intense economic relations.

The divergences in the economic structures reviewed earlier show a dichotomy in the 'Mediterranean economy' between the EU economies and all the others: high-income countries and a few large economies attract international trade flows on the northern shores; lower-income countries, many small dependent economies, characterize the other shores. Due to this dichotomy, the 'Mediterranean economy' presents unbalanced bargaining power between a set of large economic subjects (acting as one under a common market and currency) and many unrelated small economic partners. Moreover, such divergences

Table 11.3 Partners of destination and origin for the Mediterranean countries trade, 2016 (the partners are identified by the official short names in English ISO 3166-1-alpha-2)

Countries	Destin.	Origin	Countries	Destin.	Origin
EU-Mediterranean			Montenegro	RS HU	RS DE
Portugal	ES FR	ES DE	Albania	IT RS	IT DE
Spain	FR DE.	DE FR	Macedonia	DE RS	DE GB
France	DE ES	DE CN			
Italy	DE FR	DE FR	*S-E Mediterranean*		
Slovenia	DE IT	DE IT	Syria	...	...
Croatia	IT SL	DE IT	Lebanon	SA CH	CN IT
Greece	IT DE	DE IT	Jordan	AE SA	SA CH
Malta	US DE	IT KY	Israel	US HK	CN CH
Cyprus	GR UK	GR DE	West Bank and Gaza	...	...
			Egypt	AE SA	CN DE
Balkan-Anatolian			Libya	IT DE	CN IT
Turkey	DE GB	CN DE	Tunisia	FR IT	FR IT
Bosnia and Herzegovina	DE IT	DE IT	Algeria	IT ES	CN FR
Serbia	IT DE	DE IT	Morocco	ES FR	ES FR

Source: https://atlas.media.mit.edu/en/profile/country/bgd/#Destinations

are connected to the basic economic feature of this dualistic aggregation: the EU-Mediterranean countries are developed economies and those of the other shores are developing ones. Thus, considerable economic interaction (due also to the historical legacy and to the neighbouring countries) is carried out to obtain different economic aims: to continue economic growth for the first cluster of economies and to promote economic development for the others.

The migration problem: from a divergent economic performance and demographic dynamics to a common challenge and exit strategy

The structural divide in the 'Mediterranean economy' presents a further difference among the three clusters of countries due to the performance of the single economies. Between 2000 and 2016, average annual GDP growth for the EU-Mediterranean economies (excluding Malta) ranged between 1.4% (Cyprus) and 0.8% (Greece), whereas for the Balkan–Anatolian countries (excluding Bosnia and Herzegovina), it laid between 5.3% (Turkey) and 2.9% (Serbia). For the Southern Mediterranean economies, average annual GDP growth (excluding Libya) was between 6.7% in Algeria and 3.5% in Tunisia (see Table 11.4). The different rate of income growth for each cluster shows a reverse rank order for the economies, a situation that is confirmed by the trend of welfare conditions.

Table 11.4 Average annual GDP and population growth for Mediterranean countries, 2000–2016 (% values)

Countries	GDP	Pop.	Countries	GDP	Pop.
EU-Mediterranean			Montenegro	3.2	0.2
Portugal	0	0	Albania	3.6	4.2
Spain	1.1	0.8	Macedonia	3.2	0.1
France	1.1	0.6			
Italy	−0.2	0.4	*S-E Mediterranean*		
Slovenia	1.7	0.2	Syria	...	0.7
Croatia	1.1	−0.4	Lebanon	4.8	3.9
Greece	−0.8	0	Jordan	5.2	3.9
Malta	2.8	0.7	Israel	3.7	1.9
Cyprus	1.4	1.3	West Bank and Gaza		
			Egypt	4.4	2
Balkan-Anatolian			Libya	1.3	1
Turkey	5.3	1.4	Tunisia	3.5	1
Bosnia and Herzegovina	−0.7	3.1	Algeria	6.7	3.5
Serbia	2.9	−0.4	Morocco	4.5	1.3

Source: Author's elaboration from World Development Indicators, Tables 2.1 and 4.1

A concise measure of this phenomenon is obtained by the comparison between the average annual growth rates of GDP and of population: an average income growth outpacing population growth shows a welfare improvement, while the opposite trend reveals the worsening of economic conditions. The rather disappointing economic performance of EU-Mediterranean countries proves worse in the light of this index: the data recorded in Table 11.4 highlight decreased welfare in the case of Greece and Italy and a modest increase for the other countries in the cluster. By contrast, they reveal an interesting increase for the Balkan-Anatolian countries (excluding Bosnia and Herzegovina and Albania) and favourable improvements for the Southern Mediterranean economies (despite the Arab Spring). This means that most of the lower-income countries in the area succeeded in dealing with population pressure by reducing the population growth rate on the one hand, and that higher-income economies encountered difficulties overcoming the crisis on the other.

The developed and developing Mediterranean countries also diverge in the ways their economies have to allocate national income to social expenditure (healthcare, education, pensions). The reason lies in the structure of their population, that is in their 'dependency ratio'. This index measures the proportion of the non-working population (thus people depending on other wage earners) over the economically active. Traditionally the 'dependent' population includes both youth ages 0–15 years and those age 65 or over, while all those between 16 and 64 years old are considered to be of working age. Therefore, the total 'dependency ratio' (TDR) can also be decomposed into two indexes: the 'youth dependency ratio' (YDR) and the 'old dependency ratio' (ODP).

The size of the dependency ratio index and the comparative dimensions of the two indexes in which it can be decomposed characterize both the sustainability of the economic system and the income allocation to the different social requirements.[2] When the dependency ratio is close to 1 or more because of a 'baby boom' and life expectancy increase to a lesser extent than population, the economy faces in the short term a greater burden in providing the aging population with education and child healthcare. But over the medium term, the situation will be reversed because the young will become workers and the dependency ratio will decline. The situation becomes worse when the number of pensioners increase and the population experiences a below-replacement fertility rate: the dependency ratio starts to rise, and the economy faces an increasing burden due to a deficit of people entering the labour market in respect to those retiring. This phenomenon reduces the income produced and increases the social expenditure in pensions and in elderly healthcare, and in the long run leads to the country's decline. A much-debated UN study (United Nations 2001) paid close attention to the role of migration as a relief against such decline; the discussion among scholars has been heated on the solution proposed, but 'whatever the reaction to the report, it seems clear that if birth rates in the low-fertility countries do not increase, heightened immigration will hold more appeal than absolute decline' (Tarmann 2000). The scientific community, considering this prospect real according to the demographic statistics, has endeavoured to find the 'replacement migration',[3] that is 'the age-specific immigration profile that minimizes the dependency ratio in a stationary population' (Simon et al. 2012: 158).

The impact of divergent dependency ratios on social expenditure composition within the 'Mediterranean economy' emerges from Table 11.5 which presents the values of the three indexes for Mediterranean countries in 2016. The EU-Mediterranean countries present a situation with a youth dependency ratio of around 22% (excluding France), an old dependency ratio of 28%–32% (excluding Cyprus and Italy) and a total dependency ratio fluctuating between 50% and 60%. This means that the young people amount to two thirds the number of pensioners, that for every pension there are 2.5/2 workers to pay for it and that the expected decrease in the latter value will cause an increase in the financial burden for the economy. The TDR for the Balkan-Anatolian countries measures 42%–50% of those of working age and the ODR is lower than the YDR: this situation supports the economies. A better situation from this point of view is presented by the third cluster of countries which, despite the high level of income spent on childcare, will experience in the medium run the 'demographic gift'.[4] In light of these trends, there emerges the complementarity between the demographic deficit of the EU-Mediterranean economies and the excess in countries on other Mediterranean shores.

The divergent dependency ratios, as well as the specific home conditions of each economy, are causing different economic phenomena in the Mediterranean countries. In developed ones, the insufficient replacement of retirees (due to the low YDR) coupled with the economic crisis produces the need

Table 11.5 Young, old and total dependency ratios (YDR, ODR and TDR) for Mediterranean countries, 2016

Countries	YDR	ODR	TDR	Countries	YDR	ODR	TDR
EU-Mediterranean				Montenegro	27	21	48
Portugal	21	32	53	Albania	26	18	44
Spain	22	29	51	Macedonia	24	18	42
France	29	31	60				
Italy	21	36	57	*S-E Mediterranean*			
Slovenia	22	28	50	Syria	64	7	71
Croatia	22	29	51	Lebanon	35	12	47
Greece	22	31	53	Jordan	59	6	65
Malta	22	28	50	Israel	46	19	65
Cyprus	24	19	43	West Bank and Gaza			
				Egypt	54	8	62
Balkan-Anatolian				Libya	42	6	48
Turkey	38	12	50	Tunisia	35	11	46
Bosnia and Herzegovina	20	23	43	Algeria	45	9	54
Serbia	25	25	50	Morocco	42	10	52

Source: Author's elaboration from World Development Indicators

for low-cost labour: the result is youth unemployment and immigration. In the developing ones, the excess labour supply (due to the high YDR) and the insufficient growth of investments to absorb young people entering the labour market produces both youth unemployment and migration. Thus, the migration problem is an economic challenge emerging from diverging but complementary demographic dynamics, highlighted by the population 'dependency ratio'. It is a common problem calling for a common exit strategy that implements instruments both to support the development process of developing economies and to offset the shortfall in the labour force and home demand in high-income countries.

Migrants as economic agents in both receiving and sending countries

Migration is an economic phenomenon (Taylor 1999; Constant and Zimmermann 2013) intrinsic to capitalism, and specifically to the movement of the labour factor. Hence, the migrant is a member of the active population of an economy performing the economic functions of a worker, consumer and taxpayer. All things considered, also people forced to expatriate are economic subjects, although their subsistence is entrusted not only to the labour market of the hosting country but also to the public administration of the hosting state, if the country in question has signed the Convention on refugees. As admission to refugee status is costly for the granting state, some countries failed to sign the Geneva Convention: in the Mediterranean, Libya, Syria, Lebanon and Jordan are on such a list.

Due to their economic role, migrants are economic agents in both receiving and sending countries, but for different reasons and in different ways. The migration–development nexus has been analyzed in depth (Robert 2005), pointing out that the migration process provides for a lower-income country, in the long run, four kinds of capital, all crucial for development: financial capital (remittances), social capital (relational networks), cultural capital (different cultural practices and their mix with traditional ones) and symbolic capital (new roles acquired by migrants and by their families in country of origin). The most influential for economic development is the part of the income received by migrants saved and remitted to the original communities where it is then used:

- to buy goods, thereby increasing the standard of living, or to buy accommodation, thereby raising the aggregate domestic demand
- to support with investments existing entrepreneurial activities of families in the country of origin (agriculture, commerce)
- to improve the education of the members of the family and, possibly, to finance their departure.

Of course, these virtuous effects depend on the pattern of migration (temporary or permanent) and on the home support for development (administrative infrastructures, credit, institutions). On the one hand, permanent migrants exacerbate the indirect negative effects on 'human capital' ('brain and skill drain') of the lower-income country occurring in the short run: the level of education, skills and capabilities of the remaining workers could be reduced, if migrants are skilled workers, officials or students. On the other hand, temporary migrants increase their remittances when they intend to come back home to increase the available financial capital to implement new economic activities.

Economic migrants support the hosting economies through:

- the provision of a supplementary labour force to maintain the level of activity of the economy
- the supply of workers in industry and services where the number of nationals is insufficient
- contribution to the sustainability of retirement funds
- increasing engagement in entrepreneurial activities
- consumption of goods and services contributing to increase the aggregate domestic demand.

In such a framework, migrants generate positive economic effects for sending and hosting economies alike but with a trade-off for both: an increasing number of emigrants cause positive effects on the lower-income economy only if they are temporary, while in the higher-income countries, the positive effects emerge when they are permanent. This trade-off calls for shared policies to support jointly the development process of the first block of economies and the growth of the second.

Although the economic dimension of the migrant is necessary to recognize his or her social standing, it is not sufficient to define his or her legal status. In the main, the term 'migrant' identifies an undifferentiated person who leaves his or her native country and enters a foreign state, without considering either the reasons for migrating or the kind of rights he or she can benefit from in the destination country. But, for the single migrant, an exodus caused by the fear for his or her own safety or by forced displacement is different from voluntarily leaving to find a job abroad, insofar as the socio-legal status of refugee granted in the host country differs from that of mere worker. Under international law, in the former case, once the flagrant necessity is recognized, the destination state hosts and nourishes the refugee as long as the threat persists, while in the latter, national laws allow the subject to have a fixed-term settlement visa to remain in the country and to find a job. Moreover, those who come to a country illegally, that is, people crossing a border without any kind of visa or any entitlement to the status of asylum seekers or, in addition, people no longer equipped with such documents, are also usually considered migrants. Thus, the public's shallow definition of migration as people entering a state prevents both the description and understanding of the phenomenon, that is, a specific economic movement of people for different reasons.

It is not so easy to find a complete and congruent categorization either in public documents, scientific studies or reports, given that also scholars and practitioners lament migrant definitions and the estimates of the corresponding flows (Fargues 2014). This is because the phenomenon is analyzed from different points of view (political, sociological and economic) and sometimes the migrant status diverges. Thus, before presenting the statistics on the Mediterranean migration system, careful consideration of the definition is necessary.

As the economic role of migration emerges just like a constitutive feature of the migrant's status and as international and national laws govern his or her rights, the legal standing and the economic role should be the two coordinates to define this social subject. Since the definitions of *international migrant* and of *irregular migrant* respect both requirements, they can be used as starting points.

International migrants are 'persons who leave their country of origin, or the country of habitual residence, to establish themselves either permanently or temporarily in another country. An international frontier is therefore crossed' (Perruchoud and Redpath-Cross 2011: 52).[5] Thus, all such people are considered as foreign-born in the arrival or transit country (see Fargues 2014: 2 for a critique). Within this category the following can be included:

- *migrant workers*, who are 'skilled, semi-skilled or untrained workers who remain in the destination country for definite periods as determined in a work contract with an individual worker or a service contract concluded with an enterprise' (Perruchoud and Redpath-Cross 2011: 97).
- *asylum-seekers*, who are 'persons who seek safety from persecution or serious harm in a country other than their own and await a decision on the

application for refugee status under relevant international and national instruments' (Perruchoud and Redpath-Cross 2011: 12).

• *EU internal migrants*, who are EU citizens entering freely the territory of member states 'with a valid identity card or passport' (Article 5 of Directive 2004/38/EC), 'have the right of residence on the territory of another Member State for a period of up to three months without any conditions or any formalities other than the requirement to hold a valid identity card or passport' (Article 6/1 of Directive 2004/38/EC) and have 'the right of residence on the territory of another Member State for a period of longer than three months if they: (a) are workers or self-employed persons in the host Member State (Article 7 of Directive 2004/38/EC)'

Irregular migrants are by contrast

persons who, owing to unauthorized entry, breach a condition of entry or the expiry of their visa, and lack legal status in a transit or host country. The definition covers *inter alia* those persons who have entered a transit or host country lawfully but have stayed for a longer period than authorized or subsequently taken up unauthorized employment (also called clandestine/ undocumented migrants or migrants in an irregular situation).

(Perruchoud and Redpath-Cross 2011: 54)

As they are all unregistered people, the element that first distinguishes foreign-born people entering a country is their legal status.

The Mediterranean migration system: where migrants come from and where they are heading for

Migration flows represent a far from messy phenomenon: over time, they build a real set of networks called migration systems. A migration system is a set of fairly constant exchanges of people among different economies that originate a geographic network which is recognizable in space and time (Massey et al. 1998: 61). Alongside the movement of people, networks of financial resources (remittances), of technological and socio-cultural knowledge and of goods are established. Thus, real economic and social bonds connect the sending and receiving countries.

Since the Second World War, Mediterranean migration flows have grown and have become more intensive in such a way that they have woven a thick web covering both the sea and the countries fronting onto it, as well as neighbouring countries economically connected with them. Indeed, up to the 1990s, there were South–South migration flows connecting mainly the South-Eastern Mediterranean countries with the economies of the Arabian Peninsula (Baldwin-Edwards 2005) and South–North migration flows of workers linking both Turkey, Maghreb countries and EU Mediterranean countries (except for

France) to the Central and Northern European economies (including Switzerland). However, in the 1990s, the situation changed.

The changes emerging in Mediterranean migrations starting from 1990 are both dimensional and structural. As to the former aspect, in 2017 Europe received 30.22% of the world's migrants (78 million out of 258, UN 2017), about 70% of whom were non-residents living in the European Union (55 million that are the 10.8% of the 508 million of people living in the EU). This is the result of a process starting in the 1990s: Table 11.6 shows that in the receiving countries of the EU, the number of foreign-born people increased. Some countries followed trends consolidated in the previous immigration period, as in the cases of France (which increased by 1.8% between 1990 and 2017) and Switzerland (which increased from 20.9% of immigrants out of the total population to 29.6%). Numbers of immigrants more or less doubled in other countries (UK, Germany, Portugal and Greece), or quadrupled, like Italy, or

Table 11.6 International migrant stock as a percentage of the total population, 1990–2017

Countries	Year						
	1990	1995	2000	2005	2010	2015	2017
United Kingdom	6.4	7.2	8	9.8	12	12.9	13.4
Germany	7.5	9.2	11	11.5	12.1	12.5	14.8
Switzerland	20.9	21.1	21.9	24.4	26.5	29	29.6
EU-Mediterranean							
Portugal	4.4	5.2	6.3	7.3	7.2	8.3	8.5
Spain	2.1	2.6	4.1	9.3	13.4	12.7	12.8
France	10.4	10.4	10.5	11	11.4	12.3	12.2
Italy	2.5	3.1	3.7	6.7	9.7	9.8	10
Greece	6	8	10	10.5	11.5	11.1	10.9
Balkan-Anatolian							
Turkey	2.2	2.1	2	1.9	1.9	5.3	6
Bosnia and Herzegovina	1.3	1.8	2.2	1.3	1	1.1	1.1
Serbia	1	6.4	9	9.2	9.1	9.1	9.1
Albania	2	2.3	2.5	2.1	1.8	1.8	1.8
S-E Mediterranean							
Syria	5.7	5.8	5.1	4.8	8.5	5.3	5.5
Lebanon	19.4	20.1	21.4	19	18.9	33.7	31.9
Jordan	32.2	33.6	37.8	40.7	37.9	34	33.3
Israel	36.3	33.6	30.8	28.6	26.3	24.9	23.6
Egypt	0.3	0.3	0.2	0.4	0.4	0.6	0.5
Tunisia	0.5	0.4	0.4	0.3	0.4	0.5	0.5
Algeria	1.1	0.9	0.8	0.6	0.6	0.6	0.6
Morocco	0.2	0.2	0.2	0.2	0.2	0.3	0.3

Source: Author's elaboration from www.un.org/en/development/desa/population/migration/data/estimates2/estimates17.shtml

increased six-fold, like Spain. A special case of rising immigration is that of the countries on the Asian shore of the Mediterranean, where the long-lasting political crises and wars originated the exodus first of Palestinians, then of Lebanese and now of Syrians. Thus, Lebanon, Jordan and Syria present in the period highly fluctuating and sometimes striking values of foreign-born people who, together with the number of migrants living in Turkey because of the recent Syrian crisis which had increased three-fold, are, in fact, refugees.

By contrast, all the sending countries of North Africa maintained the incidence of migrants on the population at negligible percentages, even when they became transit sites. A situation at first glance similar can be found on the Balkan countries like Albania and Bosnia and Herzegovina, but in Serbia, Slovenia and Croatia the numbers of foreign-born residents have increased because they participated in the redistribution of population caused by the dismemberment of Yugoslavia. Thus, as expected, where migration can be the solution to the lack of workers a meaningful stock of migrants is registered, and where the lack of jobs drives citizens to migrate the incidence of immigrants is insignificant.

The structural changes in Mediterranean migration consist in the broadening of the web of migration, the change in the composition of migration by nationality in receiving countries. The widening of the migration system is the consequence both of accession to the European Union of the Central Eastern Europe economies that had previously generated inflows of migrant workers towards the Union, and the activation of new flows with the neighbouring countries at the borders of the Community (Ukraine, Russia, Moldova and Belarus). In addition, most of the large economies of the European Union opened their doors to those coming from far off, that is, from their ex-colonies: in 2017, 15%–20% of UK immigrants came from South Asia and 40% of those arriving in Spain came from Latin America, as occurred in Portugal. Accelerating during the last two decades, this trend has also shuffled the different national communities at the top of the foreign-born living in host countries (UN 2017). For example, in 1990 in Germany, the most numerous foreign community was the Turks, representing 26.7% of total immigrants, but in 2017, the Poles were the most numerous group (15.9% of the total) followed by Turks (13.6%) and by Russians and Kazakhs (each at 8.5%). In the United Kingdom, Indian migrants, who used to account for 22.6% of the total in the 1990s, have fallen to 9.5%, overtaken by Pakistanis (9.95%) and Poles (9.9%), while the number of the Irish decreased between 1990 and 2017 from 16% to 4.5%. In Italy, Moroccans (8% in the 1990s) have been replaced at the top by Romanians (17.6% of total immigrants) and by Albanians (7.7%). Only in France, due to the colonial legacy, have Algerians improved their position (from 13.7% to 18.4%) followed by Moroccans (11.9%).

During the last two decades, the composition by categories of immigrants also changed in the Mediterranean migration system due to the increase of refugees and the EU internal mobility permission. Table 11.7 shows values for the corresponding indexes. The importance of the refugee share on total foreigners appears in the second column of Table 11.7: the explosive situation in

Table 11.7 International migrant and refugee stock in the Mediterranean Basin, 2017

Countries	Immigration				Emigration	
	% on Pop.	Refugees % on im.	% of im. from EU	% of im. from SEM	% on Pop.	% of em. to EU
EU-Mediterranean						
Portugal	8.5	0.2	24.4	...	21.9	64.8
Spain	12.8	0.5	34.3	15.1	2.9	57.6
France	12.2	4.5	28.9	41.7	3.4	56.2
Italy	10	3.6	35.2	22.8	5.1	57.3
Greece	10.9	7.7	26.2	42	8.4	43.3
Balkan-Anatolian						
Turkey	6	63.8	22.8	70.8	4.2	80.6
Bosnia and Herzegovina	1.1	14.4	...	...	47.3	63.8
Serbia	9.1	3.9	42	56.8	10.9	76
Albania	1.8	2.6	...	...	38.9	83.7
S-E Mediterranean						
Syria	...		...	...	33.2	3.6
Lebanon	31.9	80.4	...	92.8	13.5	26
Jordan	33.3	90.6	...	88.9	7.7	...
Israel	23.6	2.3	11.3	15.6	3	...
Egypt	0.5	55.1	...	29.9	3.5	9.3
Tunisia	0.5	1.3	...	...	6.6	77
Algeria	0.6	40.2	...	...	4.3	90
Morocco	0.3	6.7	...	...	8.1	88

Source: Author's elaboration from www.un.org/en/development/desa/population/migration/data/estimates2/estimates17.shtml

Jordan and Lebanon is clear, as well as the control of Syrian fugitives by Turkey and the post-conflict situation of Bosnia and Herzegovina (Slovenia and Croatia). Instead, the incidence of refugees on migration inflows in Europe is scarce, considering also the cases of the UK (1.7%), Poland (2.0%) and Hungary (2.8%). Only the case of Germany (10.3%) is close to the Balkan situation.

The destination of the immigration flows (the last column of Table 11.7) shows that four fifths of Turkish people and over two thirds of Balkan migrants prefer EU countries, while the workers of the Mediterranean Mashrek feed the Gulf migration system. More than half of the migrants from the EU Mediterranean countries head towards the other EU Member States (except Greece, as just discussed). But considering the origin of migrants arriving in Europe from South-Eastern Mediterranean countries, only in France and Greece, they represent more than those coming from other EU members (i.e. around 40% of the total immigrants); in Portugal, Spain and Italy, the trend is the opposite, in line with the fact that 37% of the foreign-born people entering the EU were born in another EU Member State.

To conclude this overview, a few comments on irregular migration should be made. Although the phenomenon constitutes the main topic of interest for the EU, its dimension is hard to calculate. The organisms entrusted with EU border controls (like FRONTEX) provide only partial data. According to a *Briefing of the European Parliament* published in April 2015, the provisional total number of persons refused entry to the EU in 2014 was 260,375. There are only estimates for the stock of irregular migrants in the Union: between 1.9 million and 3.8 million (or 8 million).

How far does the migration problem concern Euro-Mediterranean policies?

In light of the previous analysis, the stock of migrants ascribable to the Mediterranean migration system totalled in 2017 about 55 million people feeding different geographic flows:

- EU domestic mobility accounting for 37% of regular migrants
- A share of S–E Mediterranean workers, making up 20.1% (11,054,000) of total immigrants in the EU
- An equally distributed share of European migrants from Belarus, Ukraine, Moldova and Russia, accounting for 5.3% of total EU immigrants (2,937,000)
- The remaining 37% of migrants from the rest of the world
- Many refugees, registered as migrants, form a significant share of population only on the South-Eastern Mediterranean shore and in the Balkans
- An additional flow of irregular migrants, measurable with difficulty and in any case amounting to 1% of the EU population and to 9% of regular migrants in the worst scenario.

The aforementioned statistics show that only one fifth of the Mediterranean migration flows comes from non–EU-Mediterranean shores, whose number is slightly increased if irregular migrants are added. This category accounts for slightly under half of the internal migration of the European Union and of migrants coming from the rest of the world. Thus, the migration problems extend beyond the Mediterranean Sea.

The legal framework within which the 'migration problem' has been managed by the European Union started with the 'security policies' (rejecting the economic role of migrants) and has proceeded with the idea of a 'countercyclical labour force supply' (temporary workers crossing the European Union's borders back and forth whenever 'excess labour demand' is cancelled).[6] Neither approach considers migration as a feature of modern economies that creates a trade-off both in high-income and in low-income economies. Nor do they consider that a portion of irregular migrants depend on the expiry of the settlement visa and on the lack of connection between job suppliers at destination and job applicants in sending countries. Nor do they consider citizens of other EU member states, the most important share of foreign-born people, that move as a matter of course in part of the common territory.

In the framework of the *European Agenda for the Integration of Third Country Nationals*, the most pressing challenges to manage the problem were: the prevailing low employment levels of migrants (especially for migrant women), their rising unemployment and high levels of 'over-qualification', the increasing risks of social exclusion, the gaps in educational achievement and public concerns with the lack of integration of migrants. Such challenges need to be tackled by some actions,[7] but no Community Law has yet been issued to implement them. The implementation of such measures was wished for best practices entrusted to the local administration of each country, there was no consideration for the development of the country of origin and the migrant is seen as part of only the temporary workforce.

All the aforementioned points show that the 'migration problem' requires a unified solution at the highest level: implementation of European citizenship, a shared bearing of responsibility in the case of refugees, migration policies shared with partners to manage flows and overcome the trade-offs in both low-income and high-income countries, and investments to achieve such measures. In this framework, a new Euro-Mediterranean partnership can emerge from the awareness that to promote the development of 'different level economies' requires a real multilateral approach, a shared commitment to manage all common economic problems (starting from migration) and an actively involved investment plan. In addition, all these policy suggestions entail the need for new forms of economic cooperation in the Mediterranean, graduating from a regionalized image of the Mediterranean to a multi-regional one, from the practice of joining international agreements to multilateralism, from institutional transfer (Europeanization) to institution building, and from heading for conditionality to social empowerment and human development.

Notes

1 An analysis of polarization of Mediterranean economies up to the end of the twentieth century is provided by Esteban 2002.
2 'A low dependency ratio is desirable because it indicates that there are proportionally more adults of working age who can support the young and the elderly of the population. This in turn is advantageous for the countries' health-care system and pension schemes. A downfall of the relative number of working people in a population also has negative impacts on the growth path of the Economy' (Simon et al. 2012: 158).
3 'Replacement migration' is 'the internal migration that occurs where the vacuum created by workers departing for another country is filled by workers from other parts of the country, or the international migration that a country would need to offset population decline and population ageing resulting from low fertility and mortality rates' (Perruchoud and Redpath-Cross 2011: 83).
4 The 'demographic gift' is a dividend enjoyed by an economy when the path of the demographic evolution produces advantages for the economy. This is the case of the working

population exceeding the dependent population because of young educated people entering the labour market. These new workers have a higher productivity in respect of their older counterparts.

5 The UN uses two distinct definitions for 'international migrant'. The first applies to the individual, who is defined 'as any person who changes his or her country of usual residence. A person's country of usual residence is that in which the person (. . .) normally spends the daily period of rest' (UN 1998: 17). The second applies collectively to the migrant population and defines the 'international migrant stock [as] the number of people living in a country or area other than that in which they were born' (Fargues 2014: 1–2).

6 'European legal framework for migration and asylum' Regulation (EC) No 767/2008; Regulation (EU) No 1077/2011; Directive 2011/98/EU
'The global approach to migration and mobility' COM(2011) 743 final (2012/C 191/23) and the European Agenda for the Integration of Third-Country Nationals {SEC(2011) 957 final.

7 The proposed measures were:

- Integration through participation, consisting in: the development of the socio-economic contribution of migrants, the achievement of an equal treatment and sense of belonging by rights and obligations
- More action at local level in each country by: addressing especially disadvantaged urban areas, improving a multi-level cooperation between administrations, using EU financial support to local action
- Involvement of countries of origin by the implement of: pre-departure measures in support of integration, beneficial contacts between diaspora communities and their countries of origin, circular migration and development in countries of origin.

References

Baldwin-Edwards, M., 2005. *Migration in the Middle East and Mediterranean*. Regional Study for the Global Commission of International Migration, Migration Observatory. Greece: Pantheon University, 1–18.

European Council, European Parliament and European Commission, 2017. *The New European Consensus on Development 'Our world, our dignity, our future'* 740. Strasburg: Communication COM, 22 November.

Constant, A.F., and Zimmermann, K.F., eds., 2013. *International Handbook on the Economics of Migration*. Cheltenham: Edward Elgar.

DIRECTIVE 2004/38/EC of the European Parliament and of the Council of 29 April 2004. *On the Right of Citizens of the Union and Their Family Members to Move and Reside Freely Within the Territory of the Member States.* Available from: http://eur-lex.europa.eu/legal-content/AUTO/?uri=CELEX:32004L0038&qid=1516812945405&rid=1

Esteban, J., 2002. *Economic Polarization in the Mediterranean Basin*. Barcelona: CREI Universitat Pompeu Fabra.

Fargues, F., 2014. *The Fuzzy Lines of International Migration: A Critical Assessment of Definitions and Estimates in the Arab Countries*, EUI Working Paper RSCAS No. 71.

Massey, D.S., Arango, J., Hugo, G., Kouaouci, A., Pellegrino, A., and Taylor, E.J., 1998. *World in Motion: Understanding International Migration at the End of the Millennium*. Oxford: Clarendon Press.

Perruchoud, R., and Redpath-Cross, J., eds., 2011. *Glossary on Migration*. International Migration Law No. 25. Geneva: International Organisation for Migration (IOM).

Robert, E.B., 2005. *International Migration and Economic Development: Lessons from Low-Income Countries*. Stockholm: Amkvist & Wiksell International.

Simon, C., Belyakov, A.O., and Feichtinger, G., 2012. Minimizing the Dependency Ratio in a Population with Below-Replacement Fertility through Immigration. *Theoretical Population Biology*, 82, 158–169.

Tarmann, A., 2000. *The Flap Over Replacement Migration*. Population Reference Bureau. Available from: www.prb.org/Publications/Articles/2000/TheFlapOverReplacement Migration.aspx

Taylor, J.E., 1999. The New Economics of Labour Migration and the Role of Remittances in the Migration Process. *International Migration*, 37, 65–87.

United Nations (UN), 1998. *Recommendations on Statistics of International Migration, Revision 1*, New York: UN Department of Economic and Social Affairs, Statistical Papers Series M, No. 58, Rev., ST/ESA/STAT/SER.M/58/Rev.1.

United Nations (UN), 2001. *Replacement Migration: Is It a Solution to Declining and Ageing Populations?* New York: UN Population Division, Department of Economic and Social Affairs, ST/ESA/SER.A/206.

United Nations (UN), 2017. Department of Economic and Social Affairs. Population Division. *Trends in International Migrant Stock*.

Index

Note: Page numbers in *italics* indicate figures and in **bold** indicate tables on the corresponding pages.